Electronic Music

ELECTRONIC MUSIC

A Listener's Guide

Elliott Schwartz

PRAEGER PUBLISHERS
New York • Washington

3/24/75 Eastern 8.34

Draper

66316

Published in the United States of America in 1973
by Praeger Publishers, Inc.
111 Fourth Avenue, New York, N.Y. 10003

Second printing, 1974

© 1973 by Praeger Publishers, Inc.

Library of Congress Catalog Card Number: 77–170472

Printed in the United States of America

To Nina and Jonathan

Contents

Jon H Appleton · Larry Austin · Robert Ceely · Joel Chadabe · David Cope · Lukas Foss · Kenneth Gaburo · William Hellermann · Lejaren A. Hiller, Jr. · Hubert S. Howe, Jr. · Jean Eichelberger Ivey · Gottfried Michael

Koenig · Daniel Lentz · Alvin Lucier · Otto Luening ·
Robert Moran · Gordon Mumma · Pauline Oliveros ·
Steve Reich · Gerald Shapiro · Barry Vercoe · Raymond
Wilding-White · Charles Wuorinen

A SECTION OF PHOTOGRAPHS FOLLOWS PAGE 84.

Preface

This book attempts to fill a gap in the literature on electronic music. Until now, writing on this subject has assumed a significant level of experience—either "electronic" or "musical" or both—on the reader's part. In contrast, I have tried wherever possible to avoid being overly technical in speaking of electronics or overly analytical in discussions of music, so that my subject—the most important musical development of our century—could be made accessible to the general reader. Although I assume that the book may be read by composers, engineers, and students working in the field, my primary aim has been to make the basic facts of electronic music as clear as possible for the typical "listener"—the person who cares about music and its development but has little or no background in either the art of music or the science of electronics. I hope that those who do possess such prior background in either area will judge the limitations of the book, particularly its simplifications and inevitable generalizations, in the light of this aim.

Books on music for nonmusicians hardly need any defense; it has been demonstrated beyond question that the workings of music can be explained, on a level above that of mere "appreciation," to the reader lacking the basic experience and vocabulary of a formal musical education. More importantly, though, I've tried to show the reader that *electronic* music—or, at the very least, its fundamentals—can be grasped without a sophisticated knowledge of technology. The average listener's desire to probe this area is too often thwarted by the fear that one needs a degree in engineering or mathematics to comprehend the simplest concepts. On the contrary, most composers working in the medium "know" it only in terms of its *musical* facts, its potential for use, and its results in practice, for the most part leaving the complexities of circuitry to the scientific experts.

My own experience with electronic music should offer ample comfort to any who still equate working skill and practical knowledge with technological-mechanical aptitude. I am a practicing composer, and I have worked with electronics in one form or another for a number of years. I understand what I'm about, and what my electronically minded colleagues are doing, and yet I must confess I was an indifferent science student in college and I have no mechanical ability whatsoever. I continually have trouble with simple household repairs, and the assorted gadgetry under the hood of my automobile baffles me completely. Although I have performed as pianist for at least a quarter-century, I have no real knowledge of my instrument's construction. I cannot tune it, much less repair it, and I share this deficiency with practically every other pianist I know of.

I was equally slow in my response to the "science" and technical jargon of electronic music. It took me a while to distinguish confidently between "input" and "output," for example, and terms like "impedance" and "ohm" were never really clear for quite some time. The point is that, if I and many other similarly clumsy musicians can learn to comprehend the medium—and actively perform creative work with it, as we do—its strictly *musical* aspects cannot be all that mysterious. And they are not, as I have attempted to illustrate in the following pages.

As its subtitle indicates, the book is directed to the "listener"; with this in mind, I've tried to concentrate on actual pieces of music, usually works available on commercial recordings. It follows, then, ideally that the book should be read in conjunction with a number of intensive *listening* sessions. My subject, after all, is music, and music should be heard! I don't mean to sermonize on this, but the printed word often becomes rather hypnotic, creating the delusion that a book (on whatever subject) is a self-sufficient object for study. This situation is aggravated further when the subject at hand is music; the pitches, rhythms, and sounds can be described, "explained," discussed—and inevitably misrepresented—in words, but the aural experience cannot be reproduced within the pages of a book. I've always envied people who write books about the visual arts, for example, because they can raise an important point and indicate "Figure 23," instantly referring the reader to a reproduction of the art work in question. This is impossible here: If we were to reproduce even a portion of the many compositions to be discussed, an entire shelf's worth of discs or tapes would have to accompany each copy of the book. I must place my reader on the honor system, then, and trust that each of the pieces noted in these pages will receive at least one hearing. If not, it's the reader's loss.

In a field as rapidly moving as this, no one can pretend to write an up-to-date book. Any number of developments may occur, or become passé, by the time the volume is in print. I don't claim, then, that this particular book has all the answers about "new" music or the "avant-garde." It is merely a chronicle of happenings in the recent past and events taking place while I write—a primer, perhaps, that I hope will make the future more understandable, as the future unfolds.

I have tried to describe some of the important musical developments that led to the interest in electronics, to give a brief history of "electronic" developments themselves, and to provide a basic introduction to the workings of various studio systems. With respect to the latter, the text refers to the classic tape studio, the RCA synthesizer, the use of the computer for sound generation, and the fundamentals of voltage control. I've also made a few rash observations on a number of possibilities for the future—not the strictly "electronic" future, but the ways in which the electronic revolution may alter (and may have already affected) our musical habits.

The last two sections may be of particular interest for many readers: a collection of essays by composers associated in one way or another with the electronic medium and some introductory hints for people who want to compose tape music at home with as little expensive equipment as possible.

Throughout the volume I refer to myself in the first person singular, so that allusions to "the author" and "the reader" are replaced by "I" and "you." I adopted this approach because it seemed the most relaxed way of presenting the material; it's certainly not meant to be pretentious or give the impression of speaking from on high. On the contrary, in using the first person singular I fix responsibility for any errors, hasty judgments, and dubious opinions squarely upon myself. The opinions, in particular, I hope, are few. In a book of this sort, I felt it best not to let my own preferences regarding style or method (notions of "good" or "bad," "interesting" or "dull") intrude upon the text more than was absolutely necessary; to this degree, at least, the book attempts a certain objectivity. As a composer I have very definite preferences and a particular stylistic position. I would like to think that I've found my own direction within the great gamut of twentieth-century possibilities, but, to find out what that position is, you'll have to hear my music.

Although I shoulder the blame for the inaccuracies and distortions that may lie ahead, credit for what is positive is certainly not mine alone. It must be shared with a great many people who have offered advice, suggestions, technical assistance, ideas that have proved valuable: John E. Rogers, Robert K. Beckwith, David Gamper, Marion Brown, Abelardo Morrell, Norman Cazden, Stuart Dempster, Mary Beth Burbank, and Robert Ceely. Milton Babbitt, Alvin Lucier, Pauline Oliveros, Bertram Turetzky, and Daniel Lentz supplied me with photographs that I could not have secured otherwise, and Thelma McCusker provided me with welcome typing assistance.

A special word of thanks goes to my editor, Léon King, for his patience, encouragement, and over-all contribution to the final shape of this volume. Grand Prize in all three categories is awarded to my wife, as always.

Part 1
The Musical Past, 1906–60

1. Introduction

Many people believe that there is an "electronic style" of music and that this style is duplicated invariably from piece to piece. Having convinced themselves of this, they also assume the existence of a special breed of composers who concern themselves exclusively with electronics and whose works all sound the same. Various catch-phrases are heard in attempts to describe whatever this allegedly singular quality evokes—"science fiction," "freakishness," "dehumanization"—all of them indicating that the music is, in one way or another, puzzling. Perhaps it *is*—to be more specific, perhaps one particular composition you've just recently heard is—but, to be sure, there's no guarantee that the next piece won't be entirely comprehensible, or at least puzzling in an altogether different way. It is really unfortunate that the most recent music of the twentieth century, offering the greatest variety—sonic, stylistic, aesthetic—in history, has become associated in the public mind with a single image.

Mention the phrase "electronic music," or equivalent words such as "tape" and "computer," and the image appears: a bare stage devoid of human performers, but with tape spinning efficiently and cold-bloodedly on a tape deck and an assortment of "nonmusical" sounds (hisses, pings, pops, thuds, swoops) emerging from loud-speakers. The entire scene, viewed in these terms, is truly blood-curdling. It is the final victory of the Machine over Man, the Dehumanization of Art, the triumph of Noise over Music.

Leaving aside for the moment such questions as the "musicality"

3

of any sounds out of context (noises, pitches, or what-have-you), or the mechanistic terrors of the tape deck as compared with those of, say, the harpsichord, we should ask ourselves if this singular "image" is actually representative of all that's going on in the musical world today. To be fair, we'd have to say that there are a large number of works intended solely for transmission via loud-speakers from a prerecorded tape, and that a number of these stress "noises" rather than traditional musical material. But this is hardly an accurate description of the entire electronic panorama.

For example, anyone with access to a good record collection, or within traveling distance of a university or city offering contemporary concerts, might discover Mario Davidovsky's *Synchronisms No. 1* for live performer (flutist) and tape, with its traditional cross-play between soloist and accompaniment. Or a work by Milton Babbitt for prerecorded tape, such as *Composition for Synthesizer,* which concentrates not on "noises" but on clearly defined pitches and semiorchestral timbres. Or possibly music such as Larry Austin's *Accidents* or Daniel Lentz's *ABM (Anti-Bass Music)*, featuring live performance on stage, sounds being electronically altered and distorted by ingenious arrangements of microphones, amplifiers, and other electronic gear during the performance. Or perhaps the pioneering experiments in tape music by Otto Luening and Vladimir Ussachevsky—*Fantasy in Space* and *Sonic Contours* immediately come to mind—using the often quite recognizable sounds of traditional instruments (flute, piano) and familiar patterns, but so modified that the music on tape is uniquely wedded to this medium, and unplayable by live performers.

This is only a random sampling of the diversity inherent in the electronic music scene. Our initial point of reference, then, should be *not* a hypothetical "style" but a technique—an assortment of various techniques—by means of which composers are freed (as perhaps never before) to work in whatever style they choose. Or, to alter the metaphor a bit, you might wish to think of electronic equipment collectively as a giant performing instrument, opening up new possibilities for composition in our twentieth century very much as the grand piano did in the nineteenth. It would be as absurd to speak of an electronic style, embracing the bewildering assortment of works composed for the new media, as it would be to postulate a style encompassing all music composed for, say, the clarinet. This is not to deny that instruments have their idiosyncracies; certainly the distinctive characteristics of the clarinet have stimulated the thinking of composers from Mozart to Stravinsky, and I would be influenced by some of these factors in writing a clarinet passage (so that it would very likely differ from a violin passage). But the clarinet is one instrument among many, and its unique features aren't sufficiently crucial to warrant an arbitrary categorization of all music into "works composed for clarinet" versus "works not composed for clarinet." That sort of distinction wouldn't be very useful in understanding the music, especially if it ignores all those *other* decisions made by the composer—the combination of pitches into melodic lines, chords, rhythmic activity, the succession of events in time—after the initial decision to write for the particular instrument. To divide the musical universe into "electronic" and "nonelectronic" is a similarly limited exercise, and a misleading one in that it reinforces the narrow concept of a single "style."

When we speak of electronic music, then, bear in mind that (as with the clarinet or piano) we are concentrating upon a collective "instrument"—one instrument among many. If we were discussing piano music, the question of a single approach would never arise—the divergent examples of Beethoven, Schubert, Chopin, Debussy, Bartók, and Prokofiev are too familiar to permit this sort of reasoning—and we would consider, rather, the impact of this unique instrument upon the development of music, its revolutionizing effects spread out over an array of individual styles and historical periods. In the same vein, we can agree that a sizable body of music literature has come into being within the last half-century, using electronic techniques for the creation and/or the manipulation of sounds, either processed onto recording tape for future "performance" or played on the spot by live performers in concert. Electronic techniques for the recording and transmission of sounds are also crucial to this process, but we are familiar with these anyway, as more music reaches our ears via the microphone-to-loud-speaker route than by any other means, and by "music" I now mean Mozart, Sinatra, and Hollywood film scores. We are by now so accustomed to phonograph records, Muzak, and pop singers performing on-stage with microphones that the people who most aggressively loathe "electronic music" might be the most surprised to discover that they've been listening to it for many years.

It may be worth dwelling on this last point for a moment, as it suggests at least one working definition or point of view for examining electronic music: that, through a variety of possible devices (sound generation, distortion, amplification, tape-processing, and so forth), one achieves a performance that would be *impossible* to realize without the technical assistance. In the case of the familiar examples I've just noted, "amplification" is the operative word. It enables the often untrained voice of the pop singer to whisper, sigh, and croon in perfect balance with a large instrumental ensemble; it enables the film composer to score a passage for solo flute against a weighty brass group if he wishes, knowing that microphones will balance the effect. Add to this the factor of tape-editing, and we have the situation of studio recording for the phonograph. The note-by-note perfect "performance" of Beethoven or Verdi issued on a recording is not a performance at all in the live sense, but an assortment of various "takes" spliced together on tape. I must add that there is nothing intrinsically wrong or evil about any of this. The point was raised, rather, to suggest that, if a possible starting point for discussion is this "realization of the impossible," then electronic music is more closely related to our common musical experience than we may have imagined. In fact, Milton Babbitt has stated in a lecture that anyone listening to a recording of a Tchaikovsky symphony is experiencing "electronic music." It is also no accident that the first tape experiments of the late 1940's and early 1950's were begun in European radio and recording studios. Composers there started with the given facts (of recording-reproduction-transmission) known to all of us, and used these as compositional stimuli.

The musical "realization of the impossible" is surely a laudable goal, and I doubt that anyone would object to it on principle. There must be other reasons, then, for the negative opinions voiced by certain listeners confronted with electronic music for the first time. For one thing, the music itself—the arrangement of sound patterns in time—is often surprisingly unfamiliar; the listener may "set" his mental ear for expected sounds (steady beat, singable melodies, predictable successions of chords) that never materialize. The ensuing frustration indicates, perhaps, a general unfamiliarity with any "contemporary" music—music since Wagner and Debussy—and usually dissipates when (and if) the listener acclimates himself to the various stylistic changes since 1900; the most important of these changes will be discussed later on in this book. In any event, the problem is a legitimate one, related to real musical needs and levels of listening experience and not specifically "electronic" (the same reaction might well be provoked by a Webern piano piece or Penderecki string quartet).

A much more serious kind of problem, *not* really legitimate and not related to any musical factors, is the bogus specter of "technology" that seems to haunt the entire electronic enterprise. This unfortunate misconception is apparently rooted in the belief that music "by machines" is lacking in qualities that we label "human." Press releases and articles in popular magazines during the 1950's did much to foster this sort of apprehension. It's only natural to recoil in horror upon reading headlines and articles with titles like "Sinus Tones with Nuts and Bolts" (*Harper's*), "Nothing but Us Speakers" (*New York Times*), "Union Card for a Tape Recorder" (*Music Journal*), "Canny Computers—Machines Write Music, Play Checkers . . ." (*Wall Street Journal*), "How's Petrillo Gonna Collect AFM Dues from RCA's Electronic Tooter?" (*Variety*).

To begin with, what do we mean by music "by machines"? *Composed* by machines? There is really only a very small amount of music of which this could be said, and I would estimate that over 90 per cent of the works considered "electronic" are composed by people; even those few works composed by computer have been programed to do so by mere mortals. As for music composed with the aid of machines, this concept shouldn't really trouble anybody familiar with the standard Hollywood biography in which the composer-hero tests a phrase at the piano (an intricate contraption if there ever was one), goes to his desk (certainly a man-made object), and uses both pen and paper (highly sophisticated inventions) to transcribe his ideas. Nor is the notion of music *performed* by, on, or with the aid of machines unusual; Vladimir Horowitz uses a piano, Bing Crosby a microphone, and you probably listen to either one through radio or phonograph loud-speakers.

In truth, nothing could be more wildly overstated than the popular image of music composed, performed, and presumably listened to by robots—the ultimate technological nightmare. I suppose it all depends upon one's definition of "technology." The modern piano is a masterpiece of technology, as complex an engineering achievement as an automobile; similarly, the clarinet, violin, tuba, and xylophone are examples of carefully constructed objects for music-making. Composer Mel Powell, in stressing electronic music's "logical and natural development" within the genre of nonvocal instruments, "the vast world of sonorous artifacts including anything and everything employed in the projection of musical sounds other than the human voice itself," notes that "there are no distinctions to be drawn between the strung rattle of the paleolithic hunter . . . the Renaissance shawm . . . and any of the more recent, more familiar instruments, or the transducer and playback systems that convert output of a high-speed digital computer to sounding forms." Moreover, scientific advances have for centuries paralleled important changes in the creative arts. If examples are needed, consider the invention of printing, the development of valves on brass instruments, the metronome, the evolution of the modern piano, photography, new structural materials applied to architecture, fresco painting versus oil on canvas, changes in stage design and lighting, the motion picture.

Machines, after all, serve (or should serve) very "human" purposes. More often than not, they make man's share of the work at hand easier and *less* mechanical, freeing his time for more creative pursuits and often providing stimuli for new ideas. Electronic music offers the composer not only a new "instrument" —that is, an extension of performing resources—but a new technique for composing, enabling him to work directly with sound material in a way previously unforeseen. A composer in a tape studio can, if he wishes, stand in the same relationship to the stuff of his art as the painter or sculptor, molding and shaping his

material into a finished product. He no longer has to deal with
written instructions, executants, and their possible misinterpreta-
tions, the intrusion of many different personalities into an art
work—in short, all those obstacles encountered by playwrights,
choreographers, architects, and others engaged in the "public"
(as opposed to the solitary) arts. Of course, not all electronic
composers choose this option—many prefer to write out scores
and then realize them on tape, and a large number continue to
work within the collaborative framework of the live performance
—but the very existence of the option, the availability of a variety
of options in combination, opens up fresh ways of thinking. The
composer can now redefine for himself the roles and relationships
of the twin acts of "composition" and "performance." Anything
that draws the artist further into a direct confrontation with the
materials and procedures of his art, as electronic music has done,
cannot but further "humanize" that art.

We should also distinguish between those machines that restrict
the range of human activity and those that broaden it. Here again,
then, electronic equipment has proved to be "friend" and not
"foe," widening the nature and number of choices a composer can
make. Perhaps we don't find all of these choices to our liking.
You might feel that there's something inherently wrong with a
situation in which a computer composes music (although, remember, it is programed to do so by human beings), or you may not
react well to the composer's abandonment of the traditional interaction with performers (in favor of a more "painterly" attitude,
with the reel of tape acting as canvas), or you may have spent
too many evenings watching the solitary loud-speakers sitting on
the concert stage. As far as this last complaint is concerned, the
trouble here lies not so much in the music as in the surroundings.
Perhaps it took electronic music to make us realize what an "in-
human" place the concert hall is; certainly the sounds take on a
totally different character when they emerge from loud-speakers
in an outdoor square or garden, an art gallery, a cathedral, or your
own living room. The point I wish to make about all of this,
though, is that such complaints should be aimed directly at the
composer and not at his machines. The technology is irrelevant,
in that it does not dictate the choices and does not limit the pos-

sibilities of human choice—on the contrary, it widens the possibilities.

I must stress, then, that whatever you hear in an electronic composition (whether you like it or not) can ultimately be traced to a *human* choice. The mechanism can't be blamed any more than the clarinet that plays Bartók when one wishes to hear Brahms, or the pen-on-paper notating a twelve-tone-row rather than a C-major scale. The analogies are, I hope, apt ones, because electronic equipment functions precisely in these two ways: (1) as an extension of audible sonic resources (like the clarinet or any instrument) and (2) as a tool in the composing-transcribing process (like pen, manuscript paper, and other means of making ideas tangible and thereby more controllable). Responsibility—for the sounds, for the procedures of control, for the end product—remains, as always, human responsibility.

Finally, then, consider the sounds themselves. Or, to be more accurate, consider all of the aspects by which the sounds are related and articulated: rhythm, texture, dynamics (volume), register (placement in the frequency spectrum from lowest to highest), the composer's concern for pitch and intonation versus the lack of such concern, the degree of continuity, tonality (the relation of all pitches to a single focal point) versus atonality, and so on. Taken together, these various facets constitute what might be considered a musical *language*, and it is no secret that the language of much (although not all) electronic music is radically different from that of Tchaikovsky and Verdi. The more important features of the new language will be discussed in the next chapter, and I hope that listeners who are limited in their experience of twentieth-century music will begin to grasp the changes that have taken place since the 1890's—the changes wrought by Schoenberg, Webern, Ives, Cage, Satie. Given these overwhelming changes, it is difficult to imagine a composer of the mid-twentieth century (whether writing a string quartet or creating an electronic tape) *wanting* to sound like Verdi! Too much has happened in the intervening years, and we can't escape our times except for purposes of parody or nostalgia. And, if a composer truly wants to write a traditional-sounding piece in G major, why would he want to "realize" it on an electronic synthesizer? The equipment is expensive, difficult to control without training, and would at best produce results arrived at more easily by a conventional orchestra, chorus, or chamber ensemble. The result is that the more "experimental" composers, and not the traditionalists, are most likely to be drawn to the use of the electronic media.

I should add here that, although there have been important changes in the *language* of music, there are other—equally important—aspects of music that hardly ever change, attitudes on the part of composers that have been with us for centuries and exist even in the most experimental of today's idioms. These are more difficult to label—some refer to them as the "content" of music, or the "function"—but can be observed in such typical polarities as "classic versus romantic," "abstract music versus programmatic music," "emotional versus intellectual." That is, in every age, including our own, there will be composers concerned with the sensuous and the decorative, while other composers will construct highly rational, structural narrative. There will be composers who function best within the background—incidental music for the theater, or music for dancing—while others devise strong musical argument that will demand our undivided attention. There will be composers whose work is overtly "dramatic," perhaps relying upon visual or literary associations, and composers who advance their ideas in strictly musical terms. Electronic music covers all of this ground, from one aesthetic extreme to the other. And yet not much of this diversity will come through to the listener still coping with the unfamiliar *language*; it is only after the sounds cease to be novel and strange—only after they become accessible as part of the twentieth-century musical mainstream— that the pleasures of intelligent listening really begin.

For the listener who still considers the sounds—the language —of electronic music problematic, I have one preliminary bit of advice. Don't be misled into thinking that this language is either very "new" or exclusively "electronic." On the contrary, such composers as Babbitt, Berio, Subotnick, and Stockhausen are thinking along musical lines that—no matter how unfamiliar to you—may go back to the turn of the century and have been expressed in many works for conventional instruments and voices.

To begin with the last point, there is nothing uniquely electronic about the effects and aims of this music, although electronic means may realize these more efficiently and with heightened theatricality. Pings, pops, thuds, hisses, percussive sounds of unfixed pitch? These could be found in Pauline Oliveros's *Sound Patterns*, or Bernard Rands's work of the same title. Both of these are written for chorus, the Rands specifically for schoolchildren. Dense textures and clusters, massive walls of sound articulated only by timbral changes? These are the material for Ligeti's *Atmosphères* and Penderecki's *Threnody for the Victims of Hiroshima*, both orchestral works. The tightly controlled interdependency of pitch, rhythm, attack, and timbre characterizing much of Babbitt's work can be found as convincingly in his *Composition for Twelve Instruments* as in his electronic *Ensembles for Synthesizer*; similarly, the coloristic, lyrical aspects of Berio's work are equally evident in his chamber *Circles* and electronic *Visage*.

As for "newness," we can go back in time and discover innumerable examples—by Webern, Varèse, Schoenberg, Antheil, Cowell, Cage, Bartók, Ives—which predate in one way or another the electronic music of the present. The desire for greater "control" (especially over rhythm and duration), the liberation of noise and unfamiliar sonorities, collage and montage of familiar pop/folk elements, the retuning of the octave: All of these were serious concerns years before the means of facilitating them were developed. Musical preferences have led composers to electronic possibilities for realization more often than the other way around. Electronics has, in turn, stimulated the thinking of composers, but only those composers whose aesthetic tendencies are already predisposed to such stimuli. The so-called electronic music revolution, in other words, is only one aspect of a widespread musical revolution and has brought to that larger movement new working tools and a new instrument.

Not that all composers demand or need a totally new instrument. As I've previously suggested, many composers prefer to draw unusual sounds from traditional instruments, or combine elements of live performance with electronic extensions. But, for many who had felt restricted by existing instrumental resources, particularly those composers connected with the first European studios in the 1950's, tape and sound-generating equipment served urgent musical needs. Karlheinz Stockhausen's comment of that earlier decade is most typical:

> The existing instrumental sounds are pre-formed, dependent on the way instruments are built and played: they are "objects." Did the composers of today build the piano, the violin or the trumpet? Did they determine how it should be played? . . . The structure of a given composition and the structure of the material employed in it are derived from one single musical idea.

With this statement in mind, it is essential that we reconstruct those aspects of the changing musical language that gradually (from the turn of the century through the end of World War II) led composers into electronic explorations and that caused many to embrace the new media with such conviction.

2. Some Musical Precedents

Many developments have transformed the course of music in the twentieth century, and we can't hope to go into them all here. I want specifically to note only those changes that have contributed to today's widespread interest by composers in electronic techniques, in hopes that this will finally lay to rest the myth (noted in the previous chapter) that the language of the 1970's is "new." It is anything but new, and, as suggested earlier, it is not exclusively "electronic." Rather, electronic techniques have brought to fruition, and to general public awareness, musical ideas that have been simmering below the surface for many decades.

Two ideas in particular stand out, in that they have led directly to electronic concerns. One of these is the notion of "control" or "organization," which, beginning in the 1920's with the twelve-tone technique (the control of pitch relations—the twelve tones into which our octave is usually subdivided—without the referential limits of tonality or a "key"), expanded, in the late 1940's, into the "serial" technique (in which durations, timbres, articulations, and other musical factors are organized in ways analogous to that of twelve-tone pitch organization). This is a highly rational approach to musical thinking, stressing one of music's traditional roles, that of conveying the essence of abstract "argument"—logical interrelationships among discrete, measurable bits of information.

The other central idea is the use of noise, complex sonority, and diffuse "texture" in ways that are often *un*controlled, at times spontaneous and improvisatory. For many composers working in this area, music's "logical" aspects are perhaps less important than the sensuous, "mystical" ones. This, too, is a natural outgrowth of one of music's historic roles, in this instance that of heightening our sense of ritual, ceremony, what earlier civilizations may have called "magic." Music conceived along these lines is more concerned with grand (or at least dramatic) gestures than with organizational relationships and often proceeds from theatrical rather than rational assumptions. It is also more likely to deal with "gross," diffuse effects than with "discrete" quantities.

Is either of these two notions so revolutionary? Not really. Music has always possessed a split personality, so to speak, relating to man's love of precision (mathematical, grammatical, architectural) *and* his response to the physical world of sound as an emotive, mysterious force. The two aspects have usually been fused together. Composers of the medieval and Renaissance periods, working within logical systems so intricate that scholars of the time considered music a branch of mathematics, created a body of sacred music that still retains its "magical" properties, a unique alliance of mysticism and rationality. Examples from more recent times, such as a Bach fugue or the Beethoven *Eroica Symphony*, whatever their emotional impact on us, are carefully constructed logical arguments, as intricately engineered as a cathedral or bridge.

To complicate matters further, *another* sort of dualism has existed in music for centuries: on the one hand, the precise creative workings of the composer, planning the succession of pitches and rhythms that we are to hear (analagous to the designing of a suspension bridge or building), and, on the other, the execution of this plan by an interpreter, following instructions and yet adding to them in a way that heightens our sense of music as "live," spontaneous, immediate performance. These two have also been fused together, to such a degree that most of us hardly know exactly *what* we're responding to when we witness a performance of a Brahms symphony. Is it the ordering of notes that Brahms so laboriously wrote down on manuscript paper? Or variations in tempo by one conductor as compared with another, the subtle differences in each performance, the visual "magic" of the massed violinists bowing and leaning, the tympanist bent over his drums, the horn player emptying his spit-valve between solos? The fact is that music has always appealed to many different instincts within each of us, and usually at the same time.

What makes the twentieth-century situation so fascinating is that the two aspects of music—the "rational" (with the composer assuming primary responsibility) and the "sensuous" (the live performance paramount)—have, in effect, split off from each other. Each one has become an independent organism, and each draws upon musical "tradition" in its own way. The two concerns are generally thought of as contradictory, as they usually imply different compositional working methods and appeal to different temperaments; it's fair to assume that a composer embracing either thesis would most likely reject the other. And the differences are easily evident in listening to the music itself. Compare a work ("serial") by Babbitt with one by Penderecki ("textural")—or, from an earlier generation, Webern and Varèse—and you will be presented with value systems that are literally worlds apart. To move from Babbitt–Charles Wuorinen–Charles Dodge–J. K. Randall to John Cage–Alvin Lucier–Daniel Lentz–Gordon Mumma is an even greater aesthetic leap, one that indicates how wide the split can really be.

Yet the two viewpoints, for all their surface differences, are related. The composers who serially "control" their material have expanded the notion of pitch order to cover the ordering of diverse factors–duration, timbre, and the like—in many dimensions, while other composers have turned to noise and "textures" (often improvisatory ones) as alternatives to pitch. Both, then, are proceeding from the same assumption: that the *traditional* use of pitch relationships—for generating tension and movement, for building complex structures, or for dramatic, "expressive" purposes—is no longer interesting to them. In other words, both groups of composers agree (whether they know it or not) that the *primacy* of pitch among the musical elements has ended.

That last sentence may need further explanation. It is hard to conceive of pitch, or any one aspect of music, as being predominant, especially if your musical education consisted of a traditional "appreciation course," in which the various means of articulation (pitch, rhythm, tone color, and the like) were treated as "equal."

The truth is that, for most of the music we know, the elements are *not* equal. The closest they have come to true equality, in fact, may be in today's avant-garde, and future music historians may well consider this the most significant contribution of our century. *Pitch* began to assert overwhelming primacy during the Renaissance, coinciding with the growing dominance of instruments over voices. The development of the complex system of pitch relationships known as the tonal system and the interest in "abstract" instrumental forms (rather than vocal and dance forms) led to the symphonies, sonatas, and quartets of the late eighteenth century, the period of Haydn, Mozart, and Beethoven. In such music, pitch relationships are paramount, and generations of students have "analyzed" works of the standard concert repertory by following the *pitches,* one note after another, C to E flat to D and so on—the succession of pitches (melody), the simultaneous sounding of pitches (chords), and the paths taken by these to arrive at a final goal (the tonality or "key" center of the particular passage or work). Other elements, such as rhythm, tempo, timbre, register, dynamics, and texture, were useful to composers primarily for *articulating pitch;* that is, they bring certain aspects of the note relationships into sharper relief and help to define the tonal ("key") context in which the notes function.

The most important aspect of the tonal system is the power of certain pitch successions and chord successions—the grammar of the system—to generate motion, inexorable movement toward a goal. In doing this, a necessary degree of tension is established between the incomplete or unresolved (dissonance) and its resolution (consonance). As the tonal system evolved to its high point in, some say, the nineteenth century, its cornerstone was dissonance, the force that generates tension and motion. The "direction" taken by the motion—the particular path within given key boundaries—constituted the "form" and also created the arc of dramatic intensity (the "expression," if you wish) that appeals most to the casual listener. In fact, "form" and "expression" can be thought of as virtually synonymous, particularly in nonvocal music where the drama *is* in the unfolding of form.

This developed chiefly as a German-Austrian art, with only token acceptance by French and Italian composers; the latter two continued their own—earlier—tradition of generating form through rhythm, timbre, tempo contrasts, and "theater" (including words and dance), rather than through harmonic tension. If you listen to any nineteenth-century French symphony, for example, you can observe the sonata form (a Germanic development and a natural outgrowth of a particularly dissonant language) being applied in cookbook fashion to another language to which it is really incompatible. Composers of such pieces, like their Italian and English counterparts, were much more in their element when they turned to opera, vocal and choral music, and dances. But non-Germanic music was also pitch- and key-controlled and just as susceptible to a greater and greater degree of dissonance (used for different, less doggedly driving, purposes) by the end of the nineteenth century.

And by that time the particular pitch grammar known as the tonal system, which had dominated European music for some three centuries, had reached its saturation point. There was a loss of faith by composers (if not necessarily listeners) in that power of the system to create tension and thereby to generate convincing "form." The system slowly collapsed during the years preceding World War I, not only in Germany and Austria but throughout Europe. The explorations of Debussy and Satie, for example, represented a French reaction to the decline of traditional tonality; they indicate not only an urge to liberate French music from confining Germanic influences ("music without sauerkraut," as Satie put it) but also a much broader dissatisfaction with the general state of the art. With many different composers seeking different solutions to what was basically the same problem, the first half of our century may be viewed as a series of personal, individual responses to the single question "How does one cope with *pitch* in the face of oversaturated dissonance and weakened tonality?" A number of particular features are worth noting here:

1. *New scale and pitch systems,* including the rediscovery of some old scales as well, motivated by the desire to find alternatives to the major and minor scales that had dictated the grammar of tonality. The centuries-old medieval modes are used as scalar material in works ranging from the Satie *Gymnopédies* to the

Debussy piano *Préludes* and the Vaughan Williams *Fantasia on a Theme by Tallis*. Debussy's use of the whole-tone and pentatonic scales (as, for example, in the orchestral *Nocturnes* or the opera *Pelléas et Mélisande*), Busoni's exhaustive catalogue of artificial scales, and the unusual Hungarian folk scales employed by Bartók in such works as his string quartets—all of these show this concern. At the same time, they all assume the traditional European division of the octave into twelve steps (the notes or pitches with which we're familiar). Alternative divisions of the octave include the use of "quarter tones," or pitch steps one-half the size of traditional ones; in other words, the octave is subdivided into *twenty-four* pitches. Bartók made use of quarter-tone effects, and Charles Ives's *Three Quarter-Tone Piano Pieces* (composed for two pianos, which are tuned a quarter tone apart!) is of particular interest. The American Harry Partch has further subdivided the octave into forty-three tones and created his own instruments (and notational system) for the performance of his highly evocative, atmospheric works.

2. *The expansion of dissonance and conscious avoidance of tonality* as developed primarily by Arnold Schoenberg and his pupils Alban Berg and Anton Webern. These three composers comprise what is sometimes referred to as the "Second Viennese School" of the 1920's and 1930's, which may give you some idea of their importance (since the first "Viennese School" was made up of Haydn, Mozart, and Beethoven). Schoenberg's major achievement lay in the use of pitches only in relation to one another, rather than in hierarchical reference to a focal pitch or "key" center. The dissonant, driving, and often emotionally impassioned aspects of the traditional language are uppermost, and references to tonality (the traditional point of rest) are abandoned, so that much of the music possesses an unparalleled intensity. I don't mean to imply that Schoenberg's music sounds like Webern's or Berg's or that any of the three figures resembles the others. Even a superficial hearing of some representative pieces—Schoenberg's *Fourth String Quartet*, Berg's *Violin Concerto* or *Lyric Suite,* Webern's *Concerto,* Opus 24—would instantly dispel this impression, and confirm the striking individuality of their respective personalities.

There are misleading labels attached to this general area, chief among them being "the emancipation of the dissonance," as though the music were made up *entirely* of dissonances. Dissonance levels are at a maximum, to be sure, but there are still relative states of tension and release, particularly in Berg's work. It may also be unwise to refer to *all* compositions based on these premises as "twelve-tone music." Schoenberg and his pupils did work with all twelve tones of the octave, but others have since applied the same controlling principles to rows or "sets" of any number of notes.

3. *Further reliance on the consonance, with a resulting suspension of "motion,"* is the opposite of Schoenberg's approach and leads to a totally different sense of what constitutes "movement." Forward motion may be reduced to a minimum or might be generated by rhythmic activity—as in Stravinsky's *Le Sacre du printemps* or Carl Orff's *Carmina Burana*—the sounds themselves remaining relatively static. Repeated chords or figurations often lend a physical momentum to passages, but the harmonic drive—dissonance relating to consonance—may not be present. The use of ancient scales and modes noted in 1 above naturally leads to this situation, since it is the grammatical "logic" of the major-minor scale system that produces levels of intensity and these are not offered by the more unusual scales. That is, you may hear rather familiar chords in the Satie *Parade* or Debussy *Hommage à Rameau,* but the succession of these chords—the progression from one to the next—has been disrupted and made "illogical." Similarly, the primitive-sounding scales and limited melodic figurations (a very few notes repeated again and again) of Stravinsky's *Les Noces* are essentially static and hence "consonant," even though they may be biting and discordant.

If this sounds contradictory, I must insist that the term "consonance" be used not as a synonym for "pretty sound," but simply as a point of relative *completion*; it is a sound that does not need to be followed by anything else, perhaps because there is no grammatical context that would dictate what the following sound should be. Of course, some consonances, such as Debussy's unresolved chords, may actually be rather pretty. But Satie's harmony is less so and more austere, while Varèse's brilliant clusters and melodic fragments, as in *Octandre* or *Hyperprism*, are often dense and cutting. In all cases, nonetheless, there is a minimum of tension in the consonance-dissonance equilibrium, the balance having shifted in favor of suspended states rather than inevitable forward pitch motion.

4. *Noise, unusual sonorities, avoidance of pitch as a factor* in one sense, a logical development of 3 above, with "sound" rather than pitch becoming the chosen material. Successions of noises, surprisingly enough, are often consonant; they cancel each other out, and, as with unusual scales, they are related to no particular grammar that would lead us to anticipate "resolutions." Listen to any of the once shocking piano pieces by Henry Cowell—those where clusters of notes are played by fists or arms, such as *The Tides of Manaunaun*, or in which the inner strings are stroked, rubbed, and plucked, such as his notorious *The Banshee*—and you'll find the sonorities no more "dissonant" than the cry of the wind or the rumble of thunder. Some of the sounds may remind you of gongs and bells, and the strong influence of non-Western music is evident in such moments. The Indonesian percussion ensemble, in particular, fascinated not only Cowell but Debussy, who reportedly first came in contact with the gamelan at the Paris Exposition of 1889, and John Cage, whose music for prepared piano (nuts, bolts, screws, pencils, and other items inserted between the strings) converts our most familiar instrument into a miniature percussion band. The *Ionisation* of Varèse and George Antheil's *Ballet mécanique* are perhaps more aggressive, extroverted examples of writing for "noise" instruments, including sirens and airplane propellers. Most of the above examples, by the way, were composed before 1925; the most recent of them, the Cage explorations of the prepared piano, was a product of the 1930's. This is hardly "new" music!

More recent instrumental music, or a good percentage of it, has also attempted to minimize pitch and stress sonority, often by the use of extreme "effects" on various instruments—sliding glissandi, squeals and squeaks, flutter-tonguing on wind and brass instruments, unorthodox bowings for the string players—that bring unheard-of sounds out of conventional violins, flutes, clarinets, and trumpets. Today's choral music often asks the singers to whisper, snap their fingers, cough, breathe heavily, rustle their sheet music, again all in the interests of enlarging the sound palette. Finally, many composers call for specific pitches (and not necessarily noises) but ask the performers to improvise with the pitches, choose the succession of notes, or add their individual lines *ad libitum* to complex ensemble textures. Thus pitch has been ruled out as a structural factor of major importance to the work and becomes instead a relatively unpredictable element, varying from performance to performance.

5. *"Total control" over all aspects of the material* is the logical extension of pitch organization—the method of working with the twelve tones begun by Arnold Schoenberg—now applied to the systematic control of duration, timbre, and whatever else the composer wishes. For example (and this is a crude illustration, to say the least), if I wished to relate *dynamics* to pitch, I could subdivide the dynamic spectrum—from very loudest to very softest—into twelve equidistant levels and then develop a plan whereby the organization of the one aspect of sound (the one "parameter," as some might say) parallels or responds to the organization of the other. Or I could use twelve *durational* values, to create a different sort of correspondence, or a similar organization of any other distinctly controllable element (register, timbre, articulation, to name but a few). All aspects of the musical language have become equal, and yet tightly interdependent. This way of composing is often referred to as "serialism" or "serial" technique. Strongly influenced by Webern and the experiments with rhythm and timbre of Messiaen in France, the movement developed rapidly after World War II primarily through the efforts of Pierre Boulez in Europe and Milton Babbitt in the United States.

These are the most important developments of the first half of this century, all of them, as we will see, eventually making their impact felt upon electronic music. And it is by no means a complete list. I haven't mentioned the significant use of quotations (of other people's music), such as the collages in the Ives *Second Symphony,* Stravinsky's *Pulcinella* parodies, or the work of Henry Brant in distributing sounds "spatially" around and about the performing space. These, too, have their obvious parallels in later electronic compositions.

You might inquire, at this point, why you haven't heard of these tendencies (or pieces, or composers) before or why much of this music had not been heard in concert halls. The simplest answer— which avoids a more complicated one dealing with economics, power politics, musical taste, and the market place—is that much of this work existed in a kind of "underground" and is only tangentially related (if at all) to the "mainstream" of pre–World War II music. The contemporary music that did capture a comparatively wide listening public during that period was strongly tonal, generally discordant rather than dissonant, nationalistic or archaic in its musical sources, and often mislabeled "neoclassical." While this mainstream—Prokofiev, Hindemith, Stravinsky, Shostakovich, Copland, Piston, Harris, and others with commonly related concerns—flourished into the 1940's, the more radical trends were rarely noticed. The year 1945, though, seems to have been the crucial turning point; since that date, neoclassicism has declined as an influence upon younger composers, and the former "underground" has surfaced to a position of commanding importance in the contemporary music scene, practically all of the younger composers working along lines of total control, sonority-texture, chance, collage. A number of factors may be responsible—the death, and subsequent discovery by the young, of Webern in Austria; the death, and subsequent mass popularity, of Bartók in New York; the end of World War II and the virtual explosion of activity among the young European composers—but chief among them must be the advent of the electronic revolution itself. I don't mean electronic music (this was yet to surface with any influence), but the development of the LP record and the mass marketing of wire (followed by tape) recorders.

Paradoxically, then, electronic music not only grew out of the radical tradition, but initially (in the fundamental aspects of recording and transmission) made possible the phenomenal growth of that tradition. Recordings still continue to serve this purpose. One of the chief agents in transforming any musical movement from "underground" to "establishment" must be ready accessibility to many listeners, and this has been provided in a way previously unknown. Not only for experimental music, I should add: The rediscovery and popular acceptance of Vivaldi, Berlioz, Delius, Scarlatti, the sons of Bach, Holst—the list is seemingly infinite—can be traced directly to the marketing of long-playing records. And, for the radical avant-garde, the availability of recordings, mostly tapes, has been crucial. Composers and performers interested in new music are constantly sending each other tapes, exchanging tapes, copying one another's tapes. The accelerated pace at which such information is communicated has meant unprecedented exposure of new music, and to those professionals most likely to propagate the music.

Whatever the causes, it is clear now that the second half of this century is witnessing the triumph and perhaps vindication of musical ideas that are many decades old. This brings me back to the point raised at the beginning of this chapter—that two of these ideas have led directly to electronic concerns. They were, in fact, instrumental in motivating the preliminary tape-studio experiments of the late 1940's and early 1950's. I am referring to the free use of noises, natural sounds, and sonorities of all kinds, and the diametrically opposed (some say) desire for serialized total control over all musical variables along lines hinted at by Messiaen and Webern.

Perhaps these aims need further clarification; try to imagine, then, two hypothetical, but entirely typical, composers practicing their craft in the 1950's. Composer X is a "serialist," concerned with questions of structure and interrelationships of seemingly disparate elements—correspondences of patterns, or "series," involving pitch versus duration, attack versus duration, pitch versus timbre, and the like. In this sense, his work is a logical extension of procedures found in the medieval isorhythmic motets of Machaut, the contrapuntal elaboration of minute fragments by such Renaissance composers as Ockeghem, the precise interlocking pitch networks of Bach. His music also holds with the practice of following material through (anticipating all possibilities, realignments, developments in the initial source, and then provoking these to occur) that characterizes much of European music—certainly German music—from Bach through Webern. He very likely sees his own musical role in precisely this quasi-historical way, as the stylistic heir to the "grand tradition" of Western European music, the last major contributions to which had been made by Schoenberg and Webern.

Composer X's music is, above all, rational, and he probably has little interest in such antirational figures as Cage or Ives. He might describe his music in words similar to these by Milton Babbitt:

> This music employs a tonal vocabulary which is more "efficient" than that of the music of the past, or its derivatives, [making] possible a greatly increased number of pitch simultaneities, successions and relationships. This increase in efficiency necessarily reduces the "redundancy" of the language. [Moreover,] the number of functions associated with each component of the musical event also has been multiplied . . . located in a five-dimensional musical space determined by pitch-class, register, dynamic, duration and timbre. These five components not only together define the single event, but, in the course of a work, the successive values of each component create an individually coherent structure, frequently in parallel with the corresponding structures created by each of the other components.

That is to say, the primacy of pitch among the musical elements no longer exists, and in its place we have an interlocking mesh or "grid" of equal continuities. The continuity of a durational (rhythmic) series, for example, may "reflect" upon or "comment" upon a related continuity of attacks, or perhaps pitches, one series paralleling or mirroring or inverting the other. Again, the precedents for this in the traditional music of the past two centuries should be made clear; composer X's music is ideally the apotheosis of the "working-out" process. It is unusual in that the "development" process has been extended far beyond the domain of pitch, and—as Babbitt states—the possibilities for articulating relationships have become multidimensional.

You may find in listening to the music that the many levels of coherence, often occurring simultaneously, cannot be grasped on any one hearing. The casual listener may conclude, even after a number of hearings, that this sophisticated structure is inaudible. The more "serious" or more experienced listener will be able to discern the larger shapes and most obvious relationships (the "form" in traditional jargon), while any understanding of the work on a deeper level implies not only experience but careful study of the notated score. Many people seem to be infuriated by this, although there's no logical reason why they should be. Composer X's music is, after all, "developmental" in the great tradition, and such music has always been subtle, intricate, and worthy of "study" in the best sense: Beethoven and Brahms surely do not surrender their secrets too easily. The average listener doesn't really "understand" a Beethoven symphony in the way that musicians understand it, and he accepts that fact without taking offense.

What about those who have no access to the score, or who don't read music? This shouldn't present a problem; after all, a piece is meant to be heard as well as seen and may be comprehended on the basis of what is *audible,* on whatever level one can respond to. Some—possibly those who also miss the structural aspects of the Beethoven—will find that, for them, "audibility" stops at the surface level. They will respond, perhaps with great sensitivity and discrimination, to the most obvious characteristics: the succession of registers, timbres, colors, lines, and recognizable patterns. Composer X realizes that many in his audience may listen in this manner, to the "surface," and he has most probably composed a surface that is attractive enough to hold interest. But he would prefer that we go beyond the surface, that we follow the logic of his argument and discover the rationale of his art. In fact, he would prefer that *we be composers,* or at least willing to enter into his medium with a composer's (rather than a listener's) unique concerns and expectations.

What has any of this to do with electronic music? For one thing, composer X writes music that is exceptionally difficult to perform. In serializing attack, register, duration, and the like, he requires his performers to be continually alert; rapid changes— from one octave to another, from a loud dynamic to a soft one, from staccato attack to legato—are constantly taking place. The players must also be absolutely precise—more so than they need be with a traditional piece, in fact—because a missed dynamic or wrong note will misrepresent an entire network of relationships. They must be highly sensitive to nuance and need to acquire great control over degrees of shading and articulation, because they're often called upon to play three distinctly different kinds of staccato, for example, or twelve specified dynamic levels running the gamut from *fff* to *ppp*. Given this degree of difficulty, it's no wonder, then, that performances of composer X's music are relatively few (even considering the growing number of young musicians equipped and willing to play it). Worse yet, those performances that do infrequently occur are inevitably inaccurate, ranging from utter shambles to (at best) excellent approximations of the intent. And this, ironically, in a musical style whose aesthetic rationale demands both perfection in performance *and* repeated hearings for wider comprehension!

Composer X, then, turns to the electronic studio in the 1950's —and today might well turn to the RCA synthesizer or to computer-generated sound—in order to realize an absolutely precise "performance" of a work. Because he realizes it directly on magnetic recording tape, the single medium has enabled him to cope with two problems at once: exactness *and* accessibility. There can now be as many "performances" of the piece as there are playings (and copies) of the tape, and each one is—at last— correct. He probably composes the work, with paper and pen at a desk (that is, in the old-fashioned way), long before he comes to the studio. The medium does *not* compose the work for him, nor does it assist him in the composing process. It has this potential, to be sure, and this aspect of tape technique will be exploited by composer Y (we will meet him in a moment), but composer X is too concerned with his rational decision-making processes, which, for him, are the very substance of his musical being, to delegate these to a machine. For him the studio facilities are best used to realize ideal performances and to document them via permanent recording.

Secondly, composer X, as a conscientious professional, is aware of instrumental limits and the capabilities of his performers. He could hardly compose a string quartet or a flute sonata, for example, without such awareness—the ranges of instruments, which trills are most effective, the best registers for loud dynamic levels, and so on. In this regard the electronic studio offers him another important advantage: It provides a unique, superbly versatile instrument. You might say that this is one instance in which the studio *does* aid composition, or at least influence it, even with a composer such as X, who writes out his score before he turns on the tape recorder. The influence is felt in those moments preceding the act of composition, the period of initial "conception" during which X asks himself, among other questions, "What are the capabilities of my instruments?" For the serialist, concerned with fine degrees of articulation, tape capabilities will suggest new areas that stimulate his compositional thinking—not only can his piece be "performed" as never before, but he can *compose* it as he never would have dared previously. Let's say that he is concerned with various kinds of staccato. In writing a piano piece, he would automatically be limited. Are there *really* four varieties of staccato available to a pianist? Perhaps, and perhaps not, but with tape studio techniques there may be any number of varieties. The flutist playing "live" may have great difficulty in setting many distinct dynamic levels, but these can be calibrated exactly in the studio, to a degree beyond the capabilities of any player. One can electronically "perform," for example, scales, arpeggios, and figurations more rapidly and more cleanly, with every note crystal clear, than any human instrumentalist; a fast-moving melodic line can suddenly change timbre any number of times, at a speed that defies the physical responses of live players. What we have here is no mere collection of parlor tricks, but a usable means for augmenting the composer's vocabulary—making new compositional choices possible by stretching the limits of the "performable."

At this point I should stress that none of the preceding is even remotely connected with "noise" or "sound effects." Composer X's interests are, in one sense, precisely those of Beethoven—pitch, duration, dynamics, and tone color. He wishes to relate them all, to use Babbitt's phrase, with greater "efficiency" and is primarily concerned with their degree of specificity. For this reason he most likely wants to make the sounds themselves, electronically, by using tone generators, controlling pitch, intonation, and timbre as he chooses, and would probably work in the Cologne radio studio of the 1950's (the birthplace of purely "electronic music"), *not* the Paris studio, centered about the use of natural sound sources. The original founders of the Cologne studio based their work on the firm belief that a post-Webern style of total serial control and electronic sound generation were inseparable—the perfect instrument, so to speak, for the new language. Herbert Eimert, the first director of that studio, wrote in the mid-1950's, "electronic material as a musical material completely answers to the conditions of a compositional situation . . . a new way of thought has found a new, transformed musical material." Composers with comparable interests echoed his optimism, and many of them came to work at Cologne. Later on, by the late 1950's, they would be drawn to the RCA synthesizer at Columbia University or to the possibilities of computer programing.

Some readers may wonder how relevant this discussion is to them as *listeners*: It may be interesting to consider the ways in which a particular kind of composer works, but not very helpful (you might say) when a new recording is to be heard. Does all this talk of "control" and "sound generation" have any direct bearing upon the listening experience? I can't prove that it will— each person has to answer that question for himself, on the basis of his own individual hearing—but I can offer a few general comments.

First of all, it's important to realize that *listening* intelligently to any piece of music—Beethoven, Babbitt, Verdi, Stravinsky— involves much more than simple "hearing." We listen not only with our ears, but with our experiences, memories, expectations, and a fine sense of relating all of these factors (whether we are trained musicians or not). To this degree, then, *any* "information" about a composition, or about a composer's working procedures, can be called upon during a performance of that piece; the more relationships our mental equipment can bring to bear upon the sounds of the music, the more complete our listening will be. In addition, it's always useful to have a general notion of the composer's attitude toward his music (or all music), and what he attempts to do in his work. If there is indeed a "message"

—a meaning, perhaps—to music, it is more than likely to be the *composer's*, and this is doubly so in tape composition, where there is no interpretive middleman. Knowing something about composer X's desires and aesthetic aims, then, can hopefully lead to a greater realization of what he wants us to hear.

Secondly, and more specifically, listening to composer X's music is not quite as difficult as it may seem, particularly on a recording over which you have control—that is, in your own living room or listening library. In this case, the material and the medium are ideally suited to each other: You can stop the record at any time, replay passages that really interest (or baffle) you, even listen to the ending before the beginning if you wish. That is, you can treat the work as you might a novel or any lengthy prose work—flipping pages, skimming certain chapters and returning to them later, digesting the whole in small segments. Or you can decide to hear the entire composition (a rough reading), then familiarize yourself with details, and eventually gain a more comprehensive view of the whole. (Don't people do this with Beethoven quartets and Brahms symphonies as well? I suppose that many don't. Much of our supposed problem with new music, particularly the kind composed by X, is that we haven't really learned to cope with the many complexities of the "old" music. Too many of us simply "hear," rather than listen. There may have been some excuse for this in the days of exclusively live performance, but the phonograph record has made the *study* of music available to all of us.)

This kind of approach does no disservice to composer X's work: On the contrary, it reaffirms his position that music is a highly integrated network of structures, a fixed "object" to be viewed many ways and returned to many times. And this is especially true with regard to his electronic compositions for magnetic tape (transferred to your disc recording), in that he has provided you with something exact, precise, as totally controlled as he can make it, permanent, and unchangeable. In by-passing the traditional "performer" and using the recording as his sole vehicle, composer X has not only projected his particular aesthetic in the most efficient way possible but also has enabled the listener to deal with it as never before.

Composer Y, on the other hand, has entirely different concerns. To begin with, he cares little about "control" in the serial sense, preferring instead to operate intuitively in determining form and structure. "Form" itself—at least the concept of predetermined boundaries, common to tonal and serial music—may be considered obsolete. Barney Childs, for example, proposes the idea of *open* form, "the self-generated unique form created by any series of sounds in time, or, for that matter, any series of human activities or relationships worked out in limited time and space." For other composers, the more traditional long-range plans of organization (variation, contrasting successive sections, repetition of material, a single gesture that repeats or undergoes subtle changes, and so on) are sufficient; they all implicitly reject the serialists' assumption of "form" as the working out of a fixed number of possibilities. Composer Y probably conceives of a piece in basically *dramatic* terms, not as the grammatical or structural outgrowth of a process.

There may be more than a rejection of serialism involved here. In fact, it's likely that composer Y and his colleagues have chosen to reject many aspects of the *entire* Western "concert music" tradition, substituting for these a variety of ideas drawn from ancient music, non-Western music, primitive music, popular/folk music. This makes it rather difficult to construct a "typically" representative composer Y to offset our fictitious Mr. X. Where X is single-minded and consistent in his beliefs, Y is thoroughly eclectic, altering his position from piece to piece or even within a single work. Listening to composer Y's music might reveal any of the following features, although probably not all of them for any one composer or in any single work:

1. A general disregard for pitch choices, this being left up to the performer's improvisation within set boundaries of contour and register. It is assumed that the actual pitches played will vary from one performance to another. Or there may be a preference for percussion and "noise" instruments (sirens, pistols, bowls) rather than those of exact pitch.

2. There may be a static, "motionless" sense—freely floating sonorities or endlessly repeated patterns—rather than the driving,

urgent thrust of "form" in the tonal-serial tradition. Relationships of the developmental sort are minimized or eliminated.

3. Attentive, alert listening (implicit in much of the concert repertory and demanded for comprehension of serial music) is often discouraged. For example, works based on the simplest of materials may last for an entire evening, and the audience may be invited to walk about, read, sleep, leave the hall, and return later. Repeated hearings of the same work, also encouraged within the concert tradition, are in many cases impossible, due to the improvisatory and theatrical nature of the music. You might hear a second performance of what purports to be the same composition—the same title and composer's name—but it will often turn out to be an entirely different piece. The composer's objective, then, is a unique, immediate sensory experience rather than a fixed, permanent object.

4. Distinctly "theatrical" tendencies abound. These may involve the performers in speaking and moving about, making silent visual gestures; the use of lighting and film; musical quotations of familiar passages; spatial distribution of the performers for other than acoustic reasons. In short, the composer is stressing music's function within the tradition of ritual and magic, rather than its logical, grammatical properties.

5. Many composers are fascinated by "chance" as a process by which a composition comes into being. Or for the word "composition" you could substitute performance, or activity, some composers considering all of these equivalent. The choice of instruments is often unspecified, and the musical notation itself may encourage various categories of "accidents": those of succession of events, of simultaneous juxtapositions, of rhythmic interaction. I should note here two sharp contrasts with the serial aesthetic. First of all, the notion of "precision" versus "error" is minimized. Numerous performance challenges do exist, to be sure, particularly in the area of imaginative game-playing and ensemble awareness, but interpretations are not limited by any fixed notion of accuracy. Each performance exists as given fact, an independent organism; trying to criticize a performance of John Cage's *Variations II* or Morton Feldman's *Durations* is very much like trying to assess the perfection of a tree or rock. To paraphrase Cage,

"error" is no more than failure to adjust one's preconceptions to an actuality. Secondly, the serialists' implicit wish that the ideal listener partake (however vicariously) in the process of *composition* is replaced by a demand that all parties concerned—including composer and performer—ideally respond as *listeners*. We should all accept a performance, even the second performance of the same work, as a journey into unknown regions, meeting it each time with fresh expectations. Cage, in discussing his own development, remarks, "what has happened is that I have become a listener and the music has become something to hear."

In their differing ways, these characteristics share much in common. They all reveal, for example, a tendency to concentrate upon unusual timbres, even "noises," perhaps better to free the music from traditional associations. *Sound* itself predominates the physical, tangible substance, relished for its own sake. It is important here not for its associational properties—this would be the traditional way of dealing with it—but for its own sensory, acoustical, and theatrical impact. Varèse hinted at this when he referred to music as "the corporealization of the intelligence that is in sounds" and likened his own accretions of sound masses to the formation of crystals. Barney Childs suggests psychological and theatrical implications when he writes, "If you hear an E-flat as the sixth note in the countersubject of a particular fugue that's one thing; if you hear only E-flat for five minutes, played by a particular instrument, then you can learn something about it, and about sound, and about yourself."

It takes no great leap of the imagination to realize that composers thus preoccupied with sounds *per se* would take to the new electronic medium with obvious delight. Our hypothetical composer Y of the 1950's would find the tape studio an ideal laboratory for all sorts of explorations. Unlike composer X, he would probably prefer to work with the manipulation and transformation of existing "natural" sounds—including those produced by ordinary instruments—rather than the electronic generation of pure tones. It's safe to assume, then, that he would be found working at the Paris studio associated with *musique concrète* (using as typical sound sources thunder, railway engines, water, footsteps), or perhaps following the direction set by Otto Luening and Vladimir Ussachevsky at Columbia University (stressing instrumental sources such as the flute or piano). In any event, the stylistic aims of Stockhausen at Cologne or Babbitt's use of the RCA synthesizer would hardly interest him.

This distinction between "tape" composition and "electronic" composition (or similarly partisan labels) was quite real in the 1950's, and often the subject of bitter polemic on both sides, underscoring the basic aesthetic and procedural differences between composers X and Y. Even though the intense rivalry between factions has all but disappeared—most composers now mix electronic and natural sources at will, and today's music is so eclectic that the ideological polarities of the 1950's are unthinkable—these fundamental differences still exist. Our first example, composer X, would probably find natural sonorities unsuited to his purposes. His ideas are for the most part preplanned, and, as far as sounds are concerned, he prefers to begin with *nothing*, a blank canvas, a silent reel of blank tape. He synthetically *creates* the sounds he wants and predetermines every facet of these sounds, since he "builds" them himself according to his own specifications. In doing so he must study the components of sound as a physicist might study them, reducing every aspect to its logical facts and processes. He delights in the possibility of controlling and managing all variables, this being his primary reason for using electronic means in the first place. "Electronic" composition suits his musical personality.

But not necessarily so with composer Y, most likely a "tape" composer. For him the essence of sound—of music—lies in its mysterious, "magical" qualities. Whereas his opposite number attempts to take the mystery out of sounds, composer Y may use the studio to explore the mysterious, irrational element even further. (I don't mean by this the simpleminded association of electronic music and science-fiction and horror movies. Far from it!) His great joy is in taking already *existing sounds,* often "found" natural and industrial sounds that are acoustically complex and imprecise to begin with, and then making them more so. He isolates sounds within sounds, lowers or raises the register of a sound until it takes on strange new qualities, attaches the head of one sound to the tail of the other by tape-splicing, combines sources—initially unrelated ones, perhaps—to create fascinating juxtapositions. Many of these effects are the result of spontaneous discoveries made in the studio, often accidentally. In this instance, tape technique and composing technique are one and the same. The composer works directly with sounds and *then* discovers what can be done with them. He works intuitively, he improvises, he is (as Cage suggests) a "listener." Later on, he may choose the material he wishes to preserve and edits his tape accordingly. Depending upon his fondness for chance procedures, he may let the medium guide him, following its lead rather than controlling it, creating situations where unplanned events will occur. The point is that—as Varèse stated when asked to compare himself with Babbitt—composer Y is physically *in* the sound, immersed in it, not standing "over" it and "dealing" with it.

So we have our fabricated composers X and Y, who are, of course, no more than stereotypes. As fictions of the 1950's they come close to reality, but in our eclectic, less structured 1970's they may represent, rather, the two sides of any individual composer. Composers of today have a little bit of X and Y in them; at times they're concerned with control, at times with "theater" and "magic," often choosing electronically synthesized *or* natural sounds to work with as the occasion demands. The studio, as we've seen, is equally adaptable to both. Moreover, in introducing X and Y, I don't wish to imply that issues of "control" versus "chance" are the only ones that have influenced electronic developments. There are many other motivating factors that lead composers to the medium and any number of ways of composing with electronics (including the most traditional and tonal, from the synthesized arrangements of Bach and Mozart to "Bicycle Built for Two" "sung" by a computer). Ivesian collage-quotation pieces exist in great number, and the retuning of the octave into quarter tones and microtones is of major interest to many electronic composers. But, again, none of these concerns came into being with electronic music: They have been part of the contemporary scene for a long time.

Longer than we may suspect, in fact: Busoni's writings about the future of music, electricity, and new sound resources were published in 1907; the Italian "futurists" were investigating the systematic use of noises before World War I, and in 1936 Varèse accurately predicted the course his music would take "when new instruments will allow me to write music as I conceive it." In 1937 John Cage announced:

> Wherever we are, what we hear is mostly noise. When we ignore it, it disturbs us. When we listen to it, we find it fascinating. The sound of a truck at fifty miles per hour. Static between the stations. Rain. We want to capture and control these sounds. . . . [We could] compose and perform a quartet for explosive motor, wind, heartbeat, and landslide.

Newness, in other words, is not really an issue in discussing electronic (or any other recent) music. The rationale—in fact, the unswerving logical development—behind today's music would immediately become apparent if audiences would only acquaint themselves with the music composed before 1945. As we abandon our two imaginary composers and begin to deal with real figures and actual works, I must stress this last point: Familiarize yourself, by listening and reading, with as much of the earlier twentieth century as possible. This will be especially valuable if today's music strikes you as incomprehensible, ugly, outrageous, or "strange." A recent piece by George Crumb or Witold Lutoslawski, for example, will make infinitely more sense if you know the Debussy and Bartók and Webern and others from which it draws precedents. All composers learn from one another; Wuorinen has learned as much from Webern as, say, Brahms learned from Beethoven or Schumann from Bach.

Much of the listener's problem lies not in the evolution of musical language, which is inevitable and unceasing, but in the swiftness of the rate of change. Thanks to the ready availability of scores and recordings all over the world, the learning-teaching process among composers has been greatly accelerated and is continuing at an increasing pace all the time. Composer Z's music, created in New York, can be heard and studied almost immediately in Tokyo, Stockholm, Paris, Iowa City, Berkeley, London, any place where there are other composers listening and reading. Consequently, changes that once took a century to occur now whiz by in a decade or less. There are roughly one hundred years between Bach and Schumann, twenty between Brahms and Webern, about ten between Webern and Babbitt, and the rate of change continues to grow; an entire stylistic evolution has sped past the majority of listeners.

"Evolution," by the way, does not imply "improvement," any more than we would consider the style of Brahms to be a higher stage than Bach's (or the world we live in necessarily a "better" environment than the one of Bach's time). Music does change, though, as any language changes—we don't need to be convinced that its creators are urging it forever forward, perhaps more enthusiastically than some of us would wish. What is most interesting is that composers also look *backward*. In tracing Crumb's precedents to Debussy and Webern, we would find that the latter two, in turn, had resurrected techniques and aesthetic principles from the medieval and Renaissance worlds. The past never really vanishes, but reappears stated in present terms, to be further recycled into the future—the ecology of art. Perhaps this view of a perpetual continuum will calm even those most apprehensive about our musical future.

3. Technical Precedents: The Classic Studio and the RCA Synthesizer

We have seen that musical precedents for today's avant-garde are abundant, in some instances extending back for more than a half-century. Surprisingly enough, technological precedents are also numerous, particularly if we accept the chronology offered by Otto Luening in his provocative essay "An Unfinished History of Electronic Music." Luening traces electronic developments of the recent past and also refers to our more distant forerunners, reminding us that mechanical instruments, speaking machines, and composing machines were known to Haydn and Mozart. He notes that player pianos and cylinder phonographs were first patented more than a century ago and discusses the acoustic experiments of Pythagoras and other ancients. In an uncanny reference, he even quotes a utopian passage on the music of "the new Atlantis," written by Francis Bacon in 1627, which sounds exactly like a description of a modern synthesizer! Luening's survey certainly dispels the notion that music by machine was conceived only yesterday, and even his most debatable entries are legitimately used to underscore this point. The many isolated precedents and sources, scattered about in time and place, force us to admit that there is no single "beginning," no *one* event or year or personality about which we could flatly claim, "It started here."

But, since I must choose a convenient point of departure, an admittedly arbitrary one, the year 1906 will do quite well. It was in this year that Lee De Forest invented the vacuum tube, and in 1906 Thaddeus Cahill demonstrated his new electric keyboard instrument in Holyoke, Massachusetts. Answering to the names of Dynamophone or Telharmonium, the invention used a group of dynamos run by alternating current, weighed 200 tons, and transmitted its music over telephone wires. The great European composer-pianist Ferruccio Busoni, who had read of Cahill's experiments, was moved to write at length about the potential of new music-making machines in his 1907 "Sketch of a New Aesthetic of Music." As with many of Busoni's other comments (such as his proposed artificial scales, the further subdivision of the octave, and a "neoclassic" aesthetic to offset the excesses of nineteenth-century Romanticism), his words on electrical instruments were to prove remarkably prophetic.

Cahill's work led rather quickly, in fact, to the invention of diverse electrical instruments, most notably in France and Germany. Each of these instruments had distinctive characteristics, some with keyboards tuned to the twelve-note octave, others with the potential for microtuning and sweeping glissandi. Similarly, some explored novel timbres, while others aimed at an imitation pipe-organ quality. All were developed for live performance in concert and were generally used in ensembles combined with more traditional instruments. The Theremin, introduced in the early 1920's, is perhaps the best known of these early instruments. It was performed by waving one's hands over a small box and along its attached antenna, one hand controlling pitch and the other regulating volume, thus offering a sweeping scale of possibilities rather than fixed "keyboard" degrees. A keyboard instrument known as the Ondes Martenot, also invented during the 1920's, was used in compositions by Milhaud, Honegger, Messiaen, Varèse, and Jolivet. Still another product of that decade, the Trautonium, was developed in Berlin; Hindemith and Richard Strauss were among the composers writing music for it.

An altogether different interest, concerned with means of composing rather than with live performance instruments, gained momentum during this period. By 1930 Hindemith and Ernst Toch were experimenting with the distortion of sounds and mixing of patterns on variable-speed phonographs. A number of artists at the Bauhaus were using phonograph records as "sources," altering sounds by playing the records backward and scratching into the grooves of the discs; the Bauhaus also produced experiments in the conversion of visual patterns into audible ones by using techniques developed for motion-picture sound tracks. (This has since been expanded into a highly sophisticated art by the Canadian film-maker Norman McLaren, who has created the sound for his films by scratching, painting, drawing, and cutting directly on the sound-track portion of the film itself.) In the 1930's John Cage began to produce his first works for ensembles of radios and phonographs. His *Imaginary Landscape No. 1,* for example, uses records and live instruments, the sounds to be mixed in a control booth and subsequently heard as a broadcast or recording.

These experiments in composing with electronic materials are truly impressive as pioneer efforts, especially when you realize that tape recording and the ease of tape manipulation were not known in the 1930's. Composers working during this period —in fact, until the end of World War II—had to cope with the cumbersome, relatively intractable medium of the phonograph disc recording or the "live" (and thus uncontrollable) medium of radio. What they did within these limitations is still admirable for its ingenuity.

In the late 1940's, as Europe emerged from the war with a renewal of energy in the creative arts, these earlier tentative explorations began to take on some significance. Shortly after the end of the war, Pierre Schaeffer, a Parisian engineer, made phonograph recordings of noises and musical sounds and developed these into compositions using distortion and montage. As I've noted earlier, the use of noise as a primary sound source for music is nothing new. Cage had spoken eloquently on this subject in the mid-1930's, and Luigi Russolo, a leader of the Italian futurist movement, had written about a new music of noise as early as 1913. Russolo's writings are particularly detailed, listing six categories of noises:

1. bangs, thunderclaps, explosions . . .
2. whistles, hisses, snorts . . .
3. whispers, murmurs, rustling, gurgling . . .

4. screams, buzzes, crackling, sounds produced by friction . . .
5. sounds produced by striking metal, wood, stone . . .
6. animal and human cries—roars, groans, sobs, laughter, etc. . . .

The futurists produced a number of concerts using these sounds, followed in later decades by works we've already mentioned (by Varèse, Antheil, Milhaud, and others) using such radical percussion as sirens and airplane propellers. These had been heard in Paris some twenty years before Schaeffer's experiments; moreover, the experiments of the 1930's in phonograph distortion were also known to him. Building upon these earlier models —and freely acknowledging his musical debts—Schaeffer presented a *Concert of Noises* over the French Radio in 1948. The program stimulated a great deal of interest in this comparatively unknown area, and a number of others joined Schaeffer in his work, most prominently the composer Pierre Henry. Shortly afterward, the Radiodiffusion Française installed and equipped a special studio for the newly formed group.

Their activity was named *musique concrète,* to denote its preference for "concrete" sound sources (natural environmental sounds) and the unique compositional process of working "concretely" with sonic material rather than "abstractly" via written symbols and interpretive performance. The commercial availability of magnetic tape-recording equipment shortly after 1950, offering the infinitely greater flexibility of that medium (as opposed to phonograph disc), was the movement's real catalyst. It facilitated the work of Schaeffer's group even further, and, by 1953, when the Schaeffer-Henry opera *Orpheus* was performed at the Donaueschingen Festival in Germany before a scandalized, outraged audience, examples of *musique concrète* had been heard in most of the European musical capitals. The new music had also reached the United States, in a series of presentations at the Berkshire Music Center in Tanglewood, Massachusetts.

What Schaeffer and Henry had done was basically simple in concept and straightforward in execution, especially after tape had replaced the more tedious disc procedures. The techniques of sound manipulation found in *musique concrète* draw upon the known facts of acoustics and recording characteristics; many of these techniques, in fact, are by now well known to tape-recording hobbyists and high-fidelity enthusiasts. A brief outline of these procedures would include the following:

1. Any alteration in the *speed of playback* of recorded material will alter the material. If your playback speed is slower than the original recording (a 78 rpm disc played at 45 rpm, or a 15 ips [inch per second] tape played at 7½ ips), the sound will be lower in register and slower in durations. The timbre is also considerably altered. The reverse of this is equally true: Playback of material at a faster speed raises the pitches and shortens durations, again with striking timbral changes.

2. If you play a sound *backward,* its characteristics are heard in reverse order. For example, a piano tone begins percussively, when the hammer strikes the string, and is at its loudest at the moment of striking, then faded away to silence. A recorded piano tone played backward emerges from silence, in a sudden crescendo, culminating in a surprising percussive noise.

3. It's possible (and easy, with tape splicing) to "isolate" any portion of a given sound—for example, the percussive attack of the piano tone—so that it becomes a sound object in itself. Or the isolated portion can be attached to another sound, another simple job of tape-editing, so that perhaps the piano attack-sound is affixed to an oboe note or footstep or squeaky door or violin. In this way the original sources, whatever they were, can be totally obscured, and new hybrid timbres can be created from familiar materials.

4. The original sound source (or its isolated portion, or its "wrong-speed" variant, or what have you) can be altered by adding reverberation, echo effects, filtering the sound and thus eliminating a portion of its frequencies, superimposing other sounds upon it.

5. A fairly common device is the creation of *ostinato* (repeating) patterns. This can be done by scratching into the grooves of a disc—who can forget the endlessly repeating material of a broken record?—or by splicing a portion of tape into a closed loop that repeats *ad infinitum* if you wish. By changing the tape playback speed, you can have the loop

going at a different tempo, but it will still be constantly repeating.

6. Other patterns—melodic lines, if you choose—are made
by splicing tape fragments (each containing a sound or sounds)
to each other. The rhythms of these patterns can be controlled,
if you remember that tape *length equals duration* of sound, at
the given speed of your tape playback. That is, if your tape is to
run at 7½ inches per second (ips), 7½ inches of recording
tape *is* one second's worth of duration. When such durations
are added, one to the next, rhythms are the inevitable result.
Also bear in mind that *blank* tape represents *silence;* if you have
a continuous sound of, say, ten seconds' duration (or 75 inches
of tape at 7½ ips), you could, by splicing and editing, intersperse
blank tape at different moments and convert your continuous
note into a series of repeated notes.

This is only a partial listing, to say the least. I haven't taken
into account the effects obtained by regulating volume controls,
and the fading in and out of dynamics (often used with loop
ostinato patterns, gradually bringing them into the foreground
of a texture and then slowly fading them out again). The stereophonic allocation of the musical material to various loud-speakers
is of vital importance to many composers, both for structural
reasons (to highlight contrasts and other relationships) and
acoustic ones (the sensory impact can be overwhelming). And
I have only hinted at the possibility of combining various layers
of sound onto one tape. Mixing, building up multiple-track
effects on one tape recorder, or using a number of tape recorders
for copying, rerecording, and adding material: All of these are
useful, relatively simple techniques for piling sounds upon each
other. Whichever method is used, some form of control over
simultaneous levels of activity and the mixing of timbres is
essential.

Recordings of the early *musique concrète* works are available,
and one series of discs entitled *Panorama of Musique Concrète*
—released by London Records under the sponsorship of the
UNESCO International Music Council—is well worth hunting
for. It includes a sampling of the earliest works, such as the

Railway Study of 1948, plus two important compositions of the
1950's. The *Symphonie pour un homme seul,* produced in 1949–
50, was originally intended as a multimovement exploration of
human noises, those sounds (breathing, whistling, shouting, humming) that can be made without external aids. As work on the
piece progressed, the composers added instrumental sounds and
developed a fascinating interplay between the "purely" human
and the instrumental and percussion sources, including in this
last category such "human percussion" as footsteps and claps.
Employing repeated-loop patterns much of the time, the *Symphonie* deals in amusingly incongruous juxtapositions: humming
voice against piano, rapid word patterns alternating with distorted
orchestral phrases, fragmentation of material (such as the word
absolument) into cells of varying durations. It is essentially a
humorous piece, light and buoyant, with definite ties to the
French tradition of Satie, Milhaud, and Poulenc and an irrev-
erence that is still fresh.

The *Veil of Orpheus* by Pierre Henry, drawn from the opera
that caused such a stir in 1953 at Donaueschingen, is a much
more dramatic conception—often rather grim, in fact, in its
stark contrasts of timbre. Spoken voice, chorus, słowly sweeping
glissandi (particularly the opening struck gong or cymbal) and
the use of speed changes are all highly effective. Reverberation
is used frequently and enhances the often brilliant treatment
of instrumental sources, particularly that of the harpsichord.

Parallel developments were also taking place in Germany during
this period. The revival of the twelve-tone technique, after its
total suppression during the war years, led to study groups,
seminars, festivals, and institutes designed to build up lines of
communication among the younger composers. We've noted one
such annual event, in passing: the Donaueschingen Festival. Even
more important, perhaps the strongest influences on European
composers after World War II were the International Summer
Courses held at Darmstadt. Here the works of Webern were
studied; extensions of twelve-tone procedures into those of "total"
serialism were considered; Stockhausen, Boulez, the elderly
Varèse, and others took part in lectures and demonstrations.
(Composers from many nations still continue to meet at Darmstadt,

and performances and lectures there remain an important force, although the summer festival no longer controls and dictates European "fashion" to the degree of former years. The festival at Donaueschingen continues as well but, again, without its former, often scandalous, impact.)

A number of studies in electronic tone generation, control, and application to music were made at the Bonn University Institute of Phonetics shortly after the war, and these led to a series of lectures at Darmstadt in 1950. Interest was immediate, and a number of composers began to investigate the possibilities of electronic sound production. They demonstrated their work at Darmstadt in 1951; a program of music and discussion about the new medium was broadcast over the Cologne Radio later that year, and shortly afterward an electronic music studio was formally installed at Cologne.

Activity at the Cologne Radio studio centered about the application of *concrète* techniques to the manipulation of *electronically* generated sound. The source material for composition was not drawn from the natural or instrumental environment. That would be difficult to work with in controlled, serialized fashion, and in any case pure pitches (not noises) were desired by the Cologne composers. They found their sources in sounds produced by audio generators—that is, produced electronically—and directed their energies to controlling variables of the sound (pitch, duration, dynamics, timbre) with the utmost precision. Generators produce periodic, regular, and consistent "vibrations" (waves), which, in a particular range, are audible as pitches. The waves may have a variety of forms (each of which has a distinctive shape when seen on an oscilloscope), and each waveform corresponds to a distinctive timbre or sound quality. That is, the pitch middle C will have one timbre when produced as a sine wave and a distinctly different timbre as a sawtooth wave —very much as the middle C would sound if played on a flute, then a violin, then a trumpet, and so forth. The pitch itself, middle C (irrespective of timbre), is simply the frequency of the wave—its speed.

These principles apply to musical instruments as well as electronic generators. When members of an orchestra tune to the oboe's note A, that A is in the vicinity of 440 cycles per second (frequency), usually referred to as "A 440." The special quality of the oboe's sound (its timbre) reflects, among other factors, its own characteristic waveform, which in turn represents the specific "overtone" content of that sound. If you are unfamiliar with the phenomenon of the overtone series (or "harmonic series," as it may be called), I can only note here that a vibrating sound-producing body—a violin string or column of air, for example—vibrates not only as a complete entity (the entire length of the string) but in halves, and in thirds, and so on and on, setting up a host of internally related subfrequencies. Each of these "overtones" or "harmonics" is increasingly higher in frequency (and in pitch) than the fundamental, original tone, since frequency of vibration increases as the vibrating unit becomes smaller. Each instrumental timbre is the result of a particular overtone content—some harmonics being stressed, others being suppressed—and the unique overtone content of the flute tone would hardly resemble that of, say, the xylophone or the cello. The waveforms of these tones, if observed on the oscilloscope, would certainly look different as well.

While our traditional instruments make very complex waveforms, electronic tone generators make rather simple ones: Visually, they are highly regular patterns—the sawtooth wave, for example, containing all possible harmonics, and the square wave only odd-numbered harmonics. The sine wave may be thought of as "purest" of all, perhaps, as it contains no harmonics. Composers at the Cologne electronic studio worked almost exclusively with sine tones for a number of years, for reasons that have something to do with aesthetics and philosophy (the sine tone as the ultimate building block, the "atom" of music) and a good deal more to do with practicality, in that all other timbres can be constructed from the simultaneous mixing of various sine waves.

The first director of the Cologne studio, Herbert Eimert, and his colleague Karlheinz Stockhausen produced a few sine-generated compositions by 1953 and 1954. These were presented at various festivals and then broadcast throughout Europe, attracting the interest of a great many composers. A number of these earliest works were recorded by Deutsche Grammophon, and I would recommend listening to Stockhausen's *Studie I* and *Studie II*. They are of great interest as historical documents, if not particularly stimulating listening. The prevalence of sine-wave sounds is often rather bland, especially if you come upon this after the sonic variety of *musique concrète*. On the other hand, pitch generation and control are the real points at issue here, not "sound," and in perfecting the tools and techniques for control these pieces represent a real milestone.

It was also at the Cologne studio that the term *elektronische musik* began to come into widespread use. "Electronic music" now means practically anything we want it to mean; over the past twenty years, it has been applied to a vast area of the musical scene. The term was much more restricted in its meaning then, connoting above all the use of electronic rather than "concrete" sound sources. This was the major point of distinction between the works produced at Cologne and those at the rival French studio; the difference in terminology also alluded symbolically to the more important aesthetic differences. But the distinctions, however strongly held, were short-lived. From the outset, the Cologne and Paris studios shared the same information on tape-manipulating devices, and, whatever their sound sources, the identical processes of editing, filtering, mixing, loop-making, and the like went on in both places. Pierre Henry was working with strictly controlled durations at the Paris studio by the mid-1950's, and the Cologne composers quickly recognized the need for expanding their sound sources beyond the aesthetically pure sine waveform. Stockhausen in particular made increasing use of other waveforms (such as the square wave and sawtooth wave), each with its own harmonic series and unique timbre, as well as the sound called "white noise," containing all frequencies within a given band. (Unfortunately, sounds like these simply cannot be described in a book. I can offer poor approximations, by saying that the sine tone vaguely resembles, to my ears, the sound of a flute or recorder, the square wave that of an oboe, and white noise the "shhh" of your radio dial between stations. It would be best to hear the sounds yourself on discs. Various synthesizer manufacturers have put out demonstration records, or, if these are unavailable, the *Nonesuch Guide to Electronic Music* has recorded examples of waveforms.) Even more significantly, the debate over proper source material had been resolved; both Ernst Křenek and Stockhausen, working at Cologne, were combining electronic and "natural" sounds by 1956.

Stockhausen's *Gesang der Jünglinge,* produced in that year, is a remarkable sonic experience even in the two-channel stereo version made for the phonograph. Deutsche Grammophon's recording is, in essence, a "reduction" of the original presentation on five channels and five groups of loud-speakers. Using sung and spoken vocal sounds plus electronic sources, it moves easily between areas of clarity and complexity, comprehensible words and montages of noise, shifting of direction (as the patterns wander and drift across the loud-speakers), and clearly defined antiphony. The voice of one boy is transformed, multiplied, bounced across speakers, and enveloped in a fabric that approaches the "symphonic."

The successful work done in Paris and Cologne received wide publicity, and many composers came to work at one or the other of the two studios. Messiaen, Boulez, and Jolivet came to work at the Radiodiffusion Française studios shortly after the facilities were opened; within a few years Iannis Xenakis and Varèse had visited there as well. Luciano Berio, Henri Pousseur, and Boulez were among the large number of composers working at Cologne, Berio later cofounding (with Bruno Maderna) a similar Italian studio under the sponsorship of the Milan Radio. By the mid-1950's, in fact, a great many studios had been set up throughout Europe, most of these in collaboration with state radio networks. (As we will see, the situation is quite different in the United States, where universities have assumed the primary sponsorship of electronic music facilities.)

The RAI (Radiotelevisione Italiana) Studio di Fonologia Musicale at Milan, directed by Berio and Maderna, was among the most active of these regional centers. In keeping with the changing times, composers at Milan were less doctrinaire about adhering to neat stylistic categories. Questions of "concrete" versus "electronic," or "control" versus "chance," were regarded as individual preferences to be arrived at as situations dictated —perhaps even varying from piece to piece within one composer's output—rather than as ideological absolutes. In the year 1958, for example, the Milan studio was midwife to not only Berio's *Omaggio a Joyce* (sound source primarily the human voice) but also Pousseur's *Scambi* (created exclusively from electronic white noise) and Cage's *Fontana Mix* (a random collage of a little of everything). The lyrical, surrealistic *Omaggio* and the more ascetically "patterned" *Scambi* can be heard on a two-record set produced by Mercury, also containing examples from Paris and Cologne by Kagel, Xenakis, Eimert, and others. The Cage *Fontana Mix,* a delightfully mixed bag of instrumental fragments, assorted noises, and odd juxtapositions, is available in two recorded versions: one on Turnabout; the other, combined with soprano Cathy Berberian's voice and entitled *Aria with Fontana Mix,* on Mainstream. A comparison of all these pieces should indicate the diversity of styles at the Milan studio. But, on a wider level, the range of activity reflects the greater freedom prevailing throughout Europe as the decade of the 1950's came to a close.

Not all of the European developments were "avant-garde" in style, and I should note the more conservative approach to electronics that had been developing in the Netherlands. The most important figure in this regard is the Dutch composer Henk Badings, who brought his own strongly neoclassical preferences to the studio medium. Badings's music, composed much of the time with purely electronic sources at the Philips Laboratory in Eindhoven, is solidly tonal in the dissonant style of the 1930's, with regular metric pulse and recurring melodic motives. You may ask why such a "conservative" composer bothers to work within the electronic medium at all. In retrospect, it seems that he was attracted not by any new approach to materials or procedures but by the availability of a vastly enhanced palette of tone colors. Electronic oscillators become for Badings the instruments of a unique "orchestra," an ensemble that continues to perform more or less traditional music. In his *Capriccio for Violin and Two Sound-Tracks* the effect is that of a brilliant nineteenth-century concerto "performed" by a twenty-first century group of players; this work, incidentally, is one of the first (1952) to combine live performer and taped accompaniment. The *Capriccio* can be heard on a Limelight disc that also contains Badings's *Evolutions* and *Genese*. The latter two pieces are similarly linked to the "mainstream," as witnessed by the jazz passages of *Evolutions*—not the use of prerecorded jazz fragmented and aurally transformed, as with Henry and Schaeffer, but simply jazz itself realized by electronic tone generators. (This kind of electronic music is no more and no less legitimate than any other, and there have been numerous examples besides Badings's, from Milhaud's work in the Paris studio to the *Switched-on Bach* of our own time.)

The Philips studio is also important in this narrative (apart from any Dutch works under its sponsorship) because of its connection with the *Poème électronique* of Edgard Varèse. Commissioned for presentation at the Philips Pavilion at the 1958 World's Fair in Brussels, the *Poème* is already regarded as a "classic" of the medium. It is perhaps the only important work to emerge from the *musique concrète* movement, although, ironically, Varèse refused to apply that term to his own compositions, preferring rather "organized sound."

Varèse probably deserves a chapter of this volume all to himself, since it is his career, more than any other, that foreshadows much of the electronic movement. His works of the 1920's and 1930's—such as the *Octandre* of 1924 with its brilliant interplay of sonorities, or the 1931 *Ionisation* for thirteen percussionists—seem almost prophetic; the later *Ecuatorial* does in fact make use of live electronics in performance. Equally fascinating are Varèse's lectures and writings, in which he predicts "new instruments" that will by-pass the restrictions of the more conventional ones. In this regard he echoes the earlier desires of his teacher Busoni.

By 1950 the "new instrument" came into being, in the form of the Radiodiffusion Française studio in Paris, and Schaeffer invited Varèse to work there. Encouraged further by André Malraux, Varèse finally came to Paris in 1954 and produced *Déserts,* a work combining live instrumental performance and *musique concrète,* later that year. The power of *Déserts* is unmistakable; the alternation of taped material with the instrumental sound masses, violently thrusting and piling into great blocks of sonority, add a new dimension to Varèse's own unique sound world. The *Poème électronique* was subsequently commissioned by Philips, for performance at Le Corbusier's Philips Pavilion at the 1958 Brussels World's Fair.

The *Poème* is entirely on tape and designed to be transmitted over 400 loud-speakers ringing the Pavilion's interior. "Projected" may be a better word; surely the directional angles, sweeps, and trajectories have a more explicit compositional purpose than mere "transmission" would suggest. The music grew out of direct collaboration with Le Corbusier and was meant for that specific performance site. Sound placement was also conceived as analagous to the simultaneous "projection" of diverse visual images (paintings, photographs, writing) about the interior of the hall. The aural and visual levels are entirely different and not intended for synchronization. Nevertheless, architecture and sound and pictorial imagery are allied here as they must have been in the great cathedrals of Europe many hundreds of years ago, with an awe-inspiring effect upon the vast audiences (literally thousands a day for six months) of 1958.

The massive spatial interplay is apparent even in a two-channel reduction for phonograph recording purposes, and the Columbia disc on which you can hear the *Poème* is impressive in its own right. What is more important, whether we have two loud-speakers or 400 at our disposal, is the singularly strong personality that Varèse brings to the magnetic tape medium. After two decades of inactivity, when he quietly waited for the "new instrument" of his imagination to materialize, Varèse's powers were undiminished. It is to this point that Mel Powell writes:

. . . regardless of the specialized machinery a composer works with—trained lips, lungs, and fingers, or unschooled oscillators and filters—if it happens that his essential musical mentality is endowed with a personal profile, that profile shows in all cases, despite the means that may mask it. . . . apparatus is apparatus, and Varèse is Varèse.

Electronic music developed quite differently in the United

States. For one thing, the institutional backing (and, more importantly, funding) that had facilitated studio installations in Europe was lacking here. As Luening notes, prior to the 1955 grant by the Rockefeller Foundation to Barnard College of Columbia University, tape-oriented composers in this country "had practically no foundation, institutional, governmental, or commercial support." The European alliance between electronic composers and radio stations had been ideal from a working standpoint, since radio studios contain much of the basic equipment (designed for recording and transmission but equally suitable for composition). But, unfortunately, that alliance had no parallel in the United States. There are isolated exceptions, to be sure: The earliest I know of (a Chicago station, not identified) was reported in a 1942 article by Cage describing the use of the station's frequency oscillator, recordings, and sound effects collection. In general, though, the earliest efforts in America—those of Cage, Luening, Ussachevsky, Varèse—were conducted with borrowed equipment, in living rooms of various people's homes.

When institutional support finally came, it was channeled from private foundations to the universities, rather than from government to the radio networks. The universities continue to dominate America's electronic music scene, thanks in no small measure to the great success of the first major studio (the Columbia-Princeton Electronic Music Center) under the joint directorship of Luening, Ussachevsky, Babbitt, and Roger Sessions. The prevalence of university studios also reflects the wider and more pervasive control of *all* contemporary music, electronic and instrumental, by university-based composers. The overwhelming majority of American composers will be found teaching on college and university campuses, a situation almost unknown in Europe; many performers specializing in the avant-garde and special ensembles for new music are campus-based as well. But, I must repeat, even this support from the campus was lacking in the early 1950's. Composers were working with home equipment, using their own funds, laboring under less than optimum working conditions. Worse yet, by Luening's account, they occasionally encountered obstacles to public performance in the person(s) of hostile members of the musicians' or engineers' unions! Under such circumstances, the rapid creative progress seems all the more remarkable.

A second fundamental difference between the American and European tape experiments is that of aesthetic intent. With the exception of Cage's randomly assembled noise collages, the first works in the United States (particularly those of Luening and Ussachevsky) centered upon the alteration of sounds made by traditional instruments, extending rather than disguising their natural resonance. The American contribution lies neither in the domain of *musique concrète* nor of *elektronische musik,* although it employed the tape-manipulation techniques common to both. A new term was never devised for this third position (by the mid-1950's the futility of label-mongering had become apparent to European and American alike); Luening jokingly referred to the "tapesichord," and the phrase "tape music" was at one time used frequently. The important point here is that the instrumental sources have not lost their unique character. What we sense instead is that familiar timbres have crossed over into new territory, the flute now playing as low as a contrabassoon, the strokes of the timpani carried upward into the range of the piccolo, one piano chord suddenly become many, and so on. In a number of the earliest pieces, the instruments (flute, piano, bells, drums, gongs) were played by Luening and Ussachevsky themselves. Both Otto Luening and Vladimir Ussachevsky had established solid reputations as composers in an eclectic, neo-classical idiom, and both had been known for their interest in scientific developments, when together, as faculty colleagues at Columbia University, they began tape experiments early in 1952.

In October of that year, a concert of their jointly produced tape works was given at New York's Museum of Modern Art, the first such program in the United States. Highlights of the recital can be heard on a Desto record entitled *Tape Music: An Historic Concert,* and in listening to these pieces today you can easily grasp the significance of the program, as well as its effect upon such younger composers in the audience as Luciano Berio. Berio, covering the event for an Italian journal, found Ussachevsky's *Sonic Contours* the most significant piece, while Nat Hentoff, writing for *Downbeat,* singled out Luening's *Fantasy in Space* for particular praise. The two pieces are, in fact, strikingly similar in many respects. Both are derived from, and remain faithful to, familiar instrumental sources—the Luening a multi-dimensional extension of virtuoso flute performance, Ussachevsky's work a more introspective, almost impressionistic, usage of piano sounds. In both compositions basic technical procedures are employed with great effectiveness and utmost delicacy: There are abundant instances of tape-splicing to isolate the attack or decay of individual sounds, extreme changes of speed, multiple-track overlays, reverberation, and the like. The two composers' neo-classical tendencies still ring true, however, adding an altogether charming dimension to their venture. You can't mistake the common chords, arpeggios, and scale patterns in Ussachevsky's piano source material or Luening's simple folklike tune emerging from a web of drifting sonority. The "new" and the "old" have been reconciled here, very much as in Henry Cowell's tone-cluster piano works composed before World War I. Jay Harrison, reporting on the concert for the *New York Herald-Tribune,* wrote,

> It has been a long time in coming, but music and machine are now wed. . . . The result is as nothing encountered before. It is the music of fevered dreams, of sensations called back from a dim past. It is the sound of echo. . . . It is vaporous, tantalizing, cushioned. It is in the room and yet not part of it. It is something entirely new. And genesis cannot be described.

The success of the Museum of Modern Art concert may have overshadowed other electronic experiments taking place in America. Princeton University had a long-standing record of experimentation, for example, especially in the area of the hand-drawn film sound track, which we had noted earlier in Germany and Canada. Milton Babbitt, on the Princeton faculty, was well known for his vital interest in all aspects of electronic sound production. And John Cage, working in virtual isolation (although hardly in obscurity), had assembled taped noises, tones, street sounds, and whatnot into massive collages; his *Williams Mix*—a tape-spliced panorama of sounds subdivided into six categories, such as city sounds, country sounds, electronic sounds, and small sounds requiring amplification to be heard—was, in fact, also composed in 1952. Its first major public performance, however, took place two years later, before a baffled audience at the Donaueschingen Festival in Germany. Incidentally, the *Williams Mix* and a number of other Cage compositions, including the 1939 *Imaginary Landscape No. 1* (using radio frequency phonograph records), can be heard on a three-record set issued privately by George Avakian (285 Central Park West, New York City). The recordings were originally made to commemorate the twenty-five-year retrospective Cage concert held in New York in 1958. For those interested in Cage and his unswerving creative evolution, the records are an essential document, and for some they may be a revelation.

Such relatively isolated efforts were gaining wider recognition as interest in the new medium began to rise, and it was the singular success of the Luening-Ussachevsky collaboration that made further American developments possible in a short period of time. For Luening and Ussachevsky themselves, the favorable response to their work meant a good many commissions (both jointly and individually) from 1953 onward. In many of their commissioned pieces, the two composers moved into another generally uncharted direction, that of creating music for live performers *and* taped sounds; they were among the first, along with Varèse and Bruno Maderna, to combine and synchronize these forces. The *Rhapsodic Variations* for tape and orchestra, commissioned and recorded by the Louisville Orchestra for its own Louisville Edition series, was the first piece of this kind and achieves an effective ensemble interplay of elements. But a far more interesting work is the later orchestral-tape *A Poem in Cycles and Bells,* recorded for Composers Recordings, Inc. (CRI), in which material from the *Fantasy in Space* and *Sonic Contours* is now enlarged upon and set into a convincing instrumental context.

Ussachevsky's 1956 *A Piece for Tape Recorder* is also recorded on CRI, and I note it here (apart from its own intrinsic worth as a vigorous, exciting piece) for two reasons. First of all, the work makes use of electronically generated sources as well as instrumental ones. Second, Ussachevsky has written at length about this composition in the April, 1960, issue of *Musical Quarterly*. The article, later reprinted in Paul Henry Lang's anthology *Problems of Modern Music,* offers clear, relatively non-technical descriptions of the compositional choices that precede the making of a tape piece, some of the working procedure, and the general aesthetic viewpoint that guides the whole. Younger composers can still profit from reading it.

That Ussachevsky was concerned with oscillators in 1956, or that Stockhausen was using the human voice as a sound source by this time, demonstrates that initially different approaches were all leading to the same point as the decade progressed. Any sound source was considered acceptable as basic raw material, and any sound source would most probably undergo the same "processing" (filtering, reverberation, tape-splicing, mixing of channels, and so on). Certain studio facilities were essential to this kind of manipulation, and basic similarities in studios (whether found in European radio stations or American colleges) reflected these common needs. For example, any studio would contain the following bare minimum of equipment:

1. Source material (sounds) readily available for taping, such as electronic tone generators, Theremin, Hammond organ, white-noise generator, phonograph records, microphones for recording in the studio;

2. Facilities for altering and/or controlling these sources, dials to control pitch on the generators, filters, reverberators, mixers (again, all of the latter equipped with dials to control levels), and basic paraphernalia for the editing and splicing of tape;

3. At least two, and hopefully three or more, tape recorders, for mixing, rerecording, altering material through speed changes and tape reversal, and combining channels; and

4. Amplifiers and loud-speakers, not only for the obvious aural "contact" with the material (this might also be accomplished with headphones) but also, used in conjunction with microphones, for tape delay and other effects.

In other words, *musique concrète,* "tape music," and *elektronische musik* had merged into an international phenomenon that could best be referred to, quite simply, as the "studio." We sometimes call these facilities the "classic studio," a phrase that, unfairly, implies that the techniques of the 1950's are now archaic. I suppose that some composers do use the term in this manner, pondering the incredible pace of development since that time and then mentioning "classic" techniques with a self-satisfied nod in the direction of their antiquarian forebears! But those who first applied the term "classic" were using it to connote craftsmanship, rigor, precision, rather than vintage. The studio techniques of the 1950's are anything but outdated. Even now they remain the best basic introduction to the medium for the inexperienced composer, and in many college studios "classic" technique is considered a prerequisite for further work with the more automated equipment of the 1960's.

Furthermore, there are many composers today, surrounded by the most sophisticated of synthesizers and computers, who genuinely prefer tape-splicing, the use of loops and snippets of tape (fitting these together in mosaic fashion), and the alteration of natural sounds. They enjoy "building" tape patterns with their hands, the feel of the razor blade and the splice block, the excitement of improvising with filters and mixing equipment in the studio, the happy accidents of juxtaposition that occur when unrelated channels are combined. As for the use of "environmental" and instrumental sounds, these will always have a following among composers, especially those who find the challenge of imagining what these sounds *will become* (to paraphrase Ussachevsky) a stimulating one.

For other composers, however, the classic studio presented not a challenge, in the positive sense, but a severe limitation. Those greatly concerned with serial organization of their material felt the limitation most strongly. As they preferred to work with electronically generated tones, they found it necessary to build complex timbres by rerecording and mixing; rhythmic patterns had to be created by laborious splicing, fitting one tone to the next literally by hand. Simultaneous melodic lines, even the simplest sort of counterpoint, involved careful synchronization and much rerecording. Because this kind of composer would already have plotted the details of his work (or perhaps the entire composition) in advance, direct physical contact with the sound source—a major compositional stimulus to a different sort of composer—offers no particular attractions. As I've mentioned earlier, the serially inclined composer benefits from electronics not as a stimulus to "composition" but as a mode of "performance" of an already completed composition. And, as a medium for the performance of tightly controlled, finely organized music, the classic studio was and still is inefficient.

At this point the synthesizer enters the scene, a *deus ex machina* arriving at precisely the right moment in music history. In 1955, RCA demonstrated the Olson-Belar Sound Synthesizer, an elaborate device for the direct production of sounds. More accurately, it could produce *successions* of sounds, with all varieties of timbre and duration capable of being specified by means of a coded paper input tape. The implications of that word "succession" are enormous; after all, even a generator in the classic studio could accurately produce one sound, at a given waveform (timbre), frequency (pitch), and dynamic setting. The RCA synthesizer, in automating a *series* of sounds, eliminated much of the cumbersome tape-splicing formerly involved in joining such individual sounds to each other. By punching numbers on the synthesizer's paper input roll, a composer could specify a succession of different pitches. In addition, he could control register (which given octave), timbre, articulation (varieties of staccato, legato, and the like, usually referred to in terms of "attack" and "decay" of each sound), and other such factors. Relative durations for any of these aspects would be indicated by the number of repetitions of a given instruction on the paper roll; that is, the amount of space occupied by a repeated punched number would be analogous to the duration of that indicated characteristic, relative to the speed of the paper roll moving through the machine. Since the composer could preset that speed, he could also control the tempo of the musical successions and, naturally, vary the tempo by changing the speed setting.

The synthesizer's sound sources were tuning-fork oscillators, producing sawtooth waveforms. You'll recall that these contain all harmonics. Filtering of this source (in effect, suppressing or subtracting certain overtones) could, then, result in all other possible timbres. This is the exact opposite of the technique of synthesis used in the early days of the Cologne Radio studio, when sine waveforms (no harmonics) were added—mixed together—to "build up" more complex timbres. The synthesizer could also produce white noise, and this, too, could be filtered down to required frequencies and timbres. As the resultant sounds could be heard on loud-speakers in the studio, a composer could test his effects at every stage before the actual finished "performance," which would be recorded directly onto discs.

There was great interest in the new machine, especially on the part of Milton Babbitt at Princeton University (RCA's laboratories were, in fact, located in the town of Princeton) and Luening and Ussachevsky of Columbia. Babbitt in particular had a strong compositional affinity for this kind of musical control of sustained passages. He had been a pioneer in the development of the serial method and in 1948 composed perhaps the first works to extend twelve-tone pitch relationships into other dimensions such as duration, timbre, register and dynamics. Babbitt's complex music had carried traditional instrumental resources to their limits, notably in aspects of rhythmic performance and subtlety of articulation; as a result, performances of his exacting works were necessarily limited and even then often inaccurate. The RCA synthesizer extended his resources, beyond those of live instruments, and, what is more important, made them available for use in combined interrelationships without having to resort to the incessant tape-splicing of the classic studio. From the very first, Babbitt exploited precisely that aspect of the synthesizer, transferring the preoccupations of his instrumental music directly to the electronic medium. Noises and "new sounds" were of little interest to him, and he concentrated, as before, on fantastic structural complexities.

A period of consultation and planning with the Rockefeller Foundation led eventually to a large grant and then the founding of the Columbia-Princeton Electronic Music Center. The announcement of the grant in early 1959 caused, in Luening's words, "a great deal of commotion in the world of music." The newly formed center quickly became the prime focal point for electronic activity in the United States. A number of composers were invited to work there, including Mario Davidovsky (from Argentina), Halim El-Dabh (Egypt), Bülent Arel (Turkey), and Charles Wuorinen, then a graduate student at Columbia. The RCA synthesizer was loaned to the center and soon was replaced by an even more efficient model, dubbed the "Mark II." Babbitt, with the help of resident engineers, had converted it to a tape, rather than disc, recording system.

Initial concerts of music produced at the new center were held at Columbia University in May, 1961, and that program has been recorded by Columbia Records. The recording testifies, above all, to the wide range of attitudes (aesthetic and procedural) evidenced at the center during those first two years. Those who still continue to believe that all electronic music sounds alike will have to contend with the plain fact that the widest possible spectrum of activity—*every* conceivable style— was taking place within the span of a few years, all in the same location in New York City.

The Columbia Records disc includes Arel's *Stereo Electronic Music No. 1* and Davidovsky's *Electronic Study No. 1,* both derived from wholly electronic sources and manipulated through studio techniques with maximum control and shaping of the formal structures. This may be a throwback to the "old school" of *elektronische musik,* perhaps, but this studio treatment has greater timbral variety and rhythmic urgency than any of the earlier Cologne examples I know of. Luening's *Gargoyles,* on the other hand, pits a live violinist against a tape of sound taken from the RCA synthesizer and then manipulated. It is more a traditional "concert" piece than an "electronic" one, with the tonal, quirky, often comic material giving way to contrasting sections that are alternately virtuosic and lyrical. *Leiyla and the Poet* by Halim El-Dabh offers yet another stylistic avenue: a montage of transformed live sounds (voice, drums, instruments, all subjected basically to speed changes and reverberation effects) maintaining an elusive, almost dreamlike, improvised quality, reminiscent of *musique concrète* and yet altogether different in its diffuse shapes.

Of all the works on the program, Babbitt's *Composition for Synthesizer* is perhaps the most provocative, and on two distinct levels. First, there is the music itself, almost wholly "instrumental" in its timbres and clear pitch relationships, although semi-percussive noises figure prominently as a sort of punctuation for the more organized passages. The intricacy of rhythmic, intervallic, and coloristic cross-play is utterly absorbing; distinctive melodic fragments and rhythmic sequences are tossed about, their profiles clear even when inverted, changed in tempo, reversed, intersecting one another in multidimensional space. It is, in short, virtuoso structure. Second, and equally important, is the virtuoso performance of the medium itself, the RCA synthesizer. With it, Babbitt was able to compose the work unencumbered by the labors of traditional studio technique; since an entire passage could be performed on any single run of the paper input roll, the only splicing involved the fitting together of rather lengthy "takes," analogous to the editing of motion-picture film. When you hear a motivic fragment varied in some way (increased in tempo, or reversed, or transposed, or altered in timbre), you're experiencing one of the marvels of the synthesizer in action. Babbitt may have created any of these variants by changing only one number on the input coding, or by simply altering the speed of the run. Such musical effects would have taken many hours of tedious work in the classic studio. There is, admittedly, a good deal of labor involved in programing the RCA synthesizer (ask any composer who's ever used it), much of it testing and sampling before final codings are punched. But this is meaningful compositional work, essential to the formation of a composer's musical ideas, and not mere drudgery. In short, the synthesizer had opened up the possibilities of automation, as witnessed here in Babbitt's work of the early 1960's, and was a portent of developments that would come in the following years.

I don't mean to imply that the RCA synthesizer was without its disadvantages. While not as monstrous as Cahill's 200-ton Dynamophone of 1906, it was massive (taking up at least one entire wall) and certainly not portable. Its enormous expense and size decreed that there would not be many of them installed, so that a composer had to travel to New York to use it. Even then, its own complexities were such that the composer might have to spend a lengthy period of time in learning how to control it; for many years it was said that only Babbitt truly understood the RCA synthesizer, to the point of composing at it without the aid of an engineer.

And yet the extraordinary possibilities for direct control of electronic sources—no matter what the difficulties might be in attaining that control—were fascinating and worth pursuing further. The more recent developments of the 1960's, including widespread use of small, modular, voltage-controlled synthesizers (those made by Moog are the best known) and the applications of computer-programing to the generation of sound, are the results of that pursuit. I will describe these in the next few chapters and only wish to point out here that it was the "original" synthesizer— the RCA giant, a unique machine in its time—that stimulated sufficient research to bring forth the later means of the 1960's. Whatever its limitations, the RCA synthesizer made composers and engineers acutely aware of possibilities for the future, and its value as catalyst should not be understated.

In fact, none of the achievements of the 1950's can be slighted. Our more recent "advances" may have overshadowed the methods of that earlier decade, but, when current fashions and fads have been absorbed into music's mainstream, the "old-fashioned" work done in the classic studio will be viewed in a new perspective. We certainly can't deny the great creative vitality of that period, or the worth of the major works produced at Paris, Cologne, Milan, Columbia-Princeton, and elsewhere. These earliest studios provided an international forum for the exchange of aesthetic positions and practical concerns and a stimulus for composers to examine their own intents in relation to the future and the past. (And, as we've seen, the past can be extended back many years —certainly, at least, to Busoni, who was the teacher of both Luening and Varèse and whose prophecies now seem uncanny.) The early studios also brought these developing concepts to public attention. Finally, composers of *all* stylistic, including traditional, persuasions, came to discover in the studios that their own creative goals could be furthered electronically.

These collective experiments and aspirations brought about what may be, in retrospect, the most important achievement of all: the isolation of the problem. That is, after the work of the 1950's, the musical potential of the new medium could be specified in terms of realistic goals. By 1960, composers knew what their challenges were: the electronic generation of sound, the alteration of sound (whether natural or electronic), and precise control over articulation, duration, and succession. The pioneering discoveries of the previous decade had assured that these were no longer technological challenges, but compositional ones.

Part II
The Musical Present, 1960–70

4. The Modular Synthesizer and Voltage Control

We now move directly into the 1960's, which can be classified as the "present" for the purposes of this narrative: The most important technical tools of today's electronic music have their origins in that decade, and even the very latest aesthetic attitudes of the 1970's have been a few years in the making. The modern era of electronic music began in the 1960's and hasn't ended yet. I refer here not only to important technological devices but also to the enormous *interest* in the field over the last ten years or so. Although the technical developments of the 1950's had made composition with tape a reality, composer interest in electronic music (to say nothing of general audience awareness) was a relatively isolated phenomenon. The really explosive surge of activity in the field took place in the 1960's and has continued into the present.

This is evidenced in Europe by the preponderance of electronic works in all the major contemporary festivals and in the United States by the installation of campus studios at an amazingly rapid rate. The recording industries of both continents, responding to all this activity and to the possibilities of the youth market, are also issuing a wide variety of pieces on discs. The sudden proliferation of university studios in the United States has meant a corresponding output of new works by literally hundreds of composers, many of them new to the medium. The phenomenon is particularly important in that most serious American composition is university oriented, with the great majority of composers employed on teaching faculties.

The point here is not to congratulate ourselves on this fairly recent upswing of interest but to ask why it took place so *late*— why, despite the impetus of the many impressive works produced during the earlier period, did so many composers and institutions enter the electronic field only after a decade of waiting. In part, the delay may have been due to an inevitable time lag, the passage of years before "the word" spreads from the large university centers (in this case, Columbia and the University of Illinois) to the outposts of Amherst, Grinnell, Bowdoin, or Oberlin. It's more likely, though, that the various parties involved were simply dissatisfied with existing studio possibilities. Composers were looking for a system that could reduce studio editing time *and* that would be relatively easy to operate. Institutions were concerned about the high costs of studios. Both desired, for different reasons, facilities that could be installed easily in a small space.

The startling increase in creative work and institutional support, then, is directly attributable to the answering of these needs by a single technological advance: the development of the modular, voltage-controlled synthesizer. This one device—or, to be more accurate, this collection of devices—bears little resemblance to the RCA giant machine. All they have in common is the name "synthesizer" and the ability, suggested by that name, to produce sounds. The modular, voltage-controlled synthesizer may lack the precision of the RCA namesake, and, some say, its infinite timbral versatility as well, but it has the advantages of being (1) more portable, (2) much less expensive, (3) easy to operate, and (4) readily available for installation in a small space on a limited budget. The concept of voltage control, more than any other single factor, has opened up the possibilities of electronic composition for many individuals. From the very first, it appealed to composers who could not or would not travel to the major centers for work in the highly sophisticated studios, and those who could not or would not concern themselves with the tedious procedures of classic-studio technique.

The advantages of the voltage-controlled synthesizer over the classic studio are apparent if you recall the various tasks required of a composer working during the 1950's in a vintage studio set-up. Those tasks fall roughly into three categories:

1. *The making of sounds,* using any number of oscillators, tone generators, white noise sources, and microphones for recording material, much of which required a lot of bulky equipment

2. *The altering of the sounds,* using filters, ring modulator, reverberator for echo effects, changes of tape speed, mixing facilities to build complex timbres from simple ones, which made additional hardware necessary

3. *Control over the material,* done laboriously by hand and often not very accurately

Let me stress this last area for a moment. To choose the frequency (pitch) of oscillators, or the degree of filtering, or the level of modulation, the composer would resort to twiddling dials on many different boxes scattered throughout the studio. A different sort of "control"—the succession of different pitches and durations—would entail careful splicing and editing of tape fragments. As to the accuracy of any of these, hand control may come within tolerable limits but is certainly not sufficient for various kinds of tightly organized music.

With regard to the first two of the above categories, the voltage-controlled synthesizer's advantages are perhaps minimal and involve economy and space-saving. Modules built for the execution of 1 and 2 are tiny, transistorized, and interconnected by patching plugs; this is handy, but not necessarily revolutionary. Changes in 3, though, are of far greater importance. The modular synthesizer enables a composer to alter pitch, timbre, duration, and other factors, not by fussing with knobs or splice tape but by applying control *voltages* to various electrical signals. *Control,* the massive time-waster of the classic studio, can be achieved with relative ease; many functions can be handled in one place (at the synthesizer console), and successions can be "performed" in "real time." That is to say, the duration of a given passage corresponds *exactly* to the time spent in making it, as in any live performance. While a fragment of music lasting ten seconds (to the listening ear) may have necessitated an untold period of recording and tape splicing in the classic studio, it takes a flesh-and-blood musician, performing before your very eyes, only ten seconds to make ten seconds' worth of music. In "real time," therefore, music-producing *activity* and its resultant *sounds* are simultaneous and inseparable. On the Moog synthesizer, for example, you could depress keys on a simulated organ keyboard, each key preset to activate a different control voltage. The voltages, in turn, alter the functions of various modules (oscillators, filters, amplifiers) to which they're applied. The Buchla synthesizer substitutes a touch-sensitive plate for the Moog "keyboard," but with the general principles remaining the same.

The names Moog and Buchla, in fact, dominated the electronic music scene throughout the 1960's. The instruments were named, respectively, after their inventors: Robert Moog, working in Trumansberg, New York (a small town near Ithaca), and Donald Buchla, of the San Francisco Bay area. Since the invention of the first two, a number of other small synthesizers have appeared on the market, similarly voltage controlled but not always necessarily modular: the ARP, the Putney, ElectroComp, and Neurona, to name a few. It's worth noting that, although Mr. Moog, Mr. Buchla, and subsequent synthesizer-builders were "technicians" rather than "musicians" (for whatever these antiquated distinctions are worth), their products have been designed with specifically musical ends in mind, often in collaboration with composers. This marks a significant milestone in the history of electronic music, because all equipment before this time had been originally intended to serve *other purposes*; that is, the classic studio was an assemblage of broadcast and hi-fi testing units, and the RCA synthesizer had been developed by the telephone industry to attempt speech synthesis. The 1960's witnessed the marketing of the first units designed *exclusively* for the composition and performance of electronic music. Undoubtedly, this was in response to a growing interest, and it inevitably triggered even greater interest. An important corner had been turned.

To understand the synthesizer and its functions, we might begin with a rudimentary definition of the unit itself: A voltage-controlled synthesizer is a collection of electronic devices designed to make and alter electrical signals. I should emphasize at the outset that all things in it are *electrical*; it neither makes sound (the loud-speaker at the very end of the process does that) nor alters sound. Furthermore, any material to be altered (whether generated internally by the synthesizer's own oscillators or fed in from a microphone, tape recorder, or phonograph recording) must exist in the form of an electrical signal.

Each synthesizer is composed of various modules, rather small boxes (each about the size of a tiny transistor radio) housed together in a cabinet and connected to the cabinet's internal power supply. Electrical signals can be transmitted from one module to another directly on the front panel of the synthesizer, in most cases by patch-cords and plugs. The modules for any given make of synthesizer are the same size and are thus interchangeable; you could easily remove a module from the cabinet and substitute another one in its place. Because various combinations of modules are well suited for certain functions and different combinations for others, it's advantageous to be able to juggle them about in this way. It follows, then, that no two synthesizers are necessarily alike. Each is a *particular* collection of modules to suit the needs and budget of the user. Four general classifications of modules, however, will be present: (1) sound generators, (2) sound modifiers, (3) control voltage generators, and (4) control voltage processors. Certain modules can perform more than one of these functions, as we'll see in a moment.

Sound generators produce an electrical signal that, when converted to physical vibration (by amplifiers and loud-speakers), will result in a sound. The most important of these sound generators are called oscillators; an average-sized synthesizer will have a number of them, each capable of generating a periodically changing voltage or "waveform." As I noted in the preceding chapter, there are a variety of waveforms, each having a distinctive sound (and a distinctive shape when seen on an oscilloscope). Moreover, each waveform represents the specific overtone content of that sound. The sine wave, for example, contains no harmonics, the square wave odd-numbered harmonics, the sawtooth wave all harmonics, and so forth. But we've mentioned this also before; you'll recall an earlier discussion of overtones in connection with the Cologne Radio technique of building up complex timbres by combining sine tones versus the RCA synthesizer's realization of different timbres by filtering (subtracting) harmonics from a basic sawtooth wave.

The frequency with which an oscillator produces a waveform (that is, the frequency of vibration) can be expressed in terms of "cycles per second" (cps) or hertz (hz), the note A 440 to which an orchestra tunes represented as 440 cps. Higher frequencies result in higher audible "pitches"; the note A one octave below A 440 is a frequency of 220 cps, while the A one octave above 440 is 880 cps. It's possible, of course, for frequencies to be so high or so low that they are outside of the audible range, in which case they're not experienced physically as "sounds" or "pitches" at all—and an oscillator's voltages at such frequencies would not be referred to as "signals."

A synthesizer may also contain a white noise generator, which produces a random fluctuation of voltage. This would result in a hissing sound (also alluded to in Chapter 3), very much like radio static or the "shhh" between radio stations. These two types of module, oscillator and white noise generator, are the *only* sources of sound. All other modules are present to alter, modify, process, "deal with" the signals produced by the sound-generating apparatus; they can also modify external sounds, from, say, a phonograph recording, if these have been converted to electrical signals.

Sound modifiers consist of such modules as filters, amplifiers, mixers, reverberators, ring modulators, and the like. Their names generally describe their functions. A filter, for example, will allow certain frequencies, or ranges of frequencies, to pass through it, blocking off all others. Its effect on sound is analogous to that of a photographic filter on light, and it is used to modify the timbre or tone color of a sound. An amplifier will, in effect, "amplify," by controlling the loudness or softness of the sound. A mixer combines a number of signals together in varying proportions. A reverberator, by producing a number of very short delays in a signal, can convert a single sound into echoes of varying degrees, often making sounds appear to emanate from within a large room or cave. A ring modulator, acting upon two frequencies, produces the sum and difference of the frequencies while blocking the originals—an indescribable sound effect, which, when heard, is not easily forgotten. Occasionally, when two radio signals combine in one spot on your dial, producing an eerie fuzz and near total distortion, you might begin to approach its sound.

All of the equipment noted so far could have been found in a traditional classic studio; in fact, these devices have been at the very core of electronic music since its beginnings in Paris and Cologne. The advantages of installing them within the synthesizer are twofold: first, they have been greatly reduced in size and can be dealt with in one place, and, second and more important, they exist in a state that enables them to be controlled by applied voltages.

Control voltage is, in fact, the real heart of the synthesizer, enabling the composer to alter settings of all the modules mentioned so far by applying specific voltages to them. He could, of course, also "control" these modules by twisting dials in the traditional way, if he wished, but this would be inaccurate at best (and only practical for very simple maneuvers). His tasks have been automated, to a degree, by the fact that oscillators, filters, and amplifiers can all be voltage controlled. Their functions can be made proportional to a voltage put into them; the frequency of an oscillator, for example, can be made higher by applying a control voltage (on the Moog, one volt raises the frequency by one octave), and other types of modules are similarly altered. Modules that emit a control voltage, thus effectively changing the function of *other* modules, are known as control voltage generators. We've already been introduced to a few of these: An oscillator, to name one, can be used as a control voltage generator, because it produces a periodically changing voltage; and a white noise generator, slowed down sufficiently, will produce a random control voltage that can then be used to affect other modules in appropriately random ways.

The nature of the "control" varies with the type of interacting modules: that is, an oscillator controlling another oscillator will produce "beats" that can be speeded up to a rapid vibrato; controlling an *amplifier* with an oscillator, on the other hand, creates a periodically varying loudness-softness that resembles a tremolo.

Moreover, the character of the tremolo or vibrato or whatever will be considerably altered if the periodic control voltage is changed from sine waveform to sawtooth or square wave.

There are also special control voltage generators, designed to serve only one function. When used in the most conventional way, the envelope generator, for instance, lends an articulation to the signal produced by an oscillator. It gives "shape" to a pitch (an initial attack, then a sustained sound, lastly a decay) so that the pitch takes on the quality of staccato, or legato, or portamento, or a sharp percussive sound, or whatever you wish. This is done by producing a rising voltage over a period of time (attack time) to a certain level, then decreasing the voltage over a period of time (initial decay time) to a lower level (the "sustain" level), and then dropping back to zero over another duration (the final decay time). If this total "envelope" is applied to volume, by controlling an *amplifier*, the sort of articulation of pitch I noted above will result. But, if the "envelope" is applied to pitch itself, controlling an *oscillator,* a continuum of rising and falling pitch (glissando) will be produced; using the envelope generator to control a *filter* yields equally interesting effects.

The Moog (or ARP) keyboard, a familiar sight on countless numbers of record jackets, offers another simple, straightforward means of generating control voltages. By depressing a key, you activate a voltage, and each key emits a different voltage level. Although the keyboard may control any voltage-controlled module, such as the filter or amplifier, it is more often than not linked to the oscillator, in which case the keyboard controls frequency (pitch), probably triggering the envelope generator—to articulate that pitch—every time a key is depressed. Because the standard setting of the keyboard is one key equals one-twelfth volt (and, because one volt represents an octave, that octave is divided into the twelve "traditional" parts), it is possible to "play" the keyboard as a kind of super-organ, performing familiar melodies or new ones of your own. It's also possible, however, to change the keyboard setting so that one key equals some fraction of a volt *other* than one-twelfth, thus expanding or compressing the pitch relationships within the keyed octave—in effect, creating microtones and non-Western scales. The standard keyboard setting reinforces the super-organ effect in another way: Because the voltage is changed instantly and in discrete steps with each newly depressed key, each key will result in a distinct "note." But this, too, can be changed by the flip of a switch; you could call for gradually changing voltage control from one depressed key to the next (rather than a discrete series), so that glides, swoops, and glissandi can be produced.

The great majority of keyboards supply only one control voltage at a time. That is, if you were to depress two or more keys simultaneously, you would still have the effect of one key. This means that truly polyphonic keyboard playing is impossible, except on a highly sophisticated keyboard developed by ARP. The keyboard could be preset to control three different oscillators, of course, and these could be tuned to a major chord. Then you will produce a major chord each time a key is depressed—but *each* and every key will produce a major chord, transposing it as you go up and down the keyboard. True counterpoint, line against line, can only be realized on very specialized keyboards, or by multiple recording. This latter technique is the one used for Walter Carlos's *Switched-on Bach* transcriptions: Each individual part of the complex texture is played as a solo, and then the separate lines are mixed onto a multitrack tape, with no real-time performance of the actual work ever having taken place.

Live performance of the modular synthesizer is limited not only by the single-voiced keyboard but also by the relative complexity of preparing various effects. It may be necessary to make many interconnections on the control panel to set up special timbres, and it's often difficult to change these connections at a moment's notice, especially while performing! The Moog and Buchla systems, as I've mentioned, use patch-cords and plugs for external connections among modules; the Moog, in particular, with its keyboard perched underneath a battery of phone jacks and plugs, has been described as the offspring of an electronic organ and a telephone switchboard. (One synthesizer manufacturer—Tonus, producer of the ARP—has dispensed with the "switchboard," providing a system of matrix switches instead. This allows the change of interconnections to be made with greater ease and speed.)

The Buchla synthesizer deviates from the Moog unit in one obvious, highly visible way; it substitutes a series of touch-sensitive plates for the Moog keyboard. A number of composers prefer this, usually for two reasons. First of all, it is possible to preset *each* of the touch-sensitive areas (up to sixteen of these) individually, because the control voltage from each switch is independent of the others. The Moog keyboard, by contrast, increases voltage in successive, equidistant stages, and graduated patterns (which can be a hindrance for certain kinds of compositions) are inevitable. Secondly, and this is most important for some people, the Buchla frees the compositional mentality from "keyboard" thinking. Even the very appearance of the touch-board radically changes the psychology of one's approach to the instrument, for it simply cannot be treated like a keyboard instrument. Keyboard facility is absolutely irrelevant to, and may be a drawback in, the use of the touch-plates. Furthermore, tuning the different plates to the pitches of the Western chromatic scale, which occurs automatically on the Moog or ARP keyboard unless settings are altered, is a laborious and eventually discouraging operation. The two control systems, keyboard and touch-board, appeal to very different instincts in composers. It may be more than coincidence that the Moog and ARP originated in the pitch-concerned, "control"-oriented, "academically" inclined northeastern part of the United States, while the Buchla is a product of the sound-sonority-noise-textural inclinations of the American West.

One module that does make live performance a possibility, when used in conjunction with a keyboard or touch-board, is the sequencer. Although first developed by Buchla, it can now be found in many types of synthesizers; its greatest asset is the ability to produce a sequence of control voltages that can be individually preset. Movement from one control voltage to another (that is, the "sequence") occurs at a rate, or "tempo," that can also be preset, determined by an oscillator called a clock. The rate need not be regular, and complex rhythms and varying tempi can be used. The sequence of control voltages can be applied to oscillators (creating a melodic pattern of different pitches) or to any other voltage-controlled modules and can be repeated infinitely, if one desires, creating an ostinato pattern —the equivalent of the tape loop in the classic studio—to accompany material played at the key- or touch-board. This is the most obvious use of the sequencer, and a relatively trivial one at that; as a number of composers have discovered (often to their sorrow), the "loop" effect, unless handled discreetly, borders dangerously on the cliché. A much more exciting possibility involves the sequencer's being treated as a miniature computer. It actually is one, in essence, because it can be preset or "programed" to respond in a predictable way. For example, any step in the sequence can activate a previously unused module, which might in turn further alter the sequence by virtue of its own voltage control. The clock might be programed to turn one or more envelope generators on and off; if we had two sequencers, any number of steps in one could initiate or "control" activity in the other. With an entire bank or even an entire wall of sequencers and enough voltage-controlled modules to respond to their settings, a carefully thought out program might set into motion a highly elaborate, totally controlled chain of events, without the composer's touching the control board after the initial move! The sequencer, then, is a powerful device, whether used in simple repeating ostinati or guiding various modules through detailed passages of complex music.

The foregoing is by no means a comprehensive description of a modular synthesizer, but it's about as far as I can go within the scope of this book. This is about all the information the average composer has, anyway, for his concern with the instrument is eminently practical ("musical," if you will) and he may know little of the electronics or engineering involved. With knowledge of some of this basic framework, we should be able to acquire a picture of the composer at work in such a studio.

To begin with, let's assume that he is creating a work that will ultimately exist on magnetic recording tape, either an entirely electronic piece or one for live instruments and tape, in which case his job at the synthesizer is to construct the tape "part."

In other words, he is not concerned with live performance at the synthesizer *per se*. He is therefore free to take his time in setting up connections, recording various passages on tape, stopping the tape and setting up for new situations, as often as he wishes. On the other hand, he forfeits his advantage (in using the synthesizer versus the classic studio) if he is continually stopping and resetting; it's to the composer's benefit, then, to be able to play as much of the music in "real time" as possible.

But to "play" the music he must have an "instrument," or, more accurately, he must select from the synthesizer's vast assortment of possible instruments. Any composer working at a synthesizer is, in effect, an instrument-builder as well. He's limited only by the number of oscillators, filters, and other modules available to him, and within these limits he is free to shape his sonic materials with various aims in mind:

1. *Timbre,* the waveform of an oscillator, perhaps more than one oscillator, possibly one oscillator modified by the control of another or by a noise generator
2. *Envelope* or articulation, the envelope generator being used to control the amplifier
3. The degree of *pitch stability* as opposed to vibrato, glissando, or "noise" sonority, all of the latter made possible through oscillator control, the degree of noise content, the envelope generator applied to oscillator or filter, and so on
4. *Intonation,* setting the increment of voltage control—via either keyboard or touch-board—for microtonal divisions of the octave if desired
5. *Reverberation,* or perhaps other special qualities caused by the use of filters, ring modulator, and the like, if the composer desires these
6. The degree of *automation,* or control of different levels of any of these factors, using the keyboard or touch-board and sequencer

Now the composer has *one* instrument (!), with the particular quality he desires—perhaps that of a peculiarly muted trumpet, or a deep, gonglike ensemble of bells, or something that resembles no instrument you've ever heard in the "real" world. On a synthesizer with a good number of oscillators, filters, and controlling modules, more than one such "instrument" could be set up at one time. In "performance" for the taping session, each might function independently of the other, perhaps one controlled by the sequencer and the other by a keyboard. They could also be fed into different channels of the tape recorder and emerge from different loud-speakers, if the composer wants to perform an entire passage in stereo. It's more than likely, though, that many stereophonic effects (and really intricate over-lappings of individual lines) will be created by the mixing of separately performed passages onto a final master tape. This can be done in the studio long after the actual "performance" at the synthesizer.

Although, as I mentioned, a composer must build his instrument or instruments before he can play upon the synthesizer, this doesn't necessarily imply that instrument-building must precede the *composing* of the music. Some people write out entire pieces or passages beforehand, perhaps on traditional lined-stave paper, anticipating the various timbres they wish and planning the appropriate patchings (interconnections of modules) to achieve them. Others may prefer a more spontaneous, improvisatory approach, experimenting with effects and various patchings while they play and using their time at the synthesizer to stimulate their musical thinking rather than to realize a preconceived idea. It is possible, of course, to adopt a position somewhere between these two extremes. For example, you might enter the studio with a general plan and then alter it considerably while playing. Whatever the composer's attitude, the chances are that he will *not* simply enter the studio, improvise at the synthesizer, and then regard the tape of his playing as a fully finished composition. The overwhelming majority of pieces intended for playback on magnetic tape (even those that are carefully planned beforehand and that maximize automated control in "real time") involve splicing, mixing, and other manipulations of the tape itself. It's very likely, then, that even the tape of an improvisation will be edited into a more "structured" final form, the creator choosing those passages he likes and discarding others—perhaps rearranging the order of events, perhaps mixing different "takes" from a number of sessions. For certain individuals, this becomes the real act of "composing" the work, analogous to the creative work of the film director. At any rate, there is no set rule concerning the ordering of events in the artistic process. The "composing" could be done before entering the studio, while in the studio, or after leaving it, depending on the kind of music to be made.

Finally, I might mention another sort of instrument-building, an alternative open to only a few composers in the past but one with great potential in the coming years: the active collaboration of composers and engineers in the design of synthesizers. This is the surest way of suiting the technological systems to specific compositional aims. A sort of collaboration exists any time a synthesizer is purchased, as a composer will select those modules most useful to him in his work. But the more fundamental interaction of musician and designer—creating totally *new* systems—is not as common; one must have either a sizable budget or the good fortune to work with an engineer during a period of initial conception. When the right people meet under the right circumstances, though, the results can be impressive. Notable examples include the work of James Seawright in installing the Columbia-Princeton studio equipment (and redesigning aspects of the RCA synthesizer), the special multisequencer studio built by Moog for composer Joel Chadabe at the State University of New York's Albany campus, and the collaboration of Buchla and the composers of the San Francisco Tape Music Center (particularly Morton Subotnick) during the early 1960's, which resulted in the modular synthesizer bearing Buchla's name.

The most important works for voltage-controlled synthesizer alone, intended for performance via loud-speaker playback (that is, no "live"-performance aspect to the finished product), are those of Subotnick, realized on the Buchla system. Two of these compositions were commissioned by Nonesuch Records—another intriguing form of collaboration, by the way, and a pioneering effort on the part of the recording industry. Subotnick's *Silver Apples of the Moon,* first of the commissioned efforts, is a fascinating interplay of overlapping ostinati patterns (using the sequencer most delicately) and percussive noise-filtered sonorities, which alternate with a succession of lyric, often bell-like arias. A distinct concern for subtlety of timbre pervades the whole, as well as a fine sense for the shaping of musical gestures, gradually unfolding and changing almost imperceptibly. The necessity of subdividing the work into two large movements corresponding to the two sides of a record dictates, perhaps, a form that slowly emerges and recedes. The general mood is quiet, restrained even in its most vigorous passages, and spacious in timbre. An extended crescendo of multiple ostinato fragments (side two) is the only overtly "dramatic" section in the work, and this, too, subsides to a relaxed conclusion, brilliant in its icy timbres.

The Wild Bull, Subotnick's second Nonesuch commission, is far more forceful in its timbral and dynamic contrasts. His most recent work in this medium, *Touch* (recorded for Columbia), combines elements of both preceding pieces. Often favoring the lower registers and percussive reverberations in more delicate moments, *Touch* may evoke for many listeners the images of gongs, deep drums, piano strings in vibration. Its handling of sequential patterns is highly sophisticated, creating genuine rhythmic freedom rather than simple periodicity.

These are by far the most important original works for the medium now available on commercial recording (excluding compositions for live performers and synthesized-tape part, which will be discussed in a later chapter) and illustrate the potential of the modular equipment at its best, very much as earlier pieces by Varèse, Babbitt, Schaeffer, and others stand as representative of their own respective techniques. The Subotnick works are hardly the best-*known* examples of synthesizer technique, however. That honor belongs indisputably to the transcriptions of earlier music by the gifted physicist-composer Walter Carlos. The Columbia recording *Switched-on Bach* has been Carlos's greatest success. Brilliant examples of "orchestration" on a Moog system, these are not live performances at all, but rather a superimposed studio mixing of many independently "performed" lines, specifically intended for listening over a loud-speaker system.

The choice of timbres and textures is at times highly imaginative, and the whole is certainly the work of a first-rate musician. While the initial choice of Bach as the subject for transcription is particularly apt, if only because of historical precedent (Bach's music having been revised, arranged, orchestrated, and expanded upon by composers and performers throughout the last two centuries), the validity of Carlos's approach is no less appropriate when applied to other music of the past. A number of listeners, in fact, prefer the second Carlos record, *The Well-Tempered Synthesizer,* which offers similar arrangements of Scarlatti, Handel, and Monteverdi, perhaps because these provide more innately coloristic models than the Bach pieces dealt with in the first record. Both discs capitalize upon the facts of stereo recording and tape-editing, bringing out linear distinctions in this eighteenth-century music by means of timbre contrasts and maximum separation of channels. The very qualities of Baroque music that hold our interest to begin with have been clearly articulated as never before. In this way, Carlos has asked us to re-evalute earlier music not only in terms of a new performance medium and new sound sources, but in the light of twentieth-century modes of *transmission* as well. If the interpretation is sufficiently cogent, as Carlos's is, we can hardly afford to ignore its implications for the future: The synthesizer will be put to even further use in the performance of the "classics," as an instrument for *re*composition, reconsideration, reconstruction.

All signs for the future seem to point to the further automation of the synthesizer. We'll certainly see the widespread use of multiple-voice keyboards permitting live contrapuntal performance, greater flexibility in the handling of the sequencer, and the activation of entire series of control voltages by computers. Computerized control of synthesizers is not yet available everywhere, but it's almost sure to be commonplace within a few years. The most elaborate such installation is that of the Swedish Radio studio in Stockholm, and composers who have worked there are unanimously enthusiastic about its possibilities. It offers, in effect, a synthesizer with a memory. You can recall any "patching" that you (or other composers) have made at the studio and test these aurally by consulting this central memory facility. It's also possible to program and execute lengthy chains of events and test these aurally beforehand.

Another trend for the future lies in the development of relatively portable systems specifically equipped for live performance, an area of great concern to many serious composers, rock entertainers, and theater and dance people. There are too many difficulties inherent in the standard modular setup to make flexible live performance feasible, the most crucial of these (as I've noted) being the time needed to .change interconnections. The ARP matrix-switching system, in eliminating patch-cords and plugs, does save some time, but not enough for many purposes. An assistant who alters "patches" while the soloist performs might be a possibility; organists use such assistants frequently to aid with rapid changes in registration. Or, in compositions for live-performance synthesizer and other instruments (perhaps an ensemble of synthesizers), the player may be given time to change settings, while other events are going on around him, analogous to the brass player's change of mutes (or the alteration of timpani pitches) during an orchestral *tutti*. But these are all makeshift devices at best; what we really need is a unique, "real-time" performance system. A number of units already on the market attempt this sort of flexibility: the Mini-Moog, as it is called, the compact ARP, the Putney, the ElectroComp. These are constructed not along modular lines but as single one-piece units, thus eliminating the need for complex patching. The most frequently used connections have been internally prewired, and the composer-performer can move readily from one setting to another by flipping a few switches. A keyboard may be provided (although at present not a multivoiced one), and in live performance the player rides the controls with one hand while operating the keyboard with the other.

A prototype of this sort of unit, called the Syn-Ket, was developed in Italy in the mid-1960's, the result of a collaboration between sound engineer Paolo Ketoff and the American composer, pianist, and jazz artist John Eaton, then working at the American Academy in Rome. The Syn-Ket is specifically designed for live performance and utilizes three keyboards below a master console. There has been very little marketing of the instrument, and only a few exist in the United States, but it is possible to hear some of Eaton's compositions for Syn-Ket on a Decca recording. His *Piece for Solo Syn-Ket No. 3* is quite evocative in its timbral and rhythmic cross-play, some distinctly vocal sonorities adding a touch alternately eerie and humorous. Aside from its musical qualities, though, the piece is impressive as a display of live performance, not an edited tape, but a recording of a concert by Eaton at the Hamburg Opera House. *Songs for R.P.B.,* scored for soprano voice, piano, and Syn-Ket, are dramatically charged expressionistic vehicles for three virtuoso performers. Microtonal in pitch relationships (including the piano part, played mostly on the strings, soundboard, and metal ribs of that instrument), the songs integrate electronics into the live chamber-performance situation with discretion and great musical sensitivity.

Whether constructed along the lines of these prototype models or totally new in concept, future voltage-control synthesizers must stress ease of live performance *and* greater automation. Greater precision for individual *modules* is also being emphasized. It's already obvious that there have been major improvements in pitch stability; the earliest synthesizer oscillators often tended to drift, while those being made today stay in tune for ·much longer periods of time. And, if present trends continue, more developments will occur in only a few years! Does this mean, then, technology will at last have solved all of the composer's problems? Not for a moment. Technical advances will merely change the surface of his problems, if they have any effect on them at all. The composer is concerned fundamentally with "composing"—with questions of organization, relationships, the passing of time, sounds and noises as they articulate that time, dramatic gestures, placement of sounds and events in physical space—and not with technical means. Furthermore, the average composer *enjoys* his musical "problems" and wouldn't really want to give them up; for many (especially those influenced by Stravinsky, Webern, and the European tradition), creation and problem-solving are synonymous: to attack a problem with relish is to enjoy one's work. I've raised this point here because any discussion of synthesizers, and particularly their rosy future, may lead readers to an unwarranted and certainly unrealistic optimism.

Composer Milton Babbitt, seated before the key-punch board of the RCA synthesizer at the Columbia-Princeton Music Center.

Moog Synthesizer, showing a number of modules and a keyboard but (in this photo) no patchcords for modular interconnections. *Photo: R. A. Moog, Inc.*

A fragment from the score of Davidovsky's *Synchronisms No. 1* for Flute and Electronic Sounds. Note that the tape part is not detailed, other than providing a cue (for the live player) at the start of the second tape band; the flutist must have passages carefully timed, his crescendo (ending in a loud squeal, left of example) occurring at the conclusion of a 13-second unit.

Composer David Rosenboom, seated in front of an ARP modular voltage-controlled system. Matrix switches run horizontally along the top and bottom of the ARP, taking the place of patchcords.

Pauline Oliveros's *Valentine* in performance at Mills College, 1968: A man in a black cape hitting a croquet ball, four men playing hearts (their own heart-beats amplified as well), and men building a picket fence are some of the activities involved here.   *Photo: Don W. Jones*

The "Mini-Moog," a self-contained, rather than a modular, unit; modular inter-connections are prewired, thus eliminating the need for external patchcords.

Photo: R. A. Moog, Inc.

Two examples from Elliott Schwartz's *Music for Prince Albert, on His 150th Birthday* (Piano, Assistant, and 2 Tapes). Tape B (lowest stave) is a complete entity that, once started, runs throughout the piece; Tape A must be "performed" by the Assistant. There is a continuous band of prerecorded sound on Tape A, and the Assistant makes brief snatches audible with the volume control. Upper and lower lines of the stave indicate different channels (i.e., different loudspeakers). The middle stave is for vocal activity by the pianist.

© *Bowdoin College Music Press; used by permission*

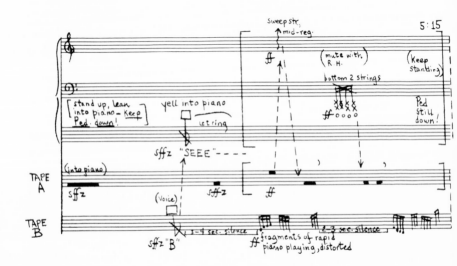

A view of the Dartmouth College Electronic Music Studio. A bank of Moog modules can be seen at the rear, and there are also tape decks, mixing console, phonograph, loudspeakers, and a Moog keyboard.   *Photo: Dartmouth College, Photographic Service*

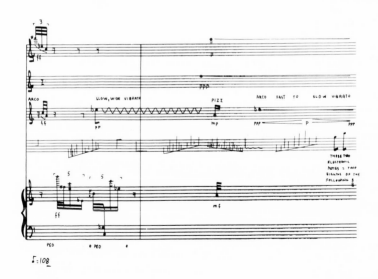

In Morton Subotnick's *Serenade No. 3* for Flute, Clarinet, and Violin, a suggestive "pictorialization" of the tape part (fourth stave down, with no clef) provides a rough indication of rhythms and pitch direction; the two electronic notes at the far right set the tempo for a highly integrated passage to follow.

Bowdoin College Music Press, used by permission

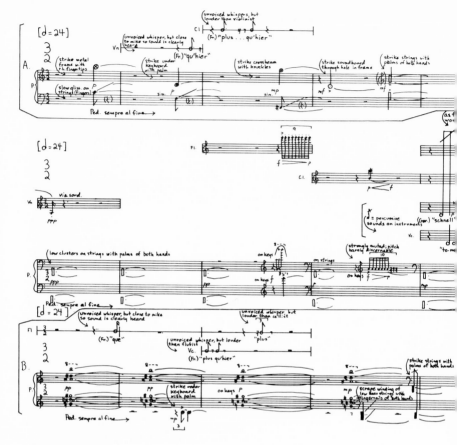

In David Burge's *Aeolian Music* there are passages
(such as the example here) in which the live ensemble
of five players performs against a prerecorded tape its
members have made themselves. Each channel of that
tape contains a separate preperformance. Note that
Flute, Cello, and Piano have made track B, while
Clarinet, Violin, and Piano are on track A. The
notation for live performance is centered on the
page between these two tape parts.

Bowdoin College Music Press, used by permission

A fragment of Lejaren Hiller's *Machine Music,* indicating the relatively great detail with which the electronic events are notated. The two staves of the part indicate left and right tape channels that, in turn, emerge from different loudspeakers.

A scene during the recording of Alvin Lucier's *North American Time Capsule 1967, using* the Sylvania Electronic Systems "Vocoder." Lucier, in the dark jacket, is monitoring material at the rear of the studio.

Photo:
Sylvania
Electronic
Systems

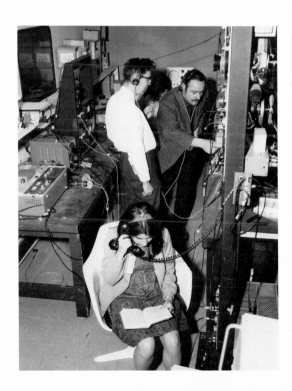

In Leslie Bassett's *Collect* for Mixed Chorus and Tape, we see a combination of indefinite graphic markings with precise rhythmic indications, all notated in strict meter.

The Sonic Arts Union, also known as the Sonic Arts Group, in concert at the U.S. Embassy in London, April 29, 1971. The performers, from left to right, are Robert Ashley, Alvin Lucier, Gordon Mumma, and David Behrman.

Photo: Mary Lucier

Newspapers and popular magazines have helped to foster this notion: After abandoning their ironic, generally skeptical stance of the 1950's, they've turned instead to a euphoric anticipation of the "limitless vistas" and "infinite possibilities" ahead. It should be stressed, then, that the electronic medium, like any other, imposes its own limits. And, in the unlikely situation that there were no limits imposed from the outside, the creator would devise his *own* challenges to restimulate his inventiveness. If the present situation is a reliable indicator, there are enough real problems to keep the composer busy for quite a while. Let me suggest a few of the questions confronting him today, seated at his Moog, ARP, or whatever and supposedly enjoying the luxury of manipulating "infinite possibilities."

To begin with, he is still dealing with an instrument. How well can he "play" that instrument? Whereas he was previously limited by the nature of traditional sound sources such as oboes and violins—their ranges and timbral possibilities—he now constructs his own sources. But he is now *his own performer,* limited by his own dexterity and skill in moving rapidly, playing the keyboard (non-pianists may be at a definite disadvantage), making fast changes of patchings, editing tape. Admittedly, this situation will improve considerably with greater automation, most likely resulting in a collaboration of computer and synthesizer.

But, secondly, there are the limitations of his listeners to consider. I don't mean their lack of experience, but the very real physical limits of the ear and human *hearing.* How many events can be heard simultaneously and still be distinctly followed? To what degree can pitches at the extremes of the audible range be registered in the listener's consciousness, and at what speed? In fact, what are the maximum and minimum tempi, in any frequency range, at which patterns will be recognized? Even if all sounds, rhythms, and relationships were possible to realize, the composer would still have to cope with these problems. We're just beginning to realize, then, that the human ear is one more "performer," with limits to its own versatility in handling the vibrations of sound.

Thirdly, the composer is faced with the necessity of creating an interesting work; even if given the solution to all of the above problems, he still has to make a piece. Unless he has consciously disavowed the cult of personality, preferring a non-Western or pre-Renaissance anonymity, he is concerned with finding the "right" gesture and the unique concept; that is, we can assume that he wants to avoid clichés. Unfortunately, however, these are becoming more noticeable in electronic music all the time. The synthesizer seems to have developed its own mannerisms, and it is ironic that the medium of "limitless possibilities" has developed a penchant for routine, predictable patterns and effects. The essence of the composer's work often lies in trying to by-pass these, to alter the ingrained habits of the instrument, and in this sense electronic composition is no more "infinite" than composition for traditional trumpets, cellos, and flutes.

Even if he can avoid all previous hurdles and come up with a work that really satisfies him musically, the composer may be faced with a final obstacle. It's a comparatively prosaic one, I admit, but some individuals think it important. If he wishes to copyright his work, through the U.S. Copyright Office, our composer will discover that—as of now—his tape alone is not sufficient for purposes of registration. It is considered a "recording" of the work (a "copy"), not the work itself. If the composer cares about this enough (many don't, but some definitely do), he must devise a *notation* for his electronic tape composition; even a piece resulting from improvisation or the studio treatment of natural sounds needs a "score," written down in some shorthand after the fact. A number of composers, sufficiently concerned about copyright, have been forced to do this, and all universally regard it as a thankless task—one problem the composer doesn't enjoy! A future change in the copyright law would solve this dilemma. To be sure, those composers who work out a written score or plan sheet before realization into sound at the studio have an advantage at the outset; even for them, though, the preparation of a finished manuscript can be a nuisance.

In other words, the millennium has not yet arrived. The job of composing is as challenging as ever, and the voltage-controlled synthesizer has merely broadened the challenge. But, again, most composers would not really want it any other way.

5. Computer-generated Sound

If the term "electronic music" causes confusion, "computer music" has proven an even more ambiguous phrase and a frequently misinterpreted one. When people speak of "computer music," they may, in fact, be referring to any one of three totally different kinds of operation: (1) the use of the computer to control various settings of synthesizer modules, (2) music actually composed by the computer itself, or (3) the computer used for "performance" of preconceived ideas, generating information that can be transformed into sound.

I've already suggested some advantages in the partnership of computer and voltage-controlled synthesizer, and there seems to be little disagreement that this will be a valuable development in future years. The second category, however, doesn't engender quite the same unanimous vote of confidence. The notion of music "created" by a computer always seems to arouse a surprising degree of hostility, usually on the part of people who find twentieth-century art increasingly "dehumanized" and "mechanical." Because these are often the same people who apply such castigating epithets to a wide range of art (from Picasso to Schoenberg to Klee to Stravinsky to Babbitt), their judgment is not entirely trustworthy. But they may, at last, be factually correct in this instance; music made up of sounds, pitches, rhythms, and articulations chosen by a nonhuman agent *is,* I suppose, "dehumanized."

But what of it? Such music can be fascinating as an art object in itself, and it can be immensely valuable as a study of musical process.

The best-known experiment involving such study was conducted in the mid-1950's by Lejaren Hiller and Leonard Isaacson at the University of Illinois and was later described comprehensively in their book *Experimental Music*. Working with the university's high-speed computer, they began with the assumption that musical composition involves the making of choices "from an essentially limitless variety of musical raw materials"; proceeding from this viewpoint, they had the computer generate its own random assortment of materials and then select information from these in accordance with specific laws of musical organization. The result was a series of short pieces for string quartet, written out on standard music paper for eventual performance by a live ensemble (that is, not intended for electronic transmission via loud-speakers at all). The two programers named the piece, appropriately enough, after the computer composer: As the computer had been dubbed the Iliac, the composition became *Iliac Suite for String Quartet*. The complete score of the work may be found at the conclusion of the Hiller-Isaacson book. It may not be a terribly "interesting" piece at first glance, and one might argue that a human creator might have produced something more "imaginative" (if anyone really knew what these two adjectives mean in this foreign context), but this would be introducing a host of issues not germane to the Illinois experiment. Hiller and Isaacson wanted to "teach" their computer to compose music, using a given range of materials and within a given (learned) style, and they succeeded. The attempt was (and still is) worth making; if only because of the questions raised and the insights gained on subjects of musical organization, "style" and—naturally—computer-programing.

But this is hardly the moment to defend the role of the computer as composer. One finds the notion either intriguing or despicable, and debate is not likely to be very fruitful. What is important here, however, is the common misconception that *all* music involving the computer must be "composed" by it. This is simply not true. The great majority of people using computers for musical purposes are composers with a definite set of musical purposes in mind; ironically, they are usually the very composers who wish to maintain the *strictest* control possible over their materials.

Contrary to any implication that they would allow a machine to make choices for them, these composers have carefully made each and every musical decision themselves, to a degree of precision often far beyond the realization in performance by live instruments. Traditional electronic techniques, whether those of the classic studio or the voltage-controlled synthesizer, may also be too crude for their specifications. The computer, then, functions for them in the last of the three ways I mentioned earlier, as a *performing* (not composing) instrument. And I must stress again that such composers are not concerned about chance, improvisation, or the happy accident; they view the computer as the surest, most expedient source of *control* they know. People concerned with the use of computers in this way often refer to their work as "computer-generated sound." This clarifies their position, and perhaps they hope it will also distinguish their compositions from those other "dehumanized" offspring of computer composer and human programer.

It should be made clear at the outset that computer-generated sound is not identical to computer control of a synthesizer. In the latter situation, the sounds have been processed from the voltage outputs of the synthesizer (its oscillators, modifiers, and so on) but are controlled by a computer program; in this way the computer functions as a super-sequencer. Computer-generated sound, on the other hand, comes directly from the information output of the computer itself. The composer's instructions for "performance," fed into the computer, result in an output on "digital" tape, which is then processed onto magnetic recording tape ("analog" tape), to be heard as sound over loud-speakers. Bear in mind that the composer programs every facet of the sound (from frequency to waveform to duration to envelope) by means of his instructions to the computer. There are no oscillators, filters, or sound-generating equipment of any kind, unless you want to think of the computer itself, used in this way, as a sound-generating device, a highly versatile "synthesizer."

It's essential in understanding this to arrive at some picture of the distinction between "digital" and "analog" apparatus. Simply stated, what is "digital" exists as a series of discrete states and can exist in only one state at a time; the most commonly used example is a light switch, which is either "on" or "off." An "analog" device exists as a continuous range and is adjustable within that range; an example is a radio dial. It is analogous (and I assume that this is the root of the term "analog") to the fluctuating, variable motion of the real world. To use one more illustration, the motion of your arm in reaching out for something or of your leg while walking is a continuously fluid movement without discrete breaks. When you take a motion picture of that action, the camera translates it into a large number of individually separated "still" frames.

As I noted earlier with reference to oscillators, all sound —any sound, whether speech, "noise," or musical tone—is made up of vibrating waves. It's obvious, then, that a representation of sound for loud-speaker transmission must be handled in an "analog" way. The average computer, though, can only accept or emit "digital" information; its output on tape, like the motion-picture film, is made up of discrete particles—in this case, magnetizations that represent numbers. That output can be converted, however, into a continuous "analog" magnetization and directly transcribed onto magnetic recording tape. The process can be reversible, analog to digital, so that a human voice or passage of music—a continuously analog voltage—is converted into a series of individual voltages, represented by separate "numbers" on a tape to be stored in a computer center. All that is needed for this translation process is a machine called a converter. There are two types of converters: one for a-to-d (analog to digital) and the other for d-to-a (digital to analog).

This technique of conversion was initially developed by the Bell Telephone System at their research laboratories in New Jersey, for the purpose of greater automation in telephone service. Two simple instances of the telephone company's use of conversion come to mind, one of these in connection with long-distance calls. When you pick up your telephone receiver in, say, New York and speak into it, the voltages of your vocal sounds are instantly converted into digital voltages, then *re-*

converted to analog form before they emerge as audible sounds through the phone receiver in, say, Los Angeles. There are a number of advantages inherent in this system, such as space-saving (more messages from more telephones being transmitted along the same number of wires). Greater accuracy is also possible, since distortion of the digital information is less damaging to the resultant sound at the other end of the line; equal distortion of an analog signal might easily garble the message. Secondly, it's more than likely that the voice you ˙hear when you've dialed a number "not in working order" is being produced by a computer. A telephone operator originally recorded the message on tape, and the tape has been converted into a series of numbers on a disc stored in some computer facility. Your dialing the unworkable number has triggered the conversion (d-to-a) to the voice you hear in your receiver.

With this equipment and expertise available at the Bell Laboratories, it is hardly surprising that a number of people concerned with musical sound synthesis began research in this area at Bell; composer James Tenney and Bell engineer Max Matthews were among the first to apply the conversion techniques to musical problems. Moreover, a few composers on the neigh-boring Princeton University faculty (in particular, J. K. Randall, Hubert Howe, and Godfrey Winham) were highly interested in these developments. A computer program for sound genera-tion was devised after intensive collaborative research; named MUSIC 4B, it was installed in the high-speed digital computer at Princeton. Similar programs were being developed at MIT and the Argonne Laboratory and, by the mid-1960's, a number of educational institutions (the universities of Michigan, New Hampshire, and Virginia, and Oberlin College, to name but a few) were using programs for musical sound generation in their computers.

How does a composer use these facilities? To begin with, he does not come into any contact with equipment that can produce a musical sound for him on demand—no oscillators, no filters, no synthesizer. In other words, there are no means of aurally testing his ideas until his program has been run through and converted onto recording tape. This means that he must know what he wants and how to program instructions for it before he uses the computer. The medium itself is musically silent, ruling out any possibility of spontaneous "improvisation." A composer could, in theory, spontaneously punch instruction cards at random, but the computer would most likely reject the run; besides, the immediate gratifications of improvising are denied him if he has to wait a few days to hear the sounds he made. Casual experimentation is also limited, not only by the nature of the machine but by the great expense of computer time: The university composer is competing with engineers, physicists, linguists, and assorted administrators who need to use the computer as urgently as he does.

To this degree, the absence of instant sound-producing equipment is a drawback. But, if we look at the same situation from another point of view, the composer working without oscillators and filters is not *limited* by any particular studio setup or any fixed number of modules. Even though the computer actually contains no physical modules, the sounds it can produce may represent an almost infinite number. Just as the composer working at the synthesizer is forced to become an instrument-builder, the composer using the computer for sound generation builds his own unique "synthesizer." He postulates the existence of oscillators and filters (as many as he wishes), envelopes of whatever characteristics he chooses, and as many other variables as he wishes; by programing instructions on punch cards, he then controls the course of his music, after his sound sources are chosen.

I should add that none of this implies the composer has any real knowledge of computer technology, and there's no reason why he must. The composer's main concern, after all, is in getting the equipment to work for his purposes, not in understanding "how" it works. He needs a basic minimum of highly specialized information, of course, even to make the computer function correctly; for example, he must be able to specify the timbres, pitches, and durations he desires in the proper coding "language" so that the computer can deal with his instructions. In addition, it's assumed that he understands the characteristics of sound, whether produced by an oscillator, flute, or computer program, and the acoustical problems he will be dealing with. But beyond this, he doesn't need the sophisticated knowledge of a computer engineer. The program, whether MUSIC 4B or a similar one, has been designed to let him function as a composer and give undivided attention to his musical, not technical, tasks.

In short, the composer approaches the computer with an entire work, or a sizable passage, already preconceived, perhaps written out on lined stave paper. He first "calls up" the MUSIC 4B (or whatever) program from the computer's "memory," if stored there, or runs it through; at this point, the computer will respond to instructions in the context of that program for sound synthesis. He then selects "instruments" and dictates, note by note, timbre by timbre, the entire course of musical events as specifically as he can, by punching cards. Then, in all probability, he waits, perhaps for hours, perhaps for days, until his program is run off, until the finished digital tape (representing a series of numbers) is brought to the d-to-a converter, and until he has a magnetic recording tape (analog) in his hands for audio playback. At this point, he may very well discover that he's made a number of crucial errors in programing. These are probably not logical errors (the computer would have rejected that category during the run), but the wrong choice of timbre, perhaps, or an articulation that's not what he really wanted. So he must then change the information on a few selected cards and run the program through once more, resulting in a further wait. It is a time-consuming process, but well worth it for those who desire the control offered by the medium. Remember, too, that the computer is being used here for "performance." Shouldn't a letter-perfect performance entail at least a few "rehearsals"? And, besides, waiting is a supremely relative affair. The few days that may elapse between the initial programing and the moment you hear your passage through loud-speakers (while interminable in comparison to the instant response of the synthesizer or the classic studio) is a trivial moment in time compared with the months and even years that go by before a live performance of your symphony or string quartet might take place.

Whether long or short, the inevitable time lag between execution and hearing is the computer studio's greatest disadvantage.

A few other problems exist as well. For one thing, the composer's usual notational language is of little use in communicating with the computer, and he must learn to specify his musical wishes in terms he's never had to consider before. Secondly, there are occasional fidelity problems in playback from the converter. The translation of isolated digital bits of information into the continuous magnetization of the analog recording tape may produce a clicking sound known as "quantization noise"; filters are used to suppress this, with varying degrees of success.

The advantages, however, are many, especially for university composers, and it's easy to see why computer studios have been activated on an increasing number of campuses during the past few years. Economy is certainly one factor, for the music school or department if not for the individual composer; a synthesizer might cost the music program many thousands of dollars, specifically charged against the music budget, while the computer is installed for the use of the institution in general, costs being shared throughout the academic community. Availability is also important, as high-speed digital computers will be found on most campuses and need only a sound-generating program to make them functional for music. Servicing is also quick and efficient: Because the computer services so many departments, the university dare not let it break down. Converters are a more specialized kind of hardware and may be difficult to find, but they, too, are becoming increasingly available at large university centers—not simply for the love of electronic music, I should add, but because more diverse uses are being found for them. For example, if the computer is being employed to process and deal with continuous information, such as light waves or heartbeats, the information must be converted, because the computer can only deal with it in the form of discrete numbers; this makes an a-to-d converter a highly useful device. Conversely, d-to-a conversion is needed whenever the computer's digital output is used to control or initiate action in the outside world, such as turning on a machine. For these reasons, converters can often be located in the university's engineering school, or science departments, or perhaps the medical center.

The greatest advantage of all, of course, is that of precise control, assuming that a composer's aesthetic demands such control. It's no secret that computer-generated sound systems are attractive mostly to composers who work from the premise of serialism and "total organization." The medium is ideal for their handling of complex rhythmic, timbral, and pitch relationships. Interesting *sounds* seem to be underplayed (their potential, in fact, is almost altogether disregarded), partly because the composers most fascinated by the medium find their ideas expressed in musical dimensions other than those of novel sonority and partly because the programing for timbral subtleties is still a complex process at this embryonic stage of the technique and is certainly, according to many composers, the most difficult process to master. In any event, why expend energy and computer time in realizing fanciful noises, many composers reason, when these can be gotten with little or no effort on a Buchla synthesizer? It would seem to be more sensible for the computer to concentrate upon those aspects of sound generation that it, more than any other medium, handles supremely well. The only remotely comparable vehicle for total composer control is the RCA synthesizer; but, if we consider that unwieldy giant in the light of all the problems I noted previously (economy, availability, ease of operation and servicing), we can see why it hasn't attracted a wide following. Significantly, those younger composers at Princeton University whose musical thinking was shaped by Milton Babbitt, master of the RCA synthesizer, nevertheless prefer to realize their own finely hewn, precise musical structures via the computer route.

It should be apparent, then, that the computer operation naturally attracts composers for whom control is a virtue. Beyond this, though, it also favors composers who prefer to make compositional decisions away from their sound sources, the actual creation of a work having taken place beforehand in the more or less traditional way (silently, at a desk). It is entirely possible that a composer could write a piece for four "players" and score it in different versions, one for live string quartet and one for computer-generated four-channel tape. And, just as the computer "rewards" such composers, it effectively "punishes" (or, at least, severely handicaps) those who need the physical stimulation of work with actual sounds in order to make their compositional decisions. If a composer considers sound his "material" rather than the surface vehicle for logical arguments concerning continuity, intimate interaction with his material is denied under present working circumstances. True improvisation—that is, guiding the flow of sonic events while they are in progress—is literally impossible. As I suggested earlier, a composer might improvise with the coding of the punch cards, but the program could (probably would) be rejected by the computer—and, in any event, this procedure is far removed in time from the resultant sounds themselves.

This isn't to say that "chance" is entirely absent from the computer music scene. The potential for certain kinds of chance operation is always there, and the rarity of its use in actual pieces (like the similar scarcity of noise effects among the sonorities) is due to lack of interest by most composers now employing the medium. Given the interest of *other* composers, then, there's nothing in the computer process that would prevent a greater degree of chance from occurring. It would be possible, for example, to build general musical "models" with many conceivable realizations, along the lines of the Hiller-Isaacson *Iliac* experiment, and then instruct the computer to perform a random selection of these. John Cage, working with Hiller on *HPSCHD* (for live harpsichords and multiple tapes), programed an extensive series of such selections. He estimates that, if he had used the traditional *I Ching,* he would have needed some 18,000 spins of three coins to arrive at the needed total of possibilities. The computer made the necessary choices in a matter of seconds.

Another sort of chance operation suggests itself: Even if all events (pitches, durations, textures, dynamics) are strictly controlled with respect to each sound in a piece of music, the *order of succession* of these sounds may vary from performance to performance. This has already been done in a vast number of live nonelectronic pieces, most notably Earle Brown's *Available Forms 1 & 2* (ranging from chamber ensemble to full orchestra) and Stockhausen's piano work *Klavierstücke XI.* Composer Charles Dodge has noted that this could also be accomplished in computer-generated music by altering the arrangement of cards prior to each computer run; each run, then, becomes a different and unique "performance" of that particular piece. It's worth noting that both sorts of chance operation—selection from multiple possibilities and rearrangement of composed material—still presuppose the existence of fixed, finite items of information. A more flexible, unpredictable kind of "improvisation" with the computer may be comparatively difficult to come by.

The most varied juxtaposition of computer-generated sound styles now available for general listening is a Nonesuch record containing works by Dodge, Barry Vercoe, and J. K. Randall. These were all realized at the computer centers of Columbia and Princeton universities (although using different sound-synthesis programs) and converted to analog tape at the Bell Telephone Laboratories. Dodge's *Changes,* as its name might imply, presents a rapidly shifting amalgam of many-layered pitch successions and highly differentiated timbres, articulated by a percussive continuity, which in turn relates to that of the pitches; dense chords interspersed among the whole reveal another aspect of the constant (and yet constantly rotating) pitch plan. It is more reminiscent of the Babbitt works for RCA synthesizer than any other composition on this record. In contrast, Barry Vercoe's *Synthesism* is stylistically akin to the "tape" music of the classic studio, employing various filtered-noise effects, reverberation, and rapid figurations of indistinct pitch succession, with a generally Romantic sweep to the over-all unfolding of ideas. Randall is represented here by two brief compositions, each less than two minutes in length (early experiments in glissandi and the elegant interplay of intersecting lines), and by the more ambitious *Mudgett: Monologues by a Mass Murderer* (computer tape with soprano voice). The textures of *Mudgett* are restrained, somber; the harmonic language is unexpectedly consonant, at times almost static—its logic gone awry. Sustained chordal sonorities and slowly moving lines are set against an aperiodic array of sharp, percussive thrusts, and the entrance of the soprano voice continues in this vein. The apparent rhythmic simplicity and regularity of beat are commanding, particularly in the vocal movement, and eventually assume a near hypnotic quality.

Set in the context of the bizarre career of Mr. Mudgett (alias H. H. Holmes, a Chicago pharmacist who may have executed literally hundreds of his lodgers—and lovers—during the late nineteenth century), the childlike lyricism may take on menacing overtones.

The presence of the soprano soloist in *Mudgett* also raises intriguing questions about the nature of "live" sound sources and their integration into a totally taped composition. The multitrack vocal counterpoint and distinctive loud-speaker separation of vocal fragments indicate that, although a live performer has been used in conjunction with the computer tape, there can never be a "live performance." The work has been designed to be heard *as a recording,* through amplifier and loud-speaker systems, and the live voice functions as an integral component of the recording, and not in opposition to it. The same relationship exists in Randall's *Lyric Variations for Violin and Computer,* recorded for Vanguard, about which the composer writes,

> Since the violin frequently plays several parts simultaneously—and anyway since the piece was conceived as sound emanating solely from two widely separated loudspeakers—there is no distinction between a "live performance" and a "recording" of this piece: in concert, a tape-recording is played through speakers.

The variations are organized so that the first five are played by violin alone, the following five for computer alone, and the remaining ten a dialogue of the two forces together. There is a gradual arc of increasing complexity, from the direct, "simplistic" solo through the subsequent multitracking and rhythmic fragmentation of the solo line and intricate tape variants; the intensity subsides during the "duo," concluding with a straightforward presentation of the subject (the "theme") upon which the variations have been built. There is little bravura virtuosity about any of this: The work reveals, rather, a careful placement of lines and artfully shaped nuances, a purposeful sort of neo-Baroque ornamentation, etched upon a plane of silence that ceases to be background and emerges as something much more positive within the whole.

The Randall, Dodge, and Vercoe works I've already mentioned

constitute, for the present, the sum total of commercially available recordings of "traditionally" composed computer-generated music. As you might guess, they all stress various aspects of control. In none of the pieces did the computer assist in the making of compositional choices, the decision-making processes having been undergone independently of the computer realization. We've seen, though, that the computer can be instructed to take a more *active* role in the composing of a work. If and when the computer becomes actively involved in the selection of events, their specifications, and their order of succession (an extreme perhaps exemplified by the *Iliac Suite*), we will arrive at an altogether different kind of music—the "music of nature," perhaps, or "music of logic" (assuming these two categories are different) at any rate, a music more detached from personal, humanistic concerns. I am sure that this will raise angry cries about the "dehumanization of art," but I would suggest that anyone feeling this way should investigate the particular piece under consideration before damning it totally; to be specific, one should consider the very real possibility of human "interference"—that is, the computer may have created the material, but the human partner still controls the analog tape. Having heard it, he may decide to edit, rearrange, and otherwise "compose" the music into its final shape. It's difficult to tell, in that case, what effects are arrived at randomly and what effects are not—which patterns and sequences are the result of overt structuring and which ones "happened." In any event, it's safe to assume that behind every art work ("dehumanized" or not) stands a living being. The one inescapable condition of art, in my view, is summed up in a phrase used in Lukas Foss's *Paradigm* (appropriately enough, spoken by various performers in a random arrangement): "Someone will be held responsible."

An example in point is *Earth's Magnetic Field,* by Charles Dodge, recorded for Nonesuch. Dodge has attempted something on the order of a "natural process" piece exploiting the computer's response to information not intrinsically "musical." The logic behind this is simple enough; once a computer is programed for sound synthesis, a composer may base his own individual program upon *any* data whatsoever. Any sequential phenomena (sociological statistics or astronomical movements of solar bodies) will do, provided they can be dealt with by the computer in the form of numbers. Punch cards may not even be necessary: It might be possible for an a-to-d converter to "read" such continuities as light waves, so that they can be handled in digital form by the computer (and an adroit human programer) for eventual reconversion into sound patterns. Dodge has chosen, as his material, the changing relationships between the rapidly expanding atmosphere of the sun ("solar wind") and the magnetic field of the earth pushing against it in turn. These data (for Dodge's piece, covering the year 1961) are recorded at various magnetic observation stations on earth at three hour intervals. With the aid of three physicists, Dodge has been able to convert the statistical information into a form suitable for use by the music program.

Was the piece composed by the computer? Not at all, because the information was selected prior to the run of the program; in this instance, the computer did not take part in that selection process. The sun and earth might well take credit for some of the music, though, and (to the degree that they supplied the data) the work might be regarded as a joint improvisation by these two bodies. Nonetheless the final "performance" is Dodge's, belongs to him and no one (or nothing) else. He has determined which successions will correspond to pitches and which data will control timbre, tempo, and dynamics; he has decided when to employ single-line interpretations, when polyphonic ones. There are countless other considerations that have gone into the shaping of the material as a *humanly* determined art work. Not that the piece might not have been equally interesting, or equally valid, had he left more of the data in their pristine untampered state. But that would be an altogether different composition; in any event, we'll never know the alternatives. What we have is a unique partnership among men, machines, and natural processes that makes for delightful listening, really quite pleasant in its folklike diatonic melodies and subtle timbral inflections.

Our last example of "computer music" brings up the subject of chance again, this time the random selection of compositional possibilities *by* the computer. I am referring to *HPSCHD,* by John Cage and Lejaren Hiller, one of the most talked-about ventures of the late 1960's. This unique work combines computer-generated analog tape music with live performance (also in part dictated by computer output), visual imagery, and "theater." In its use of the computer to perform chance operations *and* in its bold interaction of the "live" and the "electronic," then, *HPSCHD* seems the ideal vehicle for our moving directly into the next chapter.

6. Live plus Electronic

Six letters are the maximum necessary for computer-coded words, and the six-letter word HPSCHD means "harpsichord." Not that anyone witnessing the première performance of the Cage-Hiller *HPSCHD* would have doubted that fact; on May 16, 1969, at the University of Illinois, seven live harpsichordists and fifty-one computer-generated sound tapes combined in an assemblage of sound—much of it curiously reminiscent of Mozart—that lasted some five hours. A good deal of the "live" (although amplified) harpsichord sound *was* Mozart, in fact, or made up of possibilities derived from Mozart. Cage and Hiller, in creating *HPSCHD,* had used as one source Mozart's *Introduction to the Composition of Waltzes by Means of Dice.* This late eighteenth-century work had called for a flexible ordering of phrases, although all within the same key scheme and always ending on the same "fixed" measure; a computer program at the University of Illinois had generated a series of possible realizations, and these were played by three of the live harpsichordists. Two other live players performed assorted fragments of music from Mozart to the present (represented by Hiller and Cage), and a sixth player was instructed to perform any Mozart he wished.

Each of the fifty-one tapes of computer-generated sound represented a different division of the octave into microtones, from a five-tone octave (the minimum) to a fifty-six tone octave. Every division, that is, *except* the familiar one of twelve. This last was reserved for the seventh harpsichordist, who played a computer-generated "part" written on traditional music paper, designed for a conventional twelve-tone octave tuning.

But all this represents no more than a single aspect of the total "performance." Slides from fifty-two projectors flashed on the exterior of the hall, and the interior was a mass of multiple film and slide imagery—a collage of apparently unrelated visual material, from pages of Mozart's music to abstract shapes and scenes from outer space—sifting through a series of colored lights suspended from the ceiling. The audience of several thousand stood, sat, moved about the large hall as they wished, a few occasionally dancing. Richard Kostelanetz, reporting for *The New York Times,* called *HPSCHD* "one of the great artistic environments of the decade." It is not an atypical piece, either —certainly not for Cage or for Hiller, who have worked with environmental "theater" music over a period of many years, and not in light of the "mixed-media" tendencies that have been developing, in this country and abroad, with ever increasing frequency.

I've begun this chapter with reference to *HPSCHD* for two reasons. One is simply an outgrowth of some comments raised at the end of the preceding chapter, a desire to dispel any notion that computer-generated sound necessarily implies "control" at all times. In this case, we've seen the computer used to generate material "randomly"—that is, selecting from a set of possibilities—and we've also seen that material (however "fixed" it may be as computer output) being put to use *in performance* as part of a giant collage of intersecting sensory images. Secondly (and this, too, grows out of the preceding chapter), the use of electronic material as part of a live performance has not really been discussed at length until now. The one striking characteristic shared by all of the computer-generated works I've mentioned (with the exception of *HPSCHD*) is their mode of presentation, via the solitary loud-speakers. This holds true as well for most of the examples used in our brief survey of the classic studio and the voltage-controlled synthesizer: "Performance," for the most part, consists of the playing of a recording, either in a public space or privately in one's home. J. K. Randall's attitude, in particular, has eliminated live performance even in works using live instrumental sounds.

At the same time, an opposite tendency has been felt throughout the 1960's and seems likely to dominate the coming decade. This is the need for a union of electronics and the live performer, some .partnership between these two powerful forces. This interaction takes many forms and knows no one "style." *HPSCHD* presents one extreme example of a particular direction; there are other, more conservative, approaches taken by different composers. Yet I thought it best to begin this accounting of "live plus electronic" music with a particularly overwhelming, outrageous example, if only to offset the complacency we might have acquired by this point. We've examined so many works designed solely for mechanical reproduction, and the prospect of moving from that directly into a universe of "theater," lights, film, multiple tapes, and a host of live performers was too tempting to resist.

It should be noted, though, that *all* works involving live performance and electronics—whether radical or relatively traditional—have a number of characteristics in common. They all, for example, share the assumption that "performance" is necessarily changeable and spontaneous to a degree and certainly involves "interpretation." When the concepts of one man (the composer) are realized and publicly projected by another man (the performer), this kind of flexibility in playing is bound to occur: Interpretations will vary from performer to performer, and there will be differences even in the playing of the same artist on successive recitals. And this is as it should be; it is what makes the experience of the live performance so exciting to many listeners. Remember, also, that since the mid-1950's the composer doesn't have to "settle" for live performance if he doesn't want it. If a singularly fixed realization of his ideas is what he wishes, he will compose directly for magnetic recording tape. He has *chosen* the live medium because of the hazards of live performance, its immediacy, and the challenges of relating these to the "other" world of electronics. If he prefers not to, his options are open.

Another way of applying this to your own listening is to bear in mind that any recording of such a composition is *not* the composition *per se*, but one performance of that work. We've returned, then, to the original "primitive" notion of recording, whether it be of a work for cello and tape or Beethoven's *Missa Solemnis*—the record as a means of preserving a particular interpretation of a piece of music. I must stress this because most readers will experience the compositions discussed here by listening to phonograph records and should make delicate adjustments in listening when confronted with "performances" of works meant for live concert. A record of Babbitt's *Ensembles for Synthesizer* or Subotnick's *Wild Bull* is, in fact, a copy of that work, having gone through no interpretive middleman. But you can listen to Jacob Druckman's *Animus I* for trombone and tape as you would, say, the *Archduke Trio* or *Moonlight Sonata*.

With respect to live-performance pieces it's also crucial to remember that "listening" is not really the total experience. You should ideally *see* a performance by Artur Rubinstein or the Boston Symphony; when we listen to a record, many of us imagine the live performance taking place—the soloist's arms flailing, head bobbing, the lights, the audience. With much contemporary music, this visual sense is heightened even further—for example, in the Druckman trombone-tape piece I've just mentioned the soloist stalks off the stage during a violent electronic passage, to return later at a subdued moment—and in such instances a recording is not only a "mere" performance, but only a partial performance, at that. It is partial to the degree that it is not visual.

Many of the live-electronic pieces described here haven't been recorded at all, for this very reason. They are simply too theatrical in nature, involve too many diverse sense impressions, including the visual, and are often so improvisatory that to preserve any one performance would actually do the work an injustice. For those "theater" pieces that have been recorded, I'd suggest that you regard the disc version of the particular work as but one specialized performance mode—a unique performance selected from many possible performances. *HPSCHD,* to name one such composition, has been recorded by Nonesuch; to hear that version may be an awesome experience for many, but the recording is a distinctive "object" in itself, only dimly related to the totality of the 1969 Illinois extravaganza.

The pieces that suffer least from recording are those that resemble the "traditional" concert work for soloist and accompaniment. In this case, however, the accompaniment is provided by electronic tape. Such compositions are not necessarily "theatrical" (in the sense that visual action figures prominently), but they are always inherently *dramatic*. How could they be otherwise? There is the figure of the soloist, poised, proud, commanding in his bearing—appealing to all of our nineteenth-century Romantic instincts conjured up by the word "virtuoso." He represents those very qualities that we admire most in the "live," human performance. In addition, his humanity—his frailty, perhaps—is thrown into even sharper relief by the presence of the electronic gear surrounding him. We are made conscious, as never before, of the performer as human being, and the dramatic implications of the human confronting an unknown force are obvious. It is the classic situation of the concerto (the lone soloist pitted against the overwhelming ensemble) in modern guise. Much of the "drama" is illusory, of course (as it is with the concerto), and exists primarily in our imaginations; the highly stylized concert format dictates this particular sort of ritual and its more or less predictable enactment. I suppose one could also say this about a bullfight or other varieties of public spectacle. The image of the noble human engulfed by the sound of the "evil machine" is certainly stimulating, but in reality the tape is rather benign, reliable, even "comfortable" after a number of rehearsals—certainly not an antagonist.

To be fair, though, the soloist *is* faced with some unique challenges in this situation. Performing with an electronic tape is just not the same as playing with an orchestra or piano accompanist; instead of teamwork, a mutual responding between two flexible (and knowledgeable) forces of equal sensitivity, we have one pliable, mercurial human being and one inflexible machine. The inanimate object—the tape—is as predictable and unchangeable as a block of granite. It will never vary its tempo, or dynamic balances, or phrasing; it knows nothing, cannot stop or retrace its steps (unless someone pushes the right buttons), and cannot rescue the soloist in trouble as a sensitive live accompanist might. The performer's problem, then, is one of striking a balance between exact precision (being almost machine-like himself), when strict coordination with the tape is necessary, and a more flexible interpretive stance in which he works "around" and "through" the unyielding recorded sound.

I don't mean to imply that this problem of striking the balance is exclusively the performer's. The *composer* is the one initially faced with the situation, and his way of dealing with it will, in effect, determine the course of the piece. He must decide, for example, how to allow for extended solo passages by the live performer, or whether such passages should exist at all. (It's easier for the composer, in one sense, if there are no extended live solos, since his tape can then be made as a continuous, quasi-independent narrative that runs uninterruptedly throughout the performance. But then, of course, he's denied himself the traditionally useful interplay of contrasting forces and differentiated textures.) Let's assume that the composer has decided to include solo passages; he can either include a fixed duration of silence on the tape part (the tape continuing to run) or have the tape stopped during the performance and resumed later on. Either choice has its drawbacks—in the first instance because the performer's flexibility is limited (especially with regard to tempo) by the invariable parcel of silence allotted to him and in the latter case because an assistant must be found to start and stop the tape on cue (more rehearsal problems).

Secondly, the composer must indicate "cues," important events in the tape part, to the performer by means of the written score. The notation of electronic music is nearly impossible anyway, and very few composers create tapes that would lend themselves to note-by-note (or sound-by-sound) transcription in visual form; even if this could be done, it would probably look so complex that the performer would be hopelessly confused. So the composer attempts a shorthand description, on the written score, of those taped "events" (a striking sound, definite rhythmic pattern) that let the performer know where he is and that aid his coordination with the tape. There are various ways of doing this. Mario Davidovsky, in his *Synchronisms No. 1* (flute and tape), concentrates mainly upon rhythmic cues and precise points of tape entrance. In Morton Subotnick's *Prelude No. 4* (piano and tape), descriptive phrases are also used ("clicks," "fast notes on tape"), and Jacob Druckman attempts visual analogs—shapes, squiggly lines, actual notes at times—in the tape notation for his *Animus I.* Lejaren Hiller's score for *Machine Music* (piano, percussion, and tape) is the most detailed example of all, indicating all of the above plus references to the electronic sources ("filtered sawtooth tones," "banded white noise") themselves.

Notational questions are, to a degree, only mechanical; they come about after the fact of the music and grow naturally out of a composer's musical aesthetic. What, then, are some of the musical choices? A number of them, not surprisingly, deal with the options of "control" versus "chance" that we've mentioned so often before. A composer like Davidovsky structures his music very tightly, in both live and electronic parts, so that relationships are highly organized; careful synchronization of the two per- forming forces is a necessity. Other composers may allow a great deal of freedom. Cage's *Aria with Fontana Mix* offers an example of one extreme position, the vocal part functioning independently of the tape (literally so, since it can be performed as a separate work). Moreover, the tape itself is assembled from a random collage of sounds; since there is no need to synchronize live and electronic material, the singer is free to enter into the total fabric at will. There are many more pieces nearer the middle of the spectrum, in which performers are asked to improvise on selected pitches or invent rhythms and successions with given melodic phrases. Usually such pieces assume that the tape part is to be "fixed" and unchangeable, and there are definite cues on the tape that act as guides and boundaries for improvisation, setting specific limits within which various options can take place. For example, the written score of a hypothetical piece may indicate a piercing whistle on the tape part at 2 minutes 35 seconds, and a bell-like sound at 2 minute 45 seconds. The live performer has those ten seconds, between "cues," to im- provise in some manner suggested by the composer.

Or the tape part itself can be treated as a variable, rather

than as a fixed, immutable object. Robert Ashley's *The Wolfman,*
for amplified live singer-speaker and tape (a brilliantly suggestive
evocation of the sinister night-club vocalist) may be performed
with either of two markedly different tapes. Cage's *Rozart Mix*
involves its performers in the spontaneous selection of tape loops
from a vast, disorganized pile scattered in a shambles about the
playing space. My own *Options II* (clarinet, percussion, and
tape) comes with more tape than performers need in any given
concert, and the players are asked to select those bands of sound
that they prefer. All of these examples stress the factor of
multiple tape choice, but even with one tape there is considerable
freedom of *operation.* An assistant can "perform" the tape part
by manually controlling the volume or by deciding (within limits
set by the composer) *when* to make his part heard and when to
take the volume level down to silence; this presupposes a
continuously flowing band of sonic material (no silences) in
the electronic part and a tape operator with the instincts and
skills of an experienced accompanist. Many of my own compositions for instruments and tape make use of this technique.

A choice of another kind—totally unrelated to the issue of
control—involves the twin questions of texture and balance.
The live and taped forces can be viewed as opposing poles,
or as parallel aspects of a single, indivisible concept. The composer
must decide which of these extremes, or what position somewhere in the middle, is best suited to his ideas. Should the
electronic part function as an antagonist to the soloist, heightening that implicit "drama" I suggested earlier, or should the two
be closely related in timbre, dynamic level, and musical gesture,
creating a closely knit ensemble effect? That sort of choice has
been made before, of course, by composers of earlier periods
—whether to work from an attitude that focuses upon contrasts,
as in the concerto grosso, the classic concerto, and the virtuoso
showpiece, or to create the unity and "partnership" of traditional
chamber music. There are moments in Morton Subotnick's
Serenade No. 3 (flute, clarinet, violin, piano, and tape) in which
the electronic sounds blend so delicately into the entire fabric
that a balanced "quintet" sonority is felt. Mario Davidovsky's
music, although more rigorously controlled in its style, is equally

adept in integrating live and electronic material. His flute *Synchronisms No. 1* and *Synchronisms No. 3* (cello and electronic tape) are shaped so that the taped sounds emerge as subtle analogs of the performers' sounds, creating a real sense of "duet" in both pieces; *Synchronisms No. 2* expands this situation into one involving the interplay of four instruments with the electronic material. Incidentally, the three Davidovsky works are quite beautifully performed on a Columbia disc, flutist Harvey Sollberger meriting special praise.

On the other hand, Charles Whittenberg's *Electronic Study with Contrabass* is a high-tension virtuoso showpiece. It begins in confrontation—the live bassist engulfed by the taped sonorities—and is conceived as a dramatic struggle throughout. Similarly, the trombone soloist of Druckman's *Animus I* is literally overwhelmed by his electronic "adversary" in a brilliantly aggressive contest; the intensity of this is well captured in a Turnabout recording. Paradoxically, the sound sources for the two "integrated"—almost instrumental—tape parts noted above are virtually always electronic, the Subotnick a product of the Buchla voltage-control system and Davidovsky's work created by classic studio techniques. The Whittenberg and Druckman compositions, oddly enough, draw their material from sounds made by the respective live instruments. In each of these two pieces, then, the performer's "adversary" is his own alter ego, the other unexplored side of his instrument's personality.

Contrast between the live and the electronic elements doesn't always have to be this violent or demonic. Lejaren Hiller's *Machine Music* is at its best a cheerful crazy-quilt of opposing textures, drawing upon a barrage of synthesized effects *and* the battery of instruments played by the live percussionist; the latter include various drums, cymbals, glockenspiel, xylophone, bells, brake drums, ocarina (hardly percussion, though!), and alarm clock. A more relaxed, whimsical atmosphere also pervades Donald Erb's *In No Strange Land* (trombone, contrabass, and tape), in which the electronic and live materials complement one another with great coloristic variety. A Nonesuch recording of this piece also includes Erb's *Reconaissance* for four instrumentalists and two Moog synthesizers performed "live" (in "real time"), which is equally refreshing in its direct, unacademic style. By comparison, Michael Sahl's *A Mitzvah for the Dead* is nostalgic, dreamlike in nature; Sahl sets a tape fabric of half-obscured musical quotations against an overly (and intentionally so) lush solo violin part that draws heavily upon "The Last Rose of Summer." The effect is often impressionistic, and curiously static. In violinist Paul Zukofsky's recording for Vanguard the various strands combine to make up an entity that is charming, perhaps even touching, in its appeal to submerged memories.

I should add a few more words here on the entire question of musical "quotation," raised in the Sahl piece. The subject is as controversial as any in the domain of contemporary music, and not only with respect to electronic works: eyebrows are raised in consternation when Berio reconstructs Mahler in his orchestral *Sinfonia,* or when George Rochberg quotes passages from Ives, Varèse, Berg, and Bach in his chamber music. It would be sophomoric for me to quibble about the definition of "originality" or the significance of "context" here; I would note, though, that the *historical* precedents for such borrowings are great —Bach's use of everything from Lutheran chorales to Vivaldi concerti, the medieval and Renaissance paraphrases of current "popular" material, Fauré's parodies of Wagner (not to mention the famous quotes from the Wagner *Tristan* Prelude found in Berg and Debussy), and so on. The mid-twentieth century is a period in which this device can be especially useful, because we're all aware of so much more music—and greater stylistic varieties of it—than our forefathers were. We can thank the availability of recordings for this; the entire world of sonic experience, from Gregorian chant to Schubert's chamber music to Franck organ works to Buddhist liturgy, is at our disposal, at least ten centuries' and five continents' worth of it. Secondly, "quotation" is particularly well suited to *electronic* means, because of the ease of fragmenting, recombining, superimposing, and distorting (via filters, reverberators, or ring modulators) on tape. Collage was, after all, the first basic technique of the Paris *musique concrète* studio. And, even though succeeding developments, from the classic studio to the very latest computer-synthesizer system, have made it possible for composers to create "original" material on tape, collage remains a useful and legitimate aspect of the medium.

Finally, an entirely new dimension assumes importance whenever we combine live instruments and electronic means, and that is *space*. Or, perhaps even more broadly, "ambience"—the special impact, in the context of a work with live performers on stage, of sounds emanating not from the players but from loud-speakers. The use of *any* material, then, in a spatially and dramatically effective context, can be "original"—whether that taped material is filtered white noise or Palestrina or Sousa marches, whether distorted or unabashedly obvious. The drastic shifts from one image (and one space) to another, "familiar" to "unexpected" and back, create a startling frame of reference and a totally new context of listening; in this situation, even well-known quotes assume a unique character.

To illustrate: At the conclusion of Pauline Oliveros's *Double-basses at Twenty Paces,* this apparently comic theater piece (involving much speech and action by the two soloists) suddenly becomes menacing. Just at the high point of a climactic passage, the house and stage lights are extinguished, a large amorphous slide is flashed upon a backdrop, and an overpowering tape of incomprehensibly muddled sound is heard; the distortion gradually falls away, and the music comes "into focus" as the final cadence of the Beethoven Fifth Symphony, at precisely the moment when the visual image is brought into focus—and revealed as Beethoven's death mask. Or, in Sydney Hodkinson's *Organasm,* a presumably serious organ solo becomes progressively more chaotic: Assistants appear, play clusters on the keyboard, and pull the "wrong" stops; the organist's playing style changes imperceptibly from post-Webern to Bach to Radio City Music Hall to ragtime; and finally dozens of people surround the organ, blowing noise-makers and stomping on the footpedals. At the loudest point of the general pandemonium the organ power is abruptly turned off, all of the "extras" rush off stage, and all that can be heard is a recording of quiet sacred music. I have distorted familiar sources, *concrète* style, in a number of my own pieces for electronic tape and instruments, such as *Aria*

No. 4 (bassoon and tape), the focal point of which is an undisguised fragment of a Schubert trio, or *Music for Prince Albert* (piano and two tapes), which juxtaposes electronically distorted piano sounds with orchestral passages from Handel and Mendelssohn.

Works for orchestra and electronic tape are not as numerous as their solo and chamber equivalents, but this can be accounted for by the generally conservative performance policies of most orchestras, rather than any disinclination by composers. The history of compositions for this medium, though, is as long as that of tape music itself, beginning with Varèse's *Déserts* and the early Luening-Ussachevsky collaborations of the 1950's. The Belgian composer Henri Pousseur uses the two forces antiphonally, and often with great imagination, in his *Rimes pour différentes sources sonores,* available on an RCA recording; Pousseur employs a balance of textures and motivic fragments in the hard-edged style (influenced by Webern, Boulez, and the Darmstadt "school") that dominated Europe in the early postwar years, although the work is freer and more flexible in building up sustained densities. The sources of the tape are entirely electronic and used to create effects, particularly in relation to the orchestra, that are quite striking.

There are also a great many recent orchestral pieces that include tape not as a "soloistic" or special element, but merely as part of the large total ensemble. In such works, the tape part, as one voice in a complex texture, may not even be recognizable as "electronic"; perhaps a sustained tremolo on tape has been woven into a woodwind figuration, or perhaps the tape part consists of abrupt, sharp punctuations that are all but indistinguishable from the percussion battery. It's also possible that the tape role is that of presenting familiar, undistorted material (simply transmitted through the loud-speakers) rather than manipulated or synthesized sound. *The Whale,* a massive composition for chorus and orchestra by the young Englishman John Tavener, begins with recorded material, but of a most prosaic sort: an undistorted voice, reading (in even, conventional tones) a passage on whales drawn from the Collins Encyclopedia. As the voice continues to drone on, it is gradually lost in a rising crescendo of instrumental figuration. A later scene depicting Jonah in the belly of the whale includes a tape collage of popular songs, fire alarms, and a church service as part of an overpowering orchestral ostinato. My own *Island* for orchestra similarly uses recorded fragments of jazz, birdcalls, pinball machines and a shooting gallery, German drinking songs, a simple folk tune on a harmonica, and BBC London weather forecasts. Although many of these were reduced to brief spurts of a few seconds each, none was distorted or manipulated in any *concrète* way.

It should be apparent by now that "electronic" parts don't necessarily have to be synthesized or even processed from natural sources; we've certainly seen this with reference to the pieces that use quoted material. Why, then, couldn't a composer create his *own* material—that is, compose a passage for live instruments and have it recorded—and then use this tape (undisguised and undistorted) as one component of an otherwise live performance? I can foresee one possible objection from readers at this point: that this would not really be electronic composition at all. True enough, if the composer were to regard his recording as a fixed, independent "object" and declare that it—as it stands— *is* the art work, to be heard *only* in the form of a recording, then we might say, with some justification, that what he claims to be "electronic" is only the recorded performance of something "live." (But, remember, even these distinctions have become increasingly fuzzy. What of Milton Babbitt's comments about the recorded Tchaikovsky symphony, noted earlier? Or J. K. Randall's use of live performers exclusively for recorded situations?) In any event, the composer probably *doesn't* regard the recording in this way. He is using it so that the live performer *and* the tape, together, create an aura, an ambience, that neither could accomplish separately. I suggested at the outset of this volume that one possible approach to "electronic music" might be the extension of known limits: the realization of the impossible. In view of that, we have to say that the medium of "live plus live-on-tape" meets the requirement. It enables us to hear the sound of one soloist magnified many times, playing in ensemble with himself, being heard from as many spots in the hall as there are loud-speakers. Or we can hear the past recaptured, a passage previously played live now "echoed" over the sound system against something new.

The concept of "echo" has caught the imaginations of quite a few composers. Among the first to deal with it in an extended work was Mauricio Kagel, whose *Transición II* (piano, percussion, and two tapes) represents an attempt to come to grips with the problem of "recapitulation"—the past as present—while using an atonal, asymmetrical style. He asks his performers to record sections of the piece before the performance (tape 1) and then records sections of the live performance itself—material *not* performed during the preconcert recording—for use as repeating tape loops (tape 2). Speed changes in tape playback, reverberation, filtering, and other modifications may or may not be made when these two tapes are played during the course of the work, by which time, of course, the live instrumentalists have moved on to yet *another* stage of their own performance. As Kagel describes the process, "while the interpreters always play in the present, they simultaneously tape-record fragments for the future; these fragments, in turn, become the past when, later, they are made audible through loud-speakers in the hall." Adroit performances by David Tudor and Christoph Caskel, on a Mainstream recording, articulate these relationships with great clarity. Another example of prerecorded material in a chamber context occurs in David Burge's *Aeolian Music* (flute, clarinet, violin, cello, and piano); the ensemble is required to record two separate passages and then synchronize these onto the two channels of a stereo tape. In actual performance, the live group then plays a *third* passage, while spatially separated in the hall (the flutist and clarinetist having moved to far corners of the stage), as the loud-speakers join the ensemble. In effect, the five players have become fifteen. As the material itself is made up of spoken words, percussive sounds made on the instruments, and traditionally produced pitches, the total sonority is quite brilliant.

Undoubtedly the best-known passage of this kind is the finale of Lukas Foss's aptly named *Echoi* (clarinet, cello, percussion, piano), in which the past-future paradox suggested by Kagel is pursued even further. *Echoi,* throughout its four movements, deals in "echoes" of all kinds—melodic imitations, reverberating timbres (such as the clarinet being blown close to the head of a kettledrum), passages that continually repeat and revert to their beginnings like scratched record grooves. The last movement introduces a tape, previously made by the performers, which they are now required to imitate in a disjunct, distorted fashion; to complicate the fabric further, the tape finally imitates itself—the two channels simply being a rerecording of identical material separated by a fixed time duration—and a nightmarish three-part round (two parts taped, one live) advances to the work's conclusion.

The idea of "echo" is refined to an utterly perfect, self-contained art form in the work of Steve Reich. He takes the smallest recognizable units of sound—individual words, tiny instrumental phrases—and breaks them into two channels that begin together (that is, an ordinary stereo playback) and then move imperceptibly "out of phase" with one another. This began initially as a tape loop technique, using spoken words as the sound source; two of Reich's early word pieces, *Come Out* and *It's Gonna Rain,* have been recorded and are absolutely staggering listening experiences. The method proved no less commanding when he turned, later, to instrumental sources. In *Reed Phase* and *Violin Phase,* the latter recorded by Paul Zukofsky for Columbia Records, the performer makes the tape (short repeating melodic cells) beforehand and then plays against his own material in concert—gradually changing his tempo by imperceptible degrees, until he is one note out of phase with his recorded counterpart, then two, and so on. What at first appears to be great activity (rhythmic and acoustical) is the mere surface of a larger, static body at rest—a single gigantic vibration, so to speak.

Although Reich's aesthetic is uniquely his own, the concept of pitting a virtuoso soloist against a recording of himself is not new. Roman Haubenstock-Ramati's *Interpolations* for flute and recorded flutes dates back to 1958; that composer has also written a similar piece, *Liaisons,* for percussionist. Robert Erickson has coined the term "solo-ensemble piece" with reference to the genre—including music by Paul Chihara, Donald Erb, Phil Winsor, and William Duckworth—and has contributed two major works of this kind himself. Erickson's *Ricercar à 5* (trombone and four recorded trombones) and *Ricercar à 3* (contrabass and two recorded basses) were composed for two of the great virtuoso performers of avant-garde music today, trombonist Stuart Dempster and bassist Bertram Turetzky. The works are, to a degree, built about the personalities of the players and are most effective as total (visual, spatial, and aural) experiences; it's a delight to watch either performer working against his recorded images. There are excellent recorded versions of both Erickson works, however. The trombone *Ricercar,* a dazzling, aggressive, almost ferocious display, has been released on the Acoustic Research series; the contrabass piece, more somber and intro- spective, with highly resonant sitar-like textures, is issued by Ars Nova/Ars Antiqua.

This is only a sampling of works for live performers and tape, and I regret that it can't be longer. A comprehensive accounting of all the music composed for this medium would be impossible; there are simply too many works, already written and presently being written. The potential for further exploration is still great, and if our good fortune continues a number of excellent pieces now unrecorded will eventually find their way onto discs—then there will be that much more for us all to consider. Another sort of music, however, seems less likely to appear on commercial recordings. I'm referring to compositions that stress the theatrical, the multisensory, and the improvisatory. For a work of this kind, live performance in a public setting is so integral to the concept that recording is an irrelevancy. There are recorded performances of a few mixed-media "theater" pieces, such as *HPSCHD* and the *L's GA* of Salvatore Martirano, and I won't deny that they often make for exciting listening. Pure "listening," though, is only a fraction of the total experience originally intended by the composer, and a recording (even an excellent one) is a particularly limited version of a theater piece. An unavoidable reduction in scope, duration, and "environmental" abundance is often necessary before such a work can be realized for the specific "performance" space of your living room. Because of the great flexibility of this kind of piece, that is one legitimate realization (among many) and one possible mode of performance. I would guess, though, that most composers of spontaneous, multimedia, spatially extravagant works are trying their hardest to get you *out* of your living room. For many of them, the private experience of listening has been superseded by a more inclusive, communal receptivity—a taking in of diverse sounds, gestures, visual images, actions, and words.

Electronic techniques figure heavily in this new "theater music." With some composers, in fact, the theatrical aspects of their work grew out of a prior interest in electronics; the low-key, passive performance aspects of their earlier tape music didn't satisfy them, and they felt a strong need to augment these by adding human activity. Those composers interested in chance also discovered that prerecorded magnetic tape, in its very predictability, must be incorporated within a framework of *other* actions—more spontaneous ones—if the live sense of immediacy were to be preserved. The most important development within this movement, one natural outgrowth of improvisatory performance, is the virtual abandonment of the prerecorded tape. "Live electronics," the modification of sounds made on the spot in the performance place, has become one of the major directions of today's music. All manner of sounds made by the players, from the very quiet to an ear-shattering roar, can be amplified and sent directly to loud-speakers. Or the microphone signal may be rerouted and sent through filters, a ring modulator, perhaps an entire voltage-controlled synthesizer. Part of the live performance may be taped and the tape made into loops (as in the Kagel *Transición II*) or modified by playback speed changes, tape reversal, and the like. A tape of the live performance might also be run through a number of tape recorders simultaneously, creating instant effects of tape delay or echo.

Bear in mind, though, that the use of "live electronics" doesn't always have to stress the overtly theatrical, nor is improvisation essential to the process. The technique functions just as well for composers working within the concert-hall tradition. David Bedford's *Come in Here Child* (soprano voice and amplified piano) is a direct, evocative setting of a Kenneth Patchen text, and would hardly be considered "radical"; the sole novelty in this otherwise straightforward work is the use of an amplifier, controlled by the pianist, so that it catches resonances of the instrument and throws them to loud-speakers at the rear of the hall. Aside from this—and some playing on the inner strings by the pianist, which has become standard performance practice for the mid-twentieth century—the piece is well within the tradition of the art song. The virtuoso concert tradition is maintained in Druckman's *Animus III* (clarinet and tape), very much as in his earlier *Animus I* for trombone, but distorted live clarinet sounds—modified by microphone feedback—have been added to the interplay of soloist and electronic tape. As the tape itself has been made from clarinet material (including the voice of clarinetist Arthur Bloom, who performs the work on a Nonesuch recording), we now have the instrumentalist at three levels of reality, his "presence" multiplied and fragmented in different ways.

These examples demonstrate the simplest kind of live electronics, using microphone, amplifier, and loudspeakers to effect changes in sound quality. The high noise level of Robert Ashley's *The Wolfman,* noted earlier in a different connection, is caused by microphone feedback that often approaches the point of pain; the "sinister nightclub performer," improvising on vocal sounds, literally *plays* his microphone as a resonating musical instrument. Led by the numerous examples of John Cage, many composers have also investigated the use of contact microphones. These "pick up" direct friction on their surface; speaking "into" such a microphone in the traditional manner (even a few inches away from it) will not affect it at all, but, if you rub it across your clothing or skin, a wholly new spectrum of sound will materialize. Cage has pioneered in the use of contact mikes in performance: He attaches them to the surfaces of musical instruments in his orchestral *Atlas Eclipticalis,* or, in solo performances, he may affix one to his pen—or paper, or desk, or seat, or typewriter—while he answers his mail on stage. He can press one against his throat as he drinks a glass of water.

Given even this basic equipment, then, the possibilities for alteration of material during a concert are enormous. More sophisticated devices, and the presence of assistants controlling dials and settings, can lead to even more spectacular effects, as in many of Stockhausen's more recent pieces. *Mikrophonie I* and *Mikrophonie II* of the mid-1960's have exerted a special influence over the younger European composers. In these two works (the first for large gong and the second for chorus and Hammond. organ), assistants manipulate and transform the live sounds by means of directional microphones, filters, and ring modulators. During the course of *Mikrophonie II,* tapes of earlier Stockhausen compositions, including the *Gesang der Jünglinge* of his tape studio days, are heard as a distant counter-subject to the live proceedings. Both pieces, incidentally, can be heard on a Columbia recording.

In Larry Austin's *Accidents* for electronically prepared piano, the strings of the instrument are constantly in contact with vibrating membranes, and a large number of contact microphones, cartridges, and guitar pickups carry the vibrations to loud-speakers scattered about the hall. An assistant uses a ring modulator to alter the initial sounds still further. The plan of the piece is fascinating; the pianist is asked to play a series of complex passages as rapidly as possible, while *making no sounds*—any keys actually depressed ("accidents") thus triggering a barrage of sonic effects and obligating the performer to begin again. The piece ends when the pianist successfully—that is, silently—completes every gesture indicated. Alvin Lucier uses a sophis-ticated system called the "Vocoder," developed by Sylvania Electronics, in his *North American Time Capsule 1967* for chorus. The performers are asked to prepare and read state-ments descriptive of life and civilization in the twentieth century; this simultaneous word texture, fed into the Vocoder, is translated into digital information, which, in turn, is electronically processed. As recorded for Odyssey, the *Time Capsule* presents an effect that is half-garbled and half-coherent, shimmering and other-worldly. Another means of sound transformation (not always "electronic") can be found in Salvatore Martirano's brilliant theater piece *L's GA* for "gassed-masked politico, helium bomb, and two-channel tape." The solo performer, his face enclosed in a gas mask, constructs an ornate word piece, fanciful and yet bitterly ironic, from the Gettysburg Address, set against a vivid film and *concrète*-like tape; increasingly drastic distortions of the live sound, caused by everything from tape loops to helium within the mask, lead to a feverish climax that simply cannot be described. The performance for Polydor records (omitting the film, of course) is superb.

Tape loop techniques require the services of a capable assistant who (theoretically) records selected passages during a performance and then quickly splices these into continuous loops for later playback. That is, at least, the basic idea. It can be refined and simplified in one of two ways: Either the loops are recorded in advance of the performance (in which case we're dealing with "live and prerecorded live" again) or the blank tape, ready for recording in concert, has been edited into loops beforehand. To my knowledge, the most elaborate piece of this kind is Ben Johnston's *Casta* (add the performer's name to complete the title). As played by Bert Turetzky on a Nonesuch recording, *Casta Bertram* becomes a dense constellation of sounds —some vocal, some instrumental, many amplified by contact mikes—stored on three different tape loops; that accumulated material, on three simultaneous playback systems, builds in volume until it eventually drowns out the performer. The work demands tight coordination and rapid-fire execution by both soloist and recording engineer (the latter recording, mixing, and then performing all three loops on the spot), and the resulting virtuoso collaboration is in every sense a "duet."

The Johnston piece also brings us back to the notion of "echo," that intangible relationship of past and present I referred to earlier. It's evident that any live-electronic work using tape loops made during the performance touches upon this area to some degree. There is another valuable method of exploiting the unique qualities of echo in performance: the use of a single reel of tape threaded onto a number of tape recorders (at least one actually recording, the others on playback), in conjunction with a live sound source. This results in the "tape delay" of the original signal. For example, as the initial sound—a flute, perhaps—is made, it is fed through a microphone and recorded by machine 1; the sound is then played back, after a fixed time interval, by machine 2, and heard over loud-speakers. If the microphone is in a position to pick up the loud-speakers, the playback will *also* be *re*-recorded, again on machine 1, generating an infinite continuum. Meanwhile, of course, the flutist may go on playing new material against his "past" image, the combined aggregate of past and present, in turn, being added to the tape delay system. The duration of the delay is predictable and controllable, since it's determined by the distance between tape recorders at a particular playback speed. I have to admit that my illustration is oversimplified, complex as it may sound. The possibilities are enhanced enormously, for example, if the moving tape (or the initial microphone signal) can be routed through modifying devices, such as filters. Most importantly, there can be an assistant capable of controlling these variables; if we have an assistant, we may change the levels and effects of sound-modifiers, mix the sounds from different sources (if, say, we had a flute, oboe, and trumpet with separate microphones), and suppress any and all of these if an undistorted "solo" is called for. It's a formidable list of tasks, requiring a sensitive, responsive musician at the control dials. On the other hand, it may be a lot less risky than splicing tape.

The acknowledged leader in this area is Pauline Oliveros, who has done more with the technique than anyone else I can think of. Her *I of IV,* using one tape threaded between two machines, has been recorded for Odyssey, and the really haunting effects that characterize the medium are beautifully evident in the disc performance. There are other, more elaborate, systems in her music: *C(s) for Once* of 1966 (voices, flute, trumpets, and organ) uses a complex interaction of three tape decks, and a Buchla synthesizer modifies the sounds passing through four machines in her *Beautiful Soop.* Tape delay can also be heard in Martirano's *L's GA* and such pieces as my own *Interruptions* (woodwind quintet), the latter featuring a loop threaded between two machines. The technique is especially important in Daniel Lentz's *ABM (Anti-Bass Music),* where a contrabass player and actor-speaker create an overpowering wall of sound; in the two performances I've heard, the auditorium sounded as though it were under attack during an air raid. Lentz adds to this a prerecorded tape, off-stage piano, spotlights, and a number of optional endings (the use of 25 to 100 laughing machines scattered throughout the audience, a reading of the list of Vietnam war dead, a team of assistants moving through the audience and swabbing the ears of volunteers with a peroxide solution) that can be superimposed—the entire amalgam designed to alternately titillate and attack our senses. "Assault" might be an even better word; as David Cope has noted in writing about *ABM*, the work "brings to the level of equals the concert situation and a battle-field; [it is] thoroughly antagonistic to the traditions of both art and war."

In this and a number of other pieces, Lentz also uses trans-ducers, which, in effect, make any object they're placed upon (a tabletop, lamp, your arm or head, the surface of a cello) a temporary loud-speaker; the contrabass of *ABM* thus serves as the speaker system for its own echoes. The immediate effect of such a device is startling and disrupts the listener's preconceptions about space and directionality. Lentz is fond of playing upon our equilibrium, using this technique and others (transistor radios carried by assistants, walkie-talkies distributed about the audience area) in performances by his improvisational group called the California Time Machine.

(In passing, I should note that live-electronic music has made more headway in California than in any other part of the United States—an indication, perhaps, of the greater sense of freedom there with respect to chance, noise, and "theater" than the more control-oriented Eastern seaboard provides. There is no logical reason why this should be so; the facts are that the first American movement devoted to chance originated with Cage, Earle Brown, Morton Feldman, Christian Wolff, and David Tudor in New York, while the twin apostles of rationality—Schoenberg and Stravinsky—resided in Los Angeles! But that was more than twenty years ago, and today many of the "radical" avant-garde's leading figures—Subotnick, Austin, Lentz, Oliveros, Erickson, Ashley, Terry Riley, Roger Reynolds, Loren Rush—are based in California.)

Up until now, we've been discussing specific pieces—"com-positions"—by creative artists who have, so to speak, signed their names to their work. *Collaborative* enterprises are equally im-portant, especially those improvisational groups that make it their business to explore little-known areas of live electronics. The California Time Machine is a relatively recent addition to the field; a significant number of older groups are still actively flourishing: the ONCE Group of Ann Arbor, Michigan (which originally served as a springboard for Ashley, Gordon Mumma, Roger Reynolds, and others), the Sonic Arts Group based in New York (Ashley, Mumma, Alvin Lucier, and David Behrman), Cornelius Cardew's London AMM, the Musica Elettronica Viva (MEV) of Rome, and Larry Austin's New Music Ensemble of Davis, California, are but a few. Some other early groups have disbanded but, like the San Francisco Tape Music Center (comprised of Oliveros, Subotnick, and Ramon Sender; recently revived by Robert Ashley at Mills College), made their imprint on an entire "style" that emerged from their work. Or, like Lukas Foss's Improvisation Ensemble of the mid-1950's, they've seen a number of their contributions put to use in more or less traditional "compositions"; Foss's Ensemble experiences, for example, figured heavily in the writing of his *Time Cycle* and *Echoi*.

Each group has its own style, but most of them will play "composed" pieces as well as improvisations. Mumma's *Mesa* and *Horn*, for amplified (and highly altered) instrumental sounds, might be included in the Sonic Arts programs, and appearances of the Davis New Music Ensemble might well stress certain pieces by Austin, Stanley Lunetta, and other composer-performer members. Totally free, unplanned improvisation—"creation" at the moment of performance—is still the guiding principle behind the group idea, however, and prepared renditions of precomposed material are no more than secondary activities. Musica Elettronica Viva, formed by a number of young American composers in Rome, has existed since 1966 and since that time has toured throughout Europe and the United States. It's hard to describe a performance of this group, or of any of the others, but it might help to note that air microphones, contact mikes, mixers, radios, and a Moog synthesizer are standard traveling equipment for MEV and that it's membership (Frederic Rzewski, Alvin Curran, Allen Bryant, and others) may be found playing violin, piano, saxophone, harmonica, police whistles, camel bells, steel drum, glass objects, metal sheets, or Ping Pong balls (to name a few) on any given evening. The audience is invited to bring instruments and play along in a work called *Sound Pool*, or a performance of *Street Music* (players with portable sound sources—voices, objects, battery-powered electronic devices—moving in the direction of the softest "other" sounds they hear) might take place in a public square. If this engages your curiosity, you can hear a performance by MEV on a Mainstream recording, coupled with an equally provocative session by the AMM people of London. I wish both sides of the record were twice as long—my own feeling being that improvisations like this should last at least a few hours—but they do provide absorbing (often commanding) moments in the limited time available.

What next? Are there any "new directions" left in an area already extended beyond what we used to call impossible? It might seem that we've already reached our limits—live performance plus electronic tape, live plus prerecorded instrumental material, modified live sound, tapes recorded in live performance and then modified, and any and all combinations of these. Furthermore, we certainly haven't exhausted the potential *within* any of these categories. Even if nothing really "new" were to happen for quite a while, the future of live electronics would still be bright.

It seems highly likely, though, that there will be a number of radical changes within the next few years, particularly in that vast, uncharted domain known as mixed-media. For one thing, the creators of mixed-media activities generally proceed on a casual *ad hoc* basis in almost all of their work. I don't mean to imply that there's anything wrong with this; the facts are, simply, that "improvisation" means literally just that—the ability to get the maximum use out of the materials one has. By comparison, composers of more traditional persuasions usually have definite goals in mind, both for their individual pieces and for the development of the art as a whole. Someone whose main interest is in computer generation of sound, within a traditionally "controlled" context, will tell you that, over the next five years or ten, he hopes that thus and so will occur to improve the technology for his purposes. The "media" composer, improvisational by nature, has goals that are far less fixed; in fact, he may have no set goals at all, other than his determination and willingness to use *anything* the technology may devise. He will accept whatever the future has to offer and will find a way of turning it to his creative advantage. Secondly, the future contains many more options for a composer working in the area of multisensory "theater" music. I really can't venture a guess as to what will further revolutionize the synthesis of *sound* (the traditional composer's primary concern), but I'd hardly go wrong in predicting some—any—changes in the fields of videotape, laser technology, slide projection, telephone transmission, radar, medical research, ESP, stage design, synthetic fibers . . . a virtually limitless catalogue. You name it, and there's probably a composer out there somewhere who will want to *use* it in creating an "environment" of his own design.

Two important developments have already begun to attract some notice. One of these involves a turning away from the specialized reproduction-transmission equipment of electronic music, and a return to more familiar electric devices. We've already noted Daniel Lentz's use of transistor radios in performance; Pauline Oliveros also asks performers to walk across the stage carrying radios at a normal volume level—a casual, everyday action placed in another context—as part of her *Aeolian Music*. This is hardly "new" *per se;* John Cage has been drawing sounds from radios, phonograph records, toasters, typewriter bells, and every other kind of home appliance since the 1930's. More radical implications appear, however, when the familiar items are not moved into the concert hall but are played in their own natural surroundings. That is, a concert piece (played on stage) using automobile horns and headlights—whether interesting or not—is just another concert piece. A work using those elements *in* the automobiles, *in a parking lot or while moving along a roadway*, has done something on an altogether different level of importance. Robert Moran (another Californian, by the way) conducted an ensemble of cars, building lights, and radio messages in a gigantic theater piece, involving much of the city of San Francisco, a few years ago. Projects like these, and there are quite a number of them, are doing much to change our ideas about "concerts," "performances," and the proper settings for their enactment. In the following chapter, I'll take up this entire question in greater detail, noting the beginnings of a new "literature"—works that can *only* be experienced over the telephone, in your kitchen, through an automobile radio, on a moving elevator.

A second trend takes its cue, perhaps, from Cage's famous anecdote about his time spent in Harvard University's totally soundproof anechoic chamber; inexplicably, he recounts, he heard two sounds and later discovered that these were his nervous system and his blood in circulation. There are numerous such sound sources within our own bodies, capable of being tapped for use by amplification or computerized a-to-d transformations. David Rosenboom, a young composer now at York University in Toronto, has been working with brain waves, feeding impulses into a computer of his own design. He claims that performers can eventually control their output and wave type—"people can learn to recall their psychophysical states and lock in on them," as he puts it—after some practice. In this way our minds could regulate the characteristics of sound produced over loud-speakers. Rosenboom regards this as an extension of our musical traditions: in a *New York Times* interview, he advances the view of "music as an information energy system, and the human being as an input-output device. The brain is a computer—a digital-analog pattern recognizer." In the context of group performance, a number of people activating sounds along these lines discover a "meditational language," literally a dialogue of minds. A number of Rosenboom's recent works attempt something like this; the best known (if only for its title) is a seventy-two-hour piece called *How Much Better if Plymouth Rock Had Landed on the Pilgrims*, in which meditative states produce recurrent drones and repeating figurative patterns.

Alvin Lucier's *Music for Solo Performer 1965* was the innovative composition in this field and is still unique in a number of ways—for one, the impressive theatrical aspect of the performance, beginning mysteriously (only the formal title is given on the program) with various states of emerging ambiguity. An assistant cleans the soloist's scalp, applies gauze pads and electrodes to the head, tests equipment; all of this slowly builds up to the moment of sound itself, and a growing audience awareness of the actual process involved. The brain waves employed are those of the "alpha" state, present only during nonvisualizing activity; in this way, a second theatrical component has been built into the piece—the soloist's eyes must be closed before sounds can be generated, and the sounds cease whenever he opens them. Furthermore, Lucier uses the sound emerging from loud-speakers to activate *other* resonant instruments located about the hall, including timpani, bass drum, piano, bells, gongs.

The brain, while perhaps the most interesting and versatile source of waves and electrical signals, is certainly not the only one. M. L. Eaton, referring to this entire area of activity as "bio-music," mentions other possibilities: the signals generated by the heart, the movement of the eyes, involuntary muscular contractions, skin itself. It may be hard to visualize the specific uses these will be put to in performance, but the potential is already here. Pauline Oliveros has written a part for amplified heartbeats in a recent piece; Gerald Shapiro has a group improvisation called *Breath*; and there will be more to follow. Perhaps, in the future, the term "live electronics" will be more apt than ever.

7. Further Listening and Suggested Reading

You might wish to consider this chapter a kind of drawing together of some loose ends. In particular I hope that, by going further into the recorded literature, I can give a more comprehensive picture of today's electronic music scene. The variety and scope of that picture—even among the relatively few pieces that are recorded—should be apparent by now, but mention of a few dozen additional recordings will underline that point, I hope, beyond any question. I also want to set that total picture in a more accurate historical perspective. This book has been organized along two roughly parallel lines, in terms of "techniques" (the classic tape studio, the semi-automated synthesizer, electronic manipulations of live performance) *and* in a semichronological format; despite all of my protestations to the contrary, some readers may still conclude that there's a fixed relationship between the two. Because I ended the discussion of the *musique concrète* idea when the narrative moved from the 1950's into the 1960's, you might possibly assume that the idea ended then as well—or, because I began to stress live-electronic interactions in a chapter devoted to the 1960's, you may associate them exclusively with that decade. It's difficult to demonstrate by means of recordings that the second assumption is false (because many early works are simply not available on discs), but I can certainly try to wreck the first one by noting a great many recent pieces that employ "early" techniques.

This is a highly personal, selective, and therefore biased listing; it makes no attempt at being "comprehensive." I should add that, because of the whims of the recording industry and the rapid developments in this comparatively new musical area, any list of recordings is *bound* to be selective, partly incomplete, and even partly obsolete. By the time this book reaches you, new works will have been composed and recorded, some European imports may have become available in the United States, and a number of records will have undoubtedly been withdrawn from circulation. This situation is inevitable, and please keep it in mind as you read on.

For instance, it's become increasingly difficult to hear examples of the early live-performance instruments developed before World War II, as many of the recordings are no longer available. It might be possible, though, to unearth Jolivet's *Concerto for Ondes Martenot and Orchestra,* which was recorded by Westminster. Messiaen's massive *Turangalîla-Symphonie,* a monumental essay in coloristic sonority, and his more delicate chamber work *Trois petites liturgies de la présence divine* both use the Ondes Martenot in prominent roles; these are easier to obtain, on RCA Victor and Music Guild records, respectively.

There are recorded examples of *musique concrète* in abundance. Some have been realized at the Paris studios of the French Radio (ORTF) and others produced elsewhere; in view of my earlier comments, it's also worth mentioning that a good number of them have been created since 1960. Four of Iannis Xenakis's works, dating from his years in Paris, have been issued by Nonesuch. Xenakis, now teaching at Indiana University, was among the first group of young European composers to work at the Paris studio. At that time he was a practicing architect and a colleague of Le Corbusier, working closely with him, in fact, on the design of the Philips Pavilion for the 1958 Brussels World's Fair. Xenakis's *Concret P-H,* like the *Poème électronique* of Varèse, was composed for presentation at the Pavilion and similarly exploits the spatial possibilities of the 400 loud-speakers lining the interior. In *Concret P-H,* we have a beautiful example of multichannel mixing; using as source material the sound of smoldering charcoal, Xenakis brings about a gradual accretion of densities through the piling up of these minute sound particles. Great masses of small sounds are built in this way, and they, in turn, undergo gradual transformation as imperceptible changes take place within the mass. Xenakis finds this analogous to certain natural "masses" (rain, crickets at night, swarms of locusts), and the technique has been an important feature in much of his music, including nonelectronic instrumental works. The Nonesuch disc includes *Concret P-H II* .(a revised version) and other similarly conceived pieces; *Bohor I,* of 1962, a 22-minute continuum of fierce intensity, derived from the sounds of jewelry and a Laotian mouth organ, is particularly impressive.

Pierre Henry's later work, available on Limelight Records, reveals an increased dramatic sense as well as a greater freedom in combining "concrete" and "electronic" sources. His music for the theatrical production *The Green Queen* is, in fact, basically electronic, the sources being used to simulate natural and instrumental sounds much of the time. The recording of this piece also contains excerpts from Henry's *Variations for a Door and a Sigh,* a wildly inventive and often amusing fantasy derived from the sources of its title, and from the austere, mystical *Le Voyage.* The complete *Variations* and *Le Voyage* can also be heard in their entirety on separate discs. An early Folkways record offers "concrete" and "electronic" works of a more varied sort, almost all of them produced at the University of Toronto studio, which, by the way, is the second oldest studio in North America, its founding predated only by the Columbia-Princeton facility. Hugh Le Caine's *Dripsody* is perhaps the "classic" of the record, produced in 1955 and heard since, I'm sure, in nine out of every ten classroom lectures on electronic music ever given. It is an easily accessible demonstration of *concrète* technique, created from the sound of a single drop of water; the one source is recopied at various speeds, spliced into rhythmic patterns, and superimposed against itself, the whole forming a curiously traditional (and deceptively simple-sounding) "toccata." The record also includes Jean Eichelberger Ivey's *Pinball* (produced not at Toronto but at the Brandeis University studio), an impressionistic study of sounds—rattles, clicks, and bells—taken from a pinball machine in operation.

Tod Dockstadter, a New York recording engineer with former experience in painting and film, has produced for Owl Records a number of compositions using the natural sources and studio technique of *musique concrète*. He doesn't apply this term, or "electronic music," to his own work, however, preferring instead Varèse's phrase "organized sound"; as a self-confessed nonmusician, Dockstadter doesn't wish to claim that his work is necessarily "music" to anyone but himself. His contention that he is merely organizing sounds seems to be a convenient escape in the event of possible criticism, but a hardly necessary one, under the circumstances, because the work is highly "musical" in the most traditional sense. The pieces are clearly laid out in simple structures, using juxtapositions of repetition and contrast; on the larger time scale, there are neatly balanced alternations of passages or short movements. I find his *Luna Park* of 1961 and the 1963 *Water Music* the most interesting, particularly in the imaginative transformation of the sound sources.

We've already mentioned Michael Sahl in connection with *A Mitzvah for the Dead;* his *Tropes on the Salve Regina,* recorded by Lyrichord, should be heard as a part of the same memory-collage, perhaps, with its semifocused and half-familiar elements in constantly shifting relationships. A more abstract use of the "concrete" can be found in Ilhan Mimaroglu's *Bowery Bum* (the material derived from the sound of a rubber band) and *Le Tombeau d'Edgar Poe* (a reading of the Mallarmé poem). These two compositions, both quite striking in their timbral variety, are issued on a Vox Turnabout record. In contrast to Mimaroglu's dramatic thrusts, the textural fabric of Toru Takemitsu is more like that of a still painting, an artful placement of emerging and receding elements. Two of his collages, *Water Music* and *Vocalism Ai* (the sources are self-explanatory), can be heard on RCA Victor and are recommended as splendid examples of this kind of abstraction.

Ussachevsky is represented by two works on a CRI record: the 1960 *Wireless Fantasy* and *Of Wood and Brass* (1965). Both rely on natural sounds, including instrumental ones, as primary material; the sources are considerably altered (often unrecognizably) in *Of Wood and Brass* but emerge clearly and rather often in the *Wireless Fantasy*. The latter piece, in homage to the inventor and radio pioneer Lee De Forest, makes extensive use of wireless code signals and a lengthy quote from Wagner's *Parsifal,* the first music ever broadcast by De Forest. This CRI disc also contains a number of compositions by Mel Powell, including the *Second Electronic Setting*—a really dazzling display of fleeting shapes and profiles, a "virtuoso" electronic work if there ever was one—and a vocal collage called *Events.* In this piece the voices of actors Mildred Dunnock, Martha Scott, and Lee Bowman (reading Hart Crane's "Legend") are fragmented, recombined with new associations, superimposed, and set in a web of diffuse electronic sound. The two works were produced at the Yale University studio, which Powell directed for many years before assuming his present deanship at the California Institute of the Arts.

The reference here to Yale—and, earlier, to Brandeis, or Toronto, or Columbia—leads me to stress once more the pre-eminence of the American university as a central focus for electronic activity. Secondly, mention of campus studios brings to mind the recently installed and quite elaborate studio at Dartmouth College. The young director of that facility, Jon Appleton, has an unusually fluent way with "classic" studio techniques, handling them fancifully and often rather whimsically. A number of his pieces are recorded for Flying Dutchman records; a typical example might be his *Chef d'Oeuvre,* derived from the sounds of a Chef Boy-ar-dee pizza TV commercial, or the evocative subway-fantasy *Times Square Times Ten.*

Dartmouth has also sponsored an annual international competition for new electronic works. Winners of the first competition (1968) have had their works recorded on a Turnabout disc; it's worth noting that even by this late date (with so much automated synthesizing equipment available) relatively old-fashioned studio procedures figure significantly in each of the compositions—and the use of natural sound sources in more than a few of them. The 1968 winners, in order of their prizes, are: Olly Wilson (United States, University of Illinois studio), Pril Smiley (United States, Columbia-Princeton studio), Jozef Malovec (Czechoslovakia, Bratislava Radio), Eugeniusz Rudnik (Poland, Warsaw Radio), William Hellermann (United States, Columbia-Princeton), and Bohdan Mazurek (Poland, Warsaw

Radio). Their pieces vary widely in style and approach and demonstrate, each in its own way, the continued viability of traditional studio methods in the 1960's.

The Dartmouth competition record also underlines the freedom with which composers now move from *"concrète"* to "electronic" and back again—but not all composers, of course; those with a strong bent toward serial organization are still concerned with sound synthesis and its control, and many have turned to automated, computerized (rather than "classic") methods. Or you may find other composers working within the *elektronische musik* tape situation. Pieces of this kind, made at the Utrecht (Netherlands) studio, have been issued recently by Deutsche Grammophon, two of them (my particular favorites) by Cologne Radio "alumnus" Gottfried Michael Koenig. So you can see that purity of sound source is still desirable for a number of composers. In general, though, the original distinctions between the Cologne and Paris philosophies now exist only as matters of history. The WDR Radio Studio in Cologne, once the rallying point for *elektronische musik* and the primacy of the sine tone, now maintains the most flexible of positions with respect to sound sources. As we've seen, Stockhausen's *Gesang der Jünglinge* initiated this tradition in the mid-1950's, and former studio director Herbert Eimert also relaxed his post-Webernian quest for control of "pure" tones; Eimert's deeply moving, vocally derived *Epitaph* reveals the strength of his later concerns. In his most recent music, Stockhausen has abandoned the notion of control; to be more accurate, he has redefined it, not in the traditional area of notation but in the dominance of his *personality* over that of his performers. Turning more and more to the use of live electronics (occasionally with prerecorded tape as well), he often begins with purposely ambiguous playing instructions and highly eclectic sound materials, and then influences the collective "will" of the performers to transform these into a coherent whole. I've already noted two such pieces, the *Mikrophonie I* and *II*.

A few recent works of Stockhausen have been conceived directly for recorded or broadcast performance; these in particular show how the "concrete" and the "electronic" have intermingled and metamorphosed in his imagination. Two lengthy examples have been recorded for Deutsche Grammophon, both of them employing (as a starting point) highly familiar source material. *Hymnen* has been constructed from the national anthems of France, Israel, Germany, Spain, Switzerland, the United States, the Soviet Union, and various African countries, interspersed with cries, speech, crowd sounds, short-wave radio signals, and the like. The other composition, *Opus 1970,* is a colossal transmuting of Beethoven fragments in honor of the 200th anniversary of that composer's birth; electronic modifications of the material are interrelated in cryptic ways, so that the rhythm of one passage may be used to control the filtering of another, the signal of this applied to the ring modulation of that, and so on. Each piece is, by contemporary standards, staggeringly long in duration, and the "form" of each is intentionally open and rambling. Stockhausen's juxtaposition of materials is often highly evocative; the total impression, in either work, is that of an image-laden, dreamlike fantasy, without real beginning or end, a twentieth-century commentary upon the musical "environment" of past and present.

Lukas Foss's *Geod* for orchestra, recorded for Candide, also concerns itself with a fabric of intertwining, emerging, and receding quotations, similarly laden with political and nationalistic associations. Various subgroups of Foss's orchestra are required to play folk-patriotic material connected with the location of performance (the ones on the recording being distinctly American), while their degree of "participation" in the total sound web is controlled during the final mixing of channels in the recording studio. Like the Stockhausen *Hymnen, Geod* can also be realized in a live concert performance; the continual fading in and out, in that situation, would be determined by assistant conductors.

Any discussion of "early" techniques would be incomplete without reference to the RCA synthesizer. That giant machine is still alive and well as we move into the 1970's; Milton Babbitt, in particular, has continued his compositional use of this medium's virtuosity, so well matched to his own aesthetic purposes. His mid-1960's *Ensembles for Synthesizer,* on Columbia Records, typifies the unique qualities we've already observed in his earlier work: tightly knit successions of high-speed continuities (pitch, registral, rhythmic, and so on), articulated in striking detail and interacting with one another in a multilayered stereophony. The most immediately listenable of Babbitt's works, however, may be his 1964 *Philomel* (live voice, recorded vocal material, and synthesized sound), set to a text by John Hollander. The Greek legend of the girl rendered speechless and then transformed into a nightingale provides the lyric and dramatic impetus for a strong, direct statement, as accessible to the lay listener as one might wish. The suggestive, atmospheric qualities of *Philomel* are fully captured in a Deutsche Grammophon recording sponsored by the American AR (Acoustic Research) contemporary music project; the performance on disc makes an immediate impact on this "simplest" of musical levels. From another perspective, though, intricate relationships now compounded by the use of live voice and a processed voice on tape are no less fascinating.

Charles Wuorinen began working at the Columbia-Princeton center while a graduate student still in his mid-twenties. He's now a leading figure among the younger American composers, best known for his ability to extract the maximum dramatic thrust from a self-restricted body of material. Like Babbitt, he prefers to retain control over all relationships, although the surface gestures of his work are more extroverted; his earlier music is, in fact, often highly charged and intense in a manner reminiscent of Varèse. Wuorinen's major composition with the RCA synthesizer, *Time's Encomium,* was completed in 1969. His instrumental language translates easily into this particular medium: While presenting a more subdued profile here than in his youthful music, *Time's Encomium* offers a vastly richer variety of timbres and a sure means of controlling the rhythmic-durational arcs that define the work's total shape. The Nonesuch recording of the piece led to its receiving the 1970 Pulitzer Prize in music, another milestone in the history of the electronic medium: it marks the first time this award has been granted for a work existing *entirely* in recorded form.

Original compositions using a voltage-controlled synthesizer are difficult to obtain on record, except for the work of Morton

Subotnick. The only other significant recording is Andrew Rudin's *Tragoedia* (on Nonesuch), a volatile, hyperdramatic scenario created on Moog equipment. There are transcriptions galore, however, using familiar selections in "arrangements" of varying competence and taste. You can, if you wish, hear anything from "switched-on" Rachmaninoff to Verdi's "Anvil Chorus," Moog-style; I find that most of these suffer by comparison with the vastly superior work of Walter Carlos, and only further confirm Carlos's skill.

One final sort of synthesizer disc exists, and this is the "demonstration" record designed to explain various aspects of sound generation, studio setup, or composing technique. The *Nonesuch Guide to Electronic Music,* mentioned in an earlier chapter, can be very handy in this regard. I personally prefer Bent Lorentzen's *An Introduction to Electronic Music;* although the material is restricted to the simplest devices of the classic studio (sine tones, noise, reverberation, ring modulation, and so on), the recorded commentary is clear and the examples from the literature well-chosen. On the other hand, the record is a European import and may not be readily available in the United States. I'd advise your writing to J. & W. Chester, Ltd., London, for further information on this.

Two compositions by Walter Carlos for live instruments and prerecorded tape can be heard on a Turnabout record; both of these date from the mid-1960's and use the Columbia-Princeton studio facilities for the creation of the electronic parts. *Variations for Flute and Electronic Sound* is rather spritely, often witty, while Carlos's *Dialogues for Piano and Two Loudspeakers* strikes a more atmospheric note. In both pieces, the discourse between live and taped elements is one of general agreement (rather than confrontation or collision), the style economical and to the point. A more rambling, improvisational kind of free flow between instruments and electronics characterizes a collaborative record called *Human Music,* recorded by Jon Appleton and jazz virtuoso Don Cherry (for Flying Dutchman) during Cherry's stay in residence at Dartmouth College. Appleton has used the synthesizer in a variety of ways—as a foil for the live sounds, as a "lead" instrument provoking live response, as a rhythmically disjunct accompaniment—and the directions taken spontaneously by the two performers are often right on target. To turn again to a more traditional interaction, Roberto Gerhard's 1961 *Collages* (electronic tape and orchestra) is a strong, tough piece, stunning in its sonorities and inexorable in its pitch logic. The work brings to mind Messiaen, Varèse, Berg, and Webern, and yet it is all curiously its own self. The recording on Angel is well worth hearing, not only for its intrinsic qualities but as one way of introducing the late Spanish-English composer's music to an American audience largely unaware of it.

Kenneth Gaburo has composed many pieces involving electronics in one form or another, and a number of these have been issued on a single Nonesuch record. In *Antiphony II* and *Antiphony IV*, live ensembles are used in wildly inventive fashion, a perfect match for their prerecorded electronic counterparts; the musical and spatial balances (*Antiphony III* subdividing a chamber chorus into four small groups of soloists) draw the listener into a path of cross-play, imitation, and analogy. Each of the two large live-electronic pieces is concluded by an *Exit Music* of *"concrète"* tape material, to be heard entirely over loud-speakers, and in these the expressive impetus is entirely different—sustained, direct, blunt, and often grotesque in the accumulation of instrumental and electronic images. Gaburo's treatment of vocal sounds is highly imaginative; the entire record, in fact, maintains a striking level of originality.

Perhaps some of Gaburo's stylistic freedom can be traced to the fact that he worked at the University of Illinois for many years; that particular midwestern center has always been more responsive, if not actually more conducive, to musical innovation and experimentation than its counterparts on the American eastern seaboard. The university's Studio for Experimental Music has been especially flexible in encouraging a great variety of electronic activities, from the Hiller-Isaacson computer experiments to the creation of highly specialized tone generators by James Beauchamp, of the engineering faculty. The presence on campus, over the years, of composers working from every conceivable stylistic viewpoint—Harry Partch and his forty-three-tone division of the octave, Ben Johnston's similar interest in microtones, Salvatore Martirano's fusion of jazz-pop elements into an avant-garde language, the Schoenbergian organization of Herbert Brün, the more conservative neoclassicism of Gordon Binkerd—has propelled that sense of freedom even further. The studio also enjoys the advantage of being one of the oldest in America; founded in 1958, under the initial direction of Hiller, it was at one time rivaled only by Columbia-Princeton and Toronto as a major electronic center.

A number of works produced at the Illinois studio have been issued on a Heliodor record and offer a nicely balanced "sampler" of this stylistic variety. Hiller's *Machine Music* was mentioned here in an earlier chapter; the performance on this disc is delightful, quixotic in its humor but forceful when it has to be. Brün's *Futility 1964* is, by contrast, much more consistent in tone. The dogged, determined alternation of live speaker and electronic pattern-work—setting up two distinct levels of experience—conveys a sense of resignation underlining the work's title. A composition of another sort entirely is the *Underworld* of Salvatore Martirano; as a recording, this can only be considered an excerpted "reduction" because the total production involves lighting and dance, but it's still a thoroughly commanding experience in whatever form you confront it. Live instrumentalists, grim laughter that grows increasingly demonic, an electronic sound tape that intrudes and then retreats, all are welded into a fiercely cohesive unit. The "live" music is particularly disturbing in its role of intermediary between the precise electronic patterns and screaming, cackling voices; it also establishes a parallel duality of its own, vacillating between the world of strict serial control and a chaotic, "free," jazz-derived spontaneity.

One of the most intriguing records we have of live electronics was made by percussionist-composer Max Neuhaus for Columbia Records. Even if there were no considerations other than its own merits, the disc would be worth hearing; it presents a fantastic display of sonic variety, stunningly recorded. But it's also stimulating in that it reveals one possible exploitation of the "chance" aesthetic for a performer: Given the score to a work that can be realized in any number of ways (perhaps even by any kind of instrument), the player can then *choose* to make it electronic. Neuhaus has taken Earle Brown's *Four Systems*—the score consisting entirely of horizontal lines varying in thickness and length—and interpreted it as a work for four amplified cymbals. He also draws an elaborate sound palette from this deceptively "simple" setup, from rushing filtered-noise quality to a bell-like clarity.

In a similar vein, Sylvano Bussotti's *Coeur pour batteur— Positively Yes* has been transformed into a panorama of highly amplified sounds, including those of Neuhaus's body and voice. Amplification extends here even to instruments *not* to be struck during the performance; these vibrate sympathetically with other sounds and contribute their own weight to the over-all timbral ambience. Cage's *Fontana Mix* is realized as a feedback piece, in which the various instruments are placed in front of loud-speakers; contact mikes on the instruments can then initiate (and regenerate) a cyclic sound continuum. Finally, I should note that Neuhaus's performance of Morton Feldman's *The King of Denmark*—while not strictly "electronic"—derives much of its strength from the recording medium. As Neuhaus states,

> This piece is played throughout with the fingers. Like most of Feldman's music, it is extremely soft and without attacks . . . putting a magnifying glass on that area of dynamics between pianissimo and piano. . . . Because of the extremely quiet nature of this piece, much of it can only be heard (at least in one sense of the word) on a recording.

Some of Gordon Mumma's work can be heard on two separate discs. His *Mesa* is a live-performance piece for Bandoneon, an instrument that, according to the Odyssey record liner notes, belongs to the organ family, resembles an accordion, and is used in performance of the Argentine tango. Whatever timbral charac-teristics the Bandoneon may have, you won't hear many of them in this performance—except as the initial source for a wide spectrum of electronic modifications. Mumma has designed a network of circuitry (to be controlled by an assistant) that, when attached to the instrument, transforms its personality. In the recorded performance by David Tudor and the composer, we hear an amazing assortment of buzzes, noise components, vibrato states, modulation, and reverberation, and, presumably, any other performance might result in a different realization. We can also hear a prerecorded tape of Mumma's, originally composed for Milton Cohen's Space Theatre at the 1964 Venice Biennale; as presented on an Advance recording, the excerpt is entitled *Music from the Venezia Space Theatre*. Although an entirely self-sufficient tape, it's listed here with live-electronic examples because it should be heard in its original context, as one component of a total environment involving sculpture, dancers, light-projections, and live instrumentalists. The imagination will have to supply, then, what the recording cannot.

As we move further into the area of live-electronic "theater" music I should stress, once more, the important role of imagination in listening to *any* recording. It's crucial to bear in mind that you're experiencing one performance of a particular work when you hear that work on disc; try to visualize, if you can, *another* performance of that same piece, realizing that this probably means much more than a difference in articulation or tempo, as with, say, a Beethoven sonata. Playing instructions for some recent pieces may be so flexible that a second performance could entail totally different instrumentation in the live parts, or a different succession of fixed events, or new events themselves. Secondly, try to set the "environment" in your imagination: The players may be separated at distant ends of the performance space, or may be moving about, or perhaps the players and audience are freely intermingling. Are there lighting effects, slide projections, films, dance, and other physical activity to consider? Some awareness of these factors is necessary if you're to get any impression of what's "going on" in the fullest sense.

A number of examples are, in fact, recordings of live performances made on the spot in concert, allowing the immediacy of the playing to come through. A performance of Stockhausen's *Prozession* at the 1967 Darmstadt festival was recorded in this manner and has been issued by Candide records. Four instrumentalists have been "wired" via air- and contact-microphones to a control panel operated by Stockhausen; he in turn can filter the sounds, mix them in various ways, and send them to any of four loud-speakers at the corners of the hall. In performance, all of the participants, including Stockhausen, react to each other's activities in prescribed, but highly flexible, ways, using materials or techniques derived from earlier Stockhausen works; we have, then, a recurring Stockhausen feedback of reprocessed older ideas, as in *Mikrophonie I* (this is also one of the works used as a "source"), and a transmutation of quasi-familiar materials much like that of the later *Hymnen.*

Similarly, a live performance of Cage's *Variations IV* at the Feigen-Palmer Gallery in Los Angeles has led to an astounding Everest recording. The four hours of the original happening have been reduced to the duration of a single record, but it's still possible to picture Cage and David Tudor (in separate rooms of the gallery) amplifying and mixing a delicious jumble of sound material—phonographs, randomly tuned radios, pre-recorded tapes, sound generators, microphones set up around, about, and outside the gallery itself. In short, the sum total of audible experience, the banal realigned (recomposed, perhaps) into the unique. Cage's way of transforming the most depressingly trite fragments, so that they emerge as components of a wholly "original" vehicle, is uncanny. The effect may be disturbing to some, devastating for others; in any event, no one will be unmoved. Those who want to follow Cage further into his own special universe can hear the *Variations II* (recorded for Columbia Records) or *Cartridge Music* (Mainstream), in which amplification and distortion of familiar sound objects—piano strings, phonograph cartridges, microphone sound itself—can be raised to the level of virtuosity by performer David Tudor.

I hope that some of these suggestions for further listening will heighten your perspective and offer a general indication of the diversity that surrounds us. Even at best, that's all they can do; there's no one simple device that will allow us to see the *entire* creative spectrum of electronic music, because it's still unfolding at a pace almost too rapid to follow. In a few more years, with greater hindsight, we'll possibly be able to look back on this period with some understanding. Equipment not yet developed (or works not yet composed) will probably clarify the diverse strands of today's scene more succinctly than anything that could be said or written now.

This is not to imply that the future will make the present "obsolete"; we've seen that voltage control and computer synthesis haven't relegated earlier procedures to the Dark Ages, and it's equally unlikely that future directions will entirely supersede our own. Perhaps we're all guilty of "historical" reasoning in this area, especially when we refer to "advances" or "revolutionary" achievements; such phrases imply *improvement,* whereas in art things don't really "improve" at all—they just continually change. In any event, the history of electronic music is far too incomplete to be written yet. When it is written (and our present judgments prove inadequate), we'll finally discover what our "advances" really were.

At this point in our development, though, we can guess that the general directions of the present will most likely be with us for a while. It's clear enough that issues of control, chance, theater, and collage still interest composers after two decades, and it can be assumed that these concerns will remain, whatever their modes of presentation. As for techniques, we can assume that our present ones won't disappear overnight. Whatever brief "history" electronic music has should tell us this: It's obvious that the procedures of the recent past, from classic studio, to radio collage of the 1930's, to the use of the RCA synthesizer, continue to serve composers well. More than this, they still remain the models—the standards—by which we measure the newer achievements of the present and future.

In discussing readings, I must again urge those without a general background in twentieth-century music to acquire one. A basic survey of music since 1900 will lead to a more realistic understanding of this music's electronic manifestations. In other words, anyone who has come this far in the present book must be aware that the prime motivations in the new medium's development are *musical* ones and that these have their roots in the past. Unless you have a reasonable acquaintance with at least the immediate past, which extends back to Wagner and Debussy, you may view the apparently "radical" present in a wholly misleading light.

There are any number of books on the general subject of

contemporary music, some of these college texts. I prefer Eric Salzman's *Twentieth Century Music: An Introduction* (Prentice-Hall), a perceptive survey of the field by a practicing composer and one of our finest critics. You might also want to consult the more personal, informal study *Twentieth Century Music: Its Evolution from the End of the Harmonic Era into the Present Era of Sound* (Pantheon; Minerva paperback), by Peter Yates. Its general approach is implicit in its subtitle; Yates's awareness of trends leading to the "present era" is keen and enriched by personal experience. H. H. Stuckenschmidt's *Twentieth Century Music* (McGraw-Hill) is another solid text, although stronger on the European side of events than on the American.

A number of other books, while not actually comprehensive "texts," are worth reading for their unusual insights or format. The English composer-commentator Wilfrid Mellers has written a few volumes in which musical developments are seen in the light of literary, artistic, religious, or societal changes; his arguments, while often debatable, are always provocative and quite perceptive. Mellers's *Music in a New Found Land* (Knopf) deals exclusively with the American scene, and his *Caliban Reborn: Renewal in Twentieth Century Music* (Harper and Row) examines various directions common to Europe and America. You might enjoy *The New Music: The Sense Behind the Sound* by Joan Peyser (Delacorte), in which modern developments are traced through a detailed study of Schoenberg, Stravinsky, and Varèse. My own book coedited with Barney Childs, *Contemporary Composers on Contemporary Music* (Holt, Rinehart and Winston), contains essays, articles, and interviews by such individuals as Busoni, Cowell, Ives, Varèse, Cage, Henry Brant, Babbitt, and Wuorinen.

The best general reading on the subject of *electronic* music is to be found in a special issue of *Music Educators Journal* (November, 1968) devoted entirely to this area. The issue is quite remarkable on many counts, containing, for example, an interview with Milton Babbitt and articles by Randall, Ussachevsky, and Subotnick. Broadcast Music, Incorporated (BMI), put out a similar "special" issue of its journal *BMI: The Many Worlds of Music* (Summer, 1970), including a short history of electronic music by Carter Harman and a (then) comprehensive discography. For a really entertaining and thorough general history of the medium, I would suggest Otto Luening's fascinating "An Unfinished History of Electronic Music" in the *Music Educators Journal* issue noted above. The earliest decades, particularly the Cologne and Paris stages, are also well covered in the Stuckenschmidt text. The preliminary chapters of *Experimental Music* by Hiller and Isaacson (McGraw-Hill) provide excellent technical and aesthetic background to be read before one proceeds into the "body" of the Illinois computer experiments with Iliac. It's surprising that John Cage receives so little space in any of these chronicles, especially since his ground-breaking efforts in tape collage and live-electronic performance have been crucial to the events of the present. The best documentation of his early career can be found in *John Cage* (Praeger), a collection of interviews, catalogues, program notes, diagrams, photographs, and other assorted memorabilia, edited by Richard Kostelanetz; the book is heartily recommended on all counts, as a delightful introduction to Cage's unique presence.

The birth of *elektronische musik* at the Cologne studio was followed shortly after by a journal, *Die Reihe* (Universal Edition; English edition by Theodore Presser Company). A product of Cologne's most zealous period, *Die Reihe* stressed the ideological position of the studio at that time with respect to Webern, serialism, chance, spatial distribution, and numerous other far-flung topics. Issue number 1, "Electronic Music," will certainly be of interest, with articles by Eimert, Stockhausen, Boulez, Stuckenschmidt, Pousseur, Křenek, and others; unfortunately, though, much of the journal now reads as a curiously dated political manifesto, dogmatic to the extreme. Worse yet, it can often be abstruse, in its English translation, and heavily laden with mathematical-scientific data and jargon. The Yale University *Journal of Music Theory* has also produced a wide variety of articles on electronic subjects, including Milton Babbitt's "An Introduction to the RCA Synthesizer," in volume VII, number 2 (1964). This essay is clear, instructive, and surprisingly nontechnical; it is more easily readable for the layman, in fact, than the majority of *Journal of Music Theory* items (aimed, admittedly, at a professional readership). A special issue on electronic music, volume VII, number 1 (1963), can be difficult reading, although a number of items are worth while even if you understand only half of them.

A much more accessible journal was the ill-fated *Electronic Music Review,* now defunct, which mixed general background articles, technical reports, commentaries, and reviews in a random but attractive way. Back issues of these are worth searching for, particularly if you're interested in articles on programed control (issue 1), the Syn-Ket (4), Walter Carlos on multitrack recording (6)—the variety is fascinating. Issues 2 and 3, by the way, appeared as a single hefty catalog of *all* the compositions realized in all of the world's known studios by mid-1967; compiled by the English composer Hugh Davies under sponsorship of the Paris studio, this "International Electronic Music Catalog" is an excellent reference tool, although by now sadly out of date. Some of the easy-going, almost rambling flexibility of *Electronic Music Review* has been revived in a new journal called *Synthesis* (Minneapolis). Only two issues have appeared at this writing, but these include a basic article on oscillators, a comparative report on voltage-control equipment, a biographical-nostalgic tribute to Thaddeus Cahill (who, you'll remember, began it all in 1906) and the promise of a regular column by John Cage.

The list of journals is far from complete: If, for example, you want to view the opposing poles of "control" and "chance" at close range, it might be revealing to compare copies of *Perspectives of New Music* and *Source: Music of the Avant Garde.* The former represents the position of the serial—or at least highly organized—approach to composition, through the medium of a basically "scholarly" journal; it contains articles, reviews, exchanges of letters, highly detailed analyses of "classical" (that is, Webern or Stravinsky) works, and the like. *Source,* on the other hand, celebrates the theatrical and improvisational, stressing the informal interview, reproductions of manuscript scores, and spectacular pictorial layout. Often containing records, slides for projection, or bits of magnetic recording tape, *Source* is itself more of an environment, perhaps, than a journal. It's significant that *Perspectives,* issued by Princeton University, relates to the activities most associated with the American east coast, while *Source* draws its strength from California-based composers and is published in Sacramento. Although electronic music *per se* is not the prime consideration of either magazine, you can find articles by Milton Babbitt, J. K. Randall, Hubert Howe, Charles Wuorinen, and Godfrey Winham, to name a few, in *Perspectives;* *Source* has featured the work of Larry Austin, Alvin Lucier, Robert Ashley, and many others (including records of *Accidents* and *The Wolfman*), plus an extended symposium on improvisational live-electronic groups in a recent issue.

Somewhere between these two extremes, you'll find *The Composer* (Cleveland), less ideological in its presentation and offering a widely varied cross-section of aesthetic positions. *The Composer* has published an excellent article on tape delay by Pauline Oliveros, a series on new instrumental resources (including the solo-ensemble piece) by Bertram Turetzky, and a valuable introductory essay on tape by Allen Strange. Finally, I should mention the American Society of University Composers and its annual published *Proceedings;* these include quite a few articles, transcribed from sessions at the organization's national meeting, on such subjects as computer-generated sound and recent synthesizer developments. As there is very little, if any, technical jargon in the *Proceedings* (perhaps a healthy sign for the future of American composition), the articles are generally readable and often highly informative.

Mention of computer-generated sound brings to mind another recently founded journal, the *Computer Music Newsletter*. There have been only two issues as of this writing, but even in this short time the *Newsletter* (published by Purdue University) has emerged as a worth-while forum for people active in that rapidly growing field. Articles by J. K. Pulfer on recent work undertaken by the National Research Council of Canada and by Barry Vercoe on the sound-synthesis program for the IBM 360 computer are particularly interesting. The *Newsletter* has also begun listing a comprehensive bibliography on the subject, including recent books of varying technical difficulty. Perhaps the most versatile of these, covering not only sound synthesis but the use of computers in areas of music history and analysis, is *The*

Computer and Music, edited by Harry B. Lincoln (Cornell University Press). You might also want to examine Max Mathews's *The Technology of Computer Music* (MIT Press), particularly since Mathews was one of the real pioneers in this area, his work dating back to the initial experiments at the Bell Telephone Labs.

Books of a more detailed technical nature fall into the "how to" category, guides to the composition of electronic music by any one of a number of methods. The earliest of these, to my knowledge, was F. C. Judd's 1961 *Electronic Music and Musique Concrète* (Neville Spearman); Judd covers the sources and procedures of the 1950's classic studio in a clear, direct style, and refers to the best-known European works of that time (by Eimert, Stockhausen, Badings, Varèse) for his examples. Although, as we know, much has happened electronically since the book was published, it could hardly be considered out of date. Everything Judd said more than a decade ago is still true now and can be of use in building a traditional studio; on the historical level, of course, his commentary is doubly fascinating —a document from a period that some of us hardly remember! More recent manuals are concerned with voltage-control equipment and the use of modular synthesizers. If you own one, buy one, or have the opportunity to work at one, you'll naturally find an "owner's manual" published and distributed by the appropriate manufacturer. These are usually *very* detailed, but (surprisingly enough) elementally simple in the opening few chapters. The assumption here is that institutional purchasers may know nothing about the nature of sound and probably have no experience in making electronic compositions; consequently every aspect is spelled out with great care.

Anyone with access to Moog equipment will enjoy looking through Ronald Pellegrino's lengthy *An Electronic Studio Manual* (Ohio State University Publications). Pellegrino duplicates the format of the "standard" manual in his initial chapters, explaining the concept of voltage control and the function of each individual module; in his final section, though, he goes beyond this predictable outline, and it is this section that's really the most valuable. What we have, basically, is a source book of patchings, a list of the modular interconnections used by Pellegrino in one of his own compositions. This can be enormously helpful for students, especially because each particular configuration is described in three ways—by a circuit diagram drawing, by a verbal comment ("the wobbly character of this variation is due to the addition of an unprocessed triangular wave control on the filter . . ."), and by a band of sound on a prerecorded tape that accompanies the book.

A more generalized "how to" approach can be found in *Electronic Music: A Handbook of Sound Synthesis and Control* (Orcus), by M. L. Eaton. The discussion is not restricted to any specific system, electronic instrument, or composing method but rather attempts a comparative evaluation of them all. Again, the basics are emphasized at the outset ("Sound, as perceived by the ear, is a vibration of air . . ."), and here, too, an increasingly detailed picture is built up through the aid of diagrams and descriptive notes. Eaton's viewpoint, though, is one of suggestion, not prescription; the book takes you to a point where you could theoretically choose among alternative systems (or design your own), and then, in effect, it leaves you there. A concluding chapter on the *biological* potential for spontaneous electronic music—I mentioned this briefly earlier—is highly provocative and opens up staggering possibilities for the future.

Two final matters: One, simply, is that a host of articles, essays, and interviews on the subject of electronic music have appeared over the years and not always in music journals; you might acquire a wider range of knowledge from a sampling of articles in *Audio, Scientific American,* and *The New York Times,* for example, than in any single music source. If you are interested in tracking down such documents, be sure to consult *A Bibliography of Electronic Music* (University of Toronto Press), compiled by Lowell M. Cross. This lists (as of 1968) every available article or book on the subject in a variety of languages, or at least it attempts as comprehensive a listing as possible; there were no particular aesthetic requirements for entry in the *Bibliography,* and Cross covers the entire spectrum of (in his words) the "literature that ranges from highly technical works to writings of a generalized, popular, and often sensation-seeking nature." In other words, there is something for everybody, and fortunately the *Bibliography* is a reference work that can help us locate it.

Secondly, some familiarity with recent "avant-garde" music that is *not* electronic is strongly advised. We've agreed that it would be foolish to assume some unique genesis for electronic music, as though it had sprung from nowhere, and for this reason I've suggested listening to the early twentieth century. But it's equally absurd to claim, from the other side of the gallery, that all past roads lead inexorably and exclusively to electronic music and nowhere else! The newer medium is but *one* facet of the total music picture, and that picture is just as "radical" and "revolutionary" in its instrumental and vocal aspects as in any other performance mode. Besides, I don't know of a single composer who feels that tape or synthesizer has so overwhelmingly captured his interest that he now ignores traditional live music-making. The point of all this is that some reading on the "new music" (*all* of it, electronic and otherwise) might be in order, so that a Lutoslawski string quartet or Berio orchestral work can be aligned with parallel electronic activity.

The closing chapters of the Salzman and Yates books are excellent along these lines. There are also "special" issues of mass-media publications that at one time or another have concentrated on the avant-garde. Among the more popular music magazines and trade publications, there are the "New Music" issue of *High Fidelity* (September, 1968) or the "Mid-Century Music" issue of *Bandwagon* (Selmer Instrument Company, Elkhart, Indiana, 1965); both of these are filled with articles and quotations by composers, examples of scores, and a genuine awareness of recent musical activities. There is at present only one book-length treatment of developments since 1950, David Cope's *New Directions in Music* (William C. Brown), and it is a welcome addition to the literature. Concentrating heavily upon chance, "noise," theater music, and mixed-media performance, the Cope book should be of great help in locating the focus of today's music. Up until now, it's been intriguing but also misleading to concentrate on our new "instruments." Any approach to recent music must center, rather, about changed *attitudes* and aesthetic positions—whether with regard to old instruments or new ones.

Part III
Some Considerations for the Future

8. The Nature of Performance

As I've indicated in the preceding chapters, one of the distinguishing features of our century is the speed with which change occurs. In a field as dependent on technology and creative imagination as electronic music, accurate "prediction" of the future is all but impossible. The best we can do is hint at some currents that may, given the right composers and engineers at the right time, lead to interesting developments later on. Unforeseen developments have a way of advancing certain tendencies and more or less shelving other, perhaps equally exciting, projects. For example, the experiments of the 1930's and 1940's with hand-drawn film sound tracks had great potential, and few would have guessed that these would be sidetracked by the tape-recording medium in the 1950's; the first glimpse of the RCA synthesizer apparently foretold a similarly bright future, untempered by the awareness that voltage-controlled equipment and sound-generating computer programs were just around the corner. We don't need to be convinced, then, that predicting is a highly speculative and often futile game. Furthermore, it's difficult enough in this rapidly moving age to keep up with the *present,* much less venture any guesses as to what lies beyond it: By the time you read this book, anything I might "predict" now could already be with us in working form.

We have noted, of course, some general directions being taken by composers and a number of their desires with regard to the improvement and modification of equipment. If we can assume that these desires, pushed hard enough, will eventually bear fruit,

153

we might have some notion of what the future *may* be like. This still doesn't preclude the possibility of totally unexpected equipment and a corresponding change in aesthetic aims, however; creative artists are remarkably pragmatic animals, adjusting to situations as they arise. And that is about all anyone can say regarding the future of electronic music: It is comprised of creative "will" *and* blind chance, and, whatever it may be, it will probably come upon us sooner than we imagine.

It seems more profitable, at this point in our history, to comment upon some aspects of the *entire* musical process, rather than specific electronic features. That is, we can point to a number of changes in the general scene—revisions in our ways of thinking musically, and relating to *all* styles, periods, and performance media—that seem virtually irreversible over the next few decades, quite independent of any particular directions that "new" music might take. These general tendencies are certainly related to the electronic revolution and can't be fully understood except in that context: the phenomena of radio, Muzak, sound synthesis, amplification, tape-editing, phonograph recording, and video have raised a multitude of questions and stirred up a good many problems that can only be clarified in the years to come. They have already altered our musical perceptions and expectations in ways not yet fully known to us. "Tradition" has indeed been transformed and disturbed by electronic apparatus, not so much by *musique concrète* or the synthesizer (these can be ignored if you really don't like their products) as by the fact that we've unconsciously adjusted our responses to the "popular" literature as well, Bach and the Beatles and Mahler and Pete Seeger and Mozart. Most of the music we hear today has been performed, enhanced, preserved, and transmitted with the help of electronic equipment. It follows, then, that we have made subtle alterations, often without realizing it, in our own listening equipment, auditory and psychological, in such a unique way that our habits and tastes have profoundly changed, bearing little resemblance, for example, to those of the preceding few generations.

In this and the next two chapters, I will discuss three tendencies that hold out interesting prospects for the future; each of them has been influenced and accelerated by electronics, but none are specifically "electronic." First of all, we must redefine (and we've already begun to reconsider) exactly what we mean by "performance," and the various options of space, place, time, human activity, and responsibility conjured up by that one word. Secondly, it seems clear that the areas of serious music, "art" music, jazz, pop, and rock are coming closer together than ever before; stylistic distinctions that, however blurred, once existed in theory have all but disappeared in many cases, and the use of music as a social barrier, erected by groups to reinforce their culturally separate status, hardly interests the majority of younger composers. And, finally, we should look at the striking developments in music teaching, particularly at the precollege level, in which electronics and the avant-garde have begun to figure prominently.

It's already been established that a "performance" need not be "live." This is evident in the world of pop and classical recording as well as the tape-music studio, and I don't wish to belabor the point. We might note a few significant implications of that fact, however, the most important of them being that the recorded performance differs *in kind* (and not in "degree" or "quality") from the live one—that is, the recording is designed to be heard through two (soon to be four) stereophonically separated loudspeakers, usually in an informal environment—perhaps in the privacy of one's own home, experienced by a single listener or a small group at most. Visual stimuli are at a minimum, consisting of whatever you happen to look at while listening to the recording (a picture on the wall, a potted plant, a landscape through your window, the printed score of the music); in any event, such stimuli are not necessarily dictated by the piece or the "performance"— to be more accurate, neither by the *pre*performance (instruments played by musicians) in the recording studio nor the actual performance emerging from your loud-speakers. A lone exception might be the record jacket or illustrative booklet contained within an album. If it exists at all, it would constitute the only overtly visual aspect of the recorded performance.

Contrasts between this situation and that of the "live" concert —public, multifocused, highly visual, and inherently theatrical—

are obvious. Consider, also, that the *sounds* themselves—what most people would call "the music"—are equally different. What you hear on disc (unless it is a recording made at a live concert) is anything but a recaptured spontaneous "moment": it is, rather, a highly artificial assemblage of various takes, literally manufactured by editing and mixing processes. The *responsibility* for this product is a collaborative one, as a great many individuals (the musicians with their instruments, recording engineers manipulating microphones and mixers, virtuoso tape-editors) have taken part in shaping the total presentation; to stretch a point, we could also include persons not associated with the production of sounds—art directors, for example, or the writers of liner notes—as well. The point is that all of these people have, in fact, "performed"; the sounds you hear are the result of many such isolated performances, enabling you (at the final stage) to "perform" the disc —or trigger its own performance of itself—by turning on your phonograph. A carefully packaged sound product of this kind attempts to be "perfect," to the degree, at least, that the notes and markings on the printed page are meticulously observed. All of the pitches are right, the rhythms in place, dynamic contrasts scrupulously articulated, instrumental balances "enhanced." The record, then, is as faithful a realization of the composer's written score as the various performing parties can achieve within the limits of interpretation.

All of this undeniably affects our listening reactions when switching from recorded to live performance and back again, whether we realize it or not. For those of us who have grown up with the phonograph, learning about great music (*and* about great performers) via the disc medium, the initial response to live concert performance may be, "There are so many mistakes!" But what would concert-going be without "mistakes," deviations, and variations from evening to evening? It is intrinsic to the notion of public spectacle that we observe the human animal, singular or plural, confronted with overwhelming challenges and meeting these with varying degrees of success. So much of the virtuoso literature—by Liszt, Paganini, Chopin, the majority of the great concerti—has been devised precisely to provide this kind of mad challenge for the player willing to meet it head on in full public display. At whatever level of courage and skill, the musician brings an element of the erratic, the whimsical, the unpredictable —human frailty, perhaps, rather than human error—which always colors the live performance; it takes some adjusting, though, after a steady diet of recordings, to realize how integral (how necessary!) this element is to the concert environment and what a major stimulus it is to players and audience alike.

Our modes of concentration and attention are similarly affected in making the transition from one kind of performance to the other, especially when we're faced with an unfamiliar composition. In the live concert situation, the knowledge that a piece will be played only once imposes the necessity for strict, undivided, total absorption in the work; paradoxically, though, the surroundings, the mood of the moment, and the distraction of competing "theatrical" stimuli often render such utter involvement impossible. You have much wider options in hearing a recording, since you can dictate the conditions under which it will be played and eliminate as many distractions of time and place as you wish. It's possible, for example, to focus intently upon the work, partly because you don't *have* to (you can always play the disc again, thereby removing the pressure) and partly because there are fewer extraneous stimuli to contend with. Or, conversely, you can let the piece simmer in the back of your consciousness—a sort of home Muzak—while you move about and attend to other matters; there's no need to feel guilty about this, as the recorded performance can be repeated any number of times, yielding different experiences upon different hearings. The disc or tape, by the very nature of its "permanence," invites participation on all conceivable levels and with a minimum of frustration at either end of the spectrum.

There is, then, a definite dichotomy in modes of performance and one that may force us to re-examine the *meaning* of the word "performance" itself. In an earlier chapter, I had suggested that a recording of a "live" work (a Brahms symphony, say, or the Davidovsky *Synchronisms*) was categorically different from a magnetic-tape piece such as Subotnick's *Touch*. But, given the distinctions we've been dealing with now, we could just as easily say that *any* record, regardless of content, exists as a unique art "object," an immobile, fixed entity: that is, the disc can be re-garded as a work in itself, analogous to a painting, print, or piece of sculpture. And what does "performance" mean when applied to the visual arts? The creator has certainly *performed* (with brush, pencil, chisel, or whatever) so that the work could come into being, but that performance has taken place well in advance of the public display of the work—the viewing, or, in our instance, the listening. Aside from avant-garde instances of paintings being made on stage in a theatrical situation, or the public labors of the carnival caricaturist, real-time performances resulting in permanent "objects" are rare; the activity and the product would seem incon-gruous, if not contradictory. But isn't the viewing (the listening) also a *performance*? We "perform" upon an art object, no matter how seemingly permanent or fixed, by the way our eye travels about in it—perhaps even the way our bodies move toward it, away from it, or (with sculpture) around it. We "perform" architecture by moving within it. Moreover, the object itself changes with respect to our "performance," our ordering of objects in succession, the lighting, the time of day, the people we're with. So, too, with the audible recorded object: By selecting a particular sequence of records for our turntable and subjecting them to the variables of loud-speaker system, cartridge, room size, and the like (not to mention the input of our personality and musical experience), we "perform" a work that, in turn, results from the *prior* performance of instrumentalists and recording engineers. And, as in the visual analogy, that prior performance has oc-curred long before the public experience of it. In fact, as we've noted, it's not even a complete single performance, but a composite of many, assembled in the studio like a work of *musique concrète*.

Let's consider what implications this has for the instrumentalist. He may be about to give a "live" concert performance of a work that's available on disc, perhaps a piece that he has recorded himself. Does he in any sense compete with his recorded version? I can't pretend to answer this but only suggest that there's a real problem here, one that musicians must increasingly cope with in the future. We've all been led to believe—by the writings of com-posers, statements in music-appreciation texts, or whatever sources have shaped our musical preconceptions—that the performer's chief task is that of re-creating the composer's intentions as faith-fully as possible, as *exactly* as he can. If we literally subscribed to that, it might seem that the musician would be better off at the recording studio than in the concert hall; realization of the work on the RCA synthesizer might be better still. If there is justification for the live performance, as I and many others believe there is, it lies in areas other than that of "fidelity." It may have to do with the communal nature of the concert gathering itself, or the sensitive response to an "audience" (rather than to the printed notes), or the projection of mercurial, quixotic qualities that resist recording. In any event, it must entail some serious rethinking by the musician, an analysis of his own dispositions and goals, before he comprehends which of his aims are best realized through one performance medium and which through the other. For any number of reasons, a performer may decide to abandon the traditional concert format entirely: He may feel that the con-cert is a fossilized institution or realize (as a number of rock stars have) that his musical aims are inexorably linked to studio technique. The most publicized such retirement from concert activity was that of the Canadian pianist Glenn Gould, and both of the above reasons had something to do with his decision to specialize in the recorded medium. I should add, parenthetically, that many *composers* arrived at such decisions a few decades ago, choosing either to stress the recorded playback-performance (in *concrète* or synthesized works for magnetic tape) or to highlight the immediacy of the "live" by the artful use of chance, improvisa-tion and theater. Performing musicians have simply been slower to comprehend the nature of the problem.

Whether the future of performance lies more in the direction of the loud-speaker transmission or the live realization, it seems fairly likely that it *won't* reside in the traditional concert hall. Electronic music has been directly influential in this instance: The portability of speaker systems has helped to convince many listeners of a fact they should have known all along: that the recital hall is not the only (or the ideal) site for the performance of music. We've already considered the subject of private performance in your liv-ing room; of greater interest, possibly, is the spectacle of elec-tronic music heard in unusual public settings, in places where people gather for purposes other than that of "listening." The original playings of the Varèse *Poème électronique* in Le Corbusier's specially designed pavilion, or outdoor spring concerts at Columbia University's South Field, or the summer series in the courtyard of Stockholm's famous Town Hall, these have provided striking backdrops for the presentation of magnetic-tape music. In the same vein, many campus "concerts" of electronic music are held in university art galleries, quadrangles within dormitory complexes, dining halls, and similar public spaces. It hardly needs saying that rock concerts and festivals are held anywhere that electronic gear can be set up, from park to field to open beach to gymnasium.

Composers who wish to create an "environmental" music can work with such spaces as positive elements in their pieces. Robert Moran's *39 Minutes for 39 Autos,* mentioned in an earlier chapter, uses virtually the entire city of San Francisco as its "setting": On an August evening in 1969, Moran conducted an ensemble of slowly moving automobiles, directing the rhythms of their horns and headlights, while homes and office buildings blinked lights according to cues given by radio. The radio instructions, heard through hundreds of speakers, became part of the piece as well, and live television coverage (converted to semiabstract patterns for home screen viewing) added its own visual element. In this all-enveloping situation, "listening" and "performing" become almost inseparable. Max Neuhaus has devised a number of pieces in which the two activities—listening and playing—may or may not merge, but where "listening" invariably takes place in an unexpected setting. In *Public Supply*, for example, individuals are asked to telephone a local radio station and make sounds of any kind; seconds later, these will be added to a giant storage bank of sounds and heard over the radio, constantly regenerated by the feedback from your radio over the telephone (you're asked to keep the volume high while phoning, contrary to the instructions for telephoning a radio "talk show"). The sounds of Neuhaus's *Drive-in Music* can only be heard on your automobile radio, as you drive along a specially "prepared" roadway: Sound generators have been placed in trees, and lighting fixtures line the sides of the street. A computer conversion system was used in his *Telephone*

Access of 1968, in which you could make your own unique, personal "piece" by calling a designated phone number in New Jersey and then speaking; sounds would be made in response to your own words and vocal characteristics.

I have been involved in the making of one such composition to date and have plans for a second one in the near future. Both works stem from my fascination with sounds that "travel" physically within a defined space and a desire to see audiences moving in controlled patterns as well. My 1967 *Elevator Music* places the audience (ten at a time) within an elevator, moving up and down in a sixteen-story building on the Bowdoin College campus, while the performers remain situated in the lobby vestibules outside the various elevator doors on different floors. The piece I'm considering for the future, entitled *Gibson Hall* (the name of the Bowdoin music building), will be performed by keyboard sounds —practice pianos, amplified harpsichords, recordings of keyboard music—emanating from every window of the building, tracing various directional patterns (horizontal and vertical) during the music's course; the audience, naturally enough, will be outdoors, moving around the building along designated paths. In this way—although not even beginning to approach the multiplicity of the Moran auto piece—the "listener" will become an adjunct "performer."

Some electronic pieces may call for *direct* performance by the listener, going way beyond the basic listener "participation" in phonograph-playing suggested earlier. That is, the listener is instructed to maintain continuous manual control over some aspect of his electronic apparatus; the Nonesuch disc of the Cage-Hiller *HPSCHD* contains a detailed "score" for manipulation of the stereo channel controls, and a home-made performance of the piece—bringing various levels of musical activity to the surface and suppressing others—can be achieved. Jon Hassell's *MAP 2,* available in a recent copy of *Source* magazine, consists entirely of a square of prerecorded magnetic tape; you perform the work by moving a portable tape-playback-head over the square in any direction or pattern you choose, picking up material on various "tracks," often overlapped or reversed, and at the tempo of your hand movement. In this case your participation in the work is more than a mere source of variety in performance—it is required if the piece is to be activated at all.

A number of readers may wish to argue at this point that—electronic equipment aside—none of the performance options I've suggested are really "new." If anything, in fact, they're all terribly *old*, directly related to some of the most ancient traditions known in music! What can be so revolutionary about outdoor music, when street dancing, pageants of state, divertimenti for garden parties, and the like have been with us for centuries? The "performer as listener" concept is essential to the Renaissance madrigal, designed for no other audience than its participants; as for music in unconcert-like settings, the entire history of the art (certainly before the mid-eighteenth century) centers around the association of performance and highly specialized time and place—church services, festival time, dinner, afterdinner conviviality, dancing, marching, galloping on horseback, floating on the water. It is our own *concert* tradition, in fact, that seems unusual in the light of so much historical mixed media, the concert tradition that is the truly "recent" development in the history of performance.

The reply to this argument is, simply, Yes. Exactly. The whole point is that our "revolutionary," "avant-garde" propositions with regard to performance are an attempt to revive what is best in the past, substituting a host of time-honored options for a concert-hall format that (while admittedly "recent") has proved to be a short-lived experiment. The limitations of the concert are becoming apparent to composers, performers, and audiences alike; while the latter group, without necessarily knowing why, casts its vote through reduced ticket sales and lowered attendance, many composers and performers prefer a more direct attack upon the institution, breaking down its arbitrary restrictions as thoroughly as possible. It's amazing how strongly entrenched these restrictions have become in a relatively short period of time. In the space of a century or two at most, our musical sense has become habituated in a single direction, assuming the existence of certain performance "facts" and assuming them to be axiomatic:

1. To begin with, we usually assume that "serious" music, or "art" music, will be performed in a special place designated as

the "hall." This probably resembles a nineteenth-century theater, with a raised stage-platform for the performers and seating for the audience in rows separated by aisles. When we're forced to hold a concert somewhere else (for example, a campus gymnasium) we often try to make it conform to the pattern of the "hall" if we can.

2. The concert is open to the public—that is, to anyone who can pay the price of a ticket. And to help attract the attention of this amorphous potential "audience," the time and place of the concert are publicly announced in the newspapers, on wall posters, through the radio and television media.

3. We assume, in advance of the concert, that a particular soloist or ensemble will be performing, since this information has been included in the preconcert publicity noted above. Moreover, we also know what music will be played, because we're handed a printed sheet bearing this list of events (the "program") as we enter the concert hall.

4. Once the concert begins, a particular sequence of rituals is observed, from the physical placement and demeanor of the audience (all facing front, looking at the stage, and not speaking or moving about) to the manner in which the performer presents his material (not speaking to us, nor we to him, and acknowledging only those audience responses "programed" to occur at predictable moments). The musician must stand or sit still while performing, presenting an attitude of intense concentration—almost as though the audience were not there—while the public, in turn, affects the pretense of similar concentration, having been taught that the effort made to "pay attention" is of great virtue.

This, then, is the average basic routine of the "concert tradition." It is, I must repeat, relatively recent in our history. A number of the factors noted above wouldn't have existed at the beginning of our century, only a portion of them were present at the beginning of the nineteenth century, and hardly any characterized performances at the start of the eighteenth. The past few generations have witnessed this curiously cumulative formalization of our concert life for a variety of reasons, most of them social, economic, and class oriented (not musical); it's taken the intense competition of the "recorded performance," perhaps, and the spatial-theatrical-environmental experiments of our new music to make us aware of the alternatives. A great variety of options, as we've seen, can be found in the past: Apart from the obvious examples of state and church functions, our own favorite literature from the classical and Romantic periods (what we think of as the "concert" repertory) was often first presented in highly informal surroundings. Chamber music took place before small groups of friends and intimates, in medium-sized rooms of private homes and estates; the private "salon" performances of the nineteenth century resembled subdued cocktail parties or teas; orchestral works were played in an atmosphere closer to that of a restaurant (or Pops concert) than the modern formal "hall." The ritual of the concert hall is no more than *one* particular sort of "theatrical" setting, one among a staggering array of options. Its overuse during the past century or so makes it, unfortunately, the least interesting of alternatives, especially to the most recent generation of composers. Those truly concerned with environmental interplay find it a rather limited setting, its very familiarity dulling the senses, and prefer to work with the possibilities of parking lots, telephone booths, radio receivers, elevators, and the like. Other composers, whose music demands total alertness to its interrelated "grammatical" properties, have found the recorded performance an ideal vehicle for presentation.

Even those creating music for the concert hall attempt to disrupt its fixed patterns in one way or another. Why have the performers all sitting still on the stage? In Henry Brant's *Voyage Four* for orchestra (1964), only brasses, some "auxiliary" instruments (piano, harp, mandolin, glockenspiel, and so forth) and the chief conductor occupy the stage; very low strings and woodwinds are at the rear of the hall (orchestra level), while other strings and woodwinds occupy the side and rear balconies. Tympani, tuba, and chimes are placed in the *basement* of the hall, and can be heard through floor vents, these (and some of the balcony groups) being cued by subconductors. Brant has been actively concerned with this kind of spatial distribution in his pieces since the early 1950's and has attempted different "placements" in numerous chamber and orchestral works. It's also possible to have the players move about, either on stage or throughout the hall. Groups of musicians march to and from their positions, while playing, in George Crumb's Pulitzer-Prize-winning *Echoes of Time and the River* for orchestra; in my own orchestral *Magic Music*, a grand piano (placed prominently, as if for a concerto) acts as a theatrical focus, a sort of "totem" about which a number of orchestra players—and eventually the conductor, too—must move, activating the sounds of inner strings and keyboard. Performing musicians can speak as well: Morton Subotnick's *Play! No. 1* (woodwind quintet, piano, tape, film) begins as a parody of the traditional concert format, using the oboist's "tuning" note A as its starting point, and then gradually evolves into a theatrical assemblage of speech, shouting, silent visual gestures (arms and legs extended, heads swiveling, and so forth) and live-plus-electronic musical interaction. A much greater use of speech (declamation, amplified whispering, isolated syllables) pervades Lukas Foss's *Paradigm* or my own *Signals,* both recorded on a Deutsche Grammophon disc. Can the performers move among the members of the audience, leaving their perch on the stage? They do in Barney Childs's *Music for Almost Everybody,* for example, inviting the audience (and teaching them) to play specified pitches on their instruments, while these pitches are heard on tapes made at previous performances. The audience itself contributes to a performance comprised of speech, movement, gesture, and musical tone.

Nor does the audience have to remain fixed in its collective chairs. Certain kinds of pieces—notably those in which a purposely limited area of material is explored for great lengths of time—invite informal movement by the listeners; performances of such works resemble continuous-run film presentations and the "hall" itself is a kind of concourse, gallery, or waiting-room with some people sitting, others standing or walking about, a few sleeping or reading or conversing with friends. Cage's *HPSCHD* suggests a format of this type, as does Erik Satie's eighteen-hour *Vexations* or the meditative "drone" aesthetic of La Monte Young, David Rosenboom, Steve Reich. Terry Riley's massive *In C,* which takes up an entire Columbia record but could conceivably last much longer than that, is often performed in this informal manner; in two separate playings that I've witnessed, loud-speakers (amplifying the live music) have also been set up outside the hall itself—in lobbies and courtyards—so that people could wander in and out without missing the sounds. It's also worth noting that *another* performance of *In C* that I've seen (at Darmstadt in 1969) proved to be a disaster, mostly because it retained all of the artificial concert-hall restrictions; forced to remain immobile, seated, and in an attitude of feigned "concentration," the audience reacted by leaving the hall—it was emptied, in fact, within some thirty minutes. The work and its mode of presentation were in that case totally mismatched.

The listening audience can, of course, actively "perform" in a piece, and in more positive ways than that of leaving the auditorium. There are a variety of recent works in which the sounds and gestures made by the audience are integral to a complete performance. In *Contactics* by Udo Kasamets, each musician in a chamber ensemble is instructed to "play" the actions of a selected member of the audience (chosen without that member's initial knowledge). A number of simultaneously played games are taking place, then, as individuals in the audience try to test their guesses (Have I been chosen? Haven't I been chosen?) by moving, changing physical positions, and eventually walking directly to a musician they believe has, in fact, "picked" them. Robert Ashley's *Public Opinion Descends upon the Demonstrators* offers an elaborate variant of this plan. A single performer, seated and surrounded by a battery of electronic sound-producing equipment (generators, radios, tape decks with prerecorded material, or whatever else he wishes) confronts an audience. The first few minutes are usually fairly silent, punctuated by only a few electronic sounds; it takes a while before the audience realizes that the soloist is "performing" their actions, triggering specific sounds in response to definite physical indications, such as coughing, or switching position in one's chair, or a sign of inattention. As the audience—collectively and individually—comprehends the nature of the situation, it symbolically turns on the soloist ("playing" him, in effect, as he has been previously "playing" all of them), making rapid gestures, testing his reaction times. Gradually, then, the performance becomes a wild shambles—though always *con-*

trolled by the activities of the audience; it ends, in effect, whenever public and soloist both decide it should.

These are only a few of the methods composers have used to fight the limitations of the concert format. Aside from these more experimental ventures, *performers*—even those specializing in music of earlier periods—are coping, too, with the problems of concert-giving, each in his or her own way. Some, as we've seen, have abandoned live performance altogether, preferring the medium of the recording studio (with *its* unique problems, I should add). Other musicians retain the traditional setting for their work —that is, the hall itself—but have altered so many of the familiar procedures that the listener's experience becomes fresh again: The program may not necessarily be announced in advance, or the instrumentalist may speak to his audience (introducing and commenting upon various pieces), or the pianist may decide to plan his evening not as a solo effort but as part solo, part piano plus chamber ensemble, part piano plus orchestra. Perhaps the concert will be planned for an unfixed duration of time—half a day, for example—and the public invited to spend as much of its time in attendance as it wishes, staying, leaving and returning later. Most importantly, why should live performance take place in the hall? If we face the fact that *all* music can be considered and presented as "theater music," it becomes obvious that the right setting for any given piece is its original setting, or the closest approximation we can find. Works of the Middle Ages and Renaissance intended for banquet halls, town squares, towers, and cathedrals, classical and Romantic pieces meant for drawing rooms and gardens—all of these function beautifully in their own spaces, as a growing number of performers (and listeners) have finally discovered.

To summarize briefly, then: The advent of the recording has helped to bring this all about, not only through its usefulness as a medium for preservation and transmission of the traditionally "performed" music (this has been important, too, introducing us to a greater variety of music than we've ever known before) but as an unprecedented performance medium in itself. We're coming to realize that the playing of a record entails a unique kind of experience for both listeners and performers—an experience with spatial, acoustical, theatrical, and technological implications that have yet to be unraveled. It may be "false" to the intended experience of, say, a Haydn string quartet, but, then, as we're also beginning to admit, so is the concert hall presentation of that quartet. It may be best to concede that, with few exceptions, any performance is a compromise, and that, whether we like it or not, the "present" has at all times reinterpreted the "past" for its own purposes.

Or, if you don't wish to concede, remain a purist. But that may be more difficult than it appears at first. You would have to insist, for example, that the recorded music you hear consist only of works *intended* solely for the recorded "experience." All compositions for magnetic-tape playback (whether *musique concrète,* computer-generated sound, or synthesizer pieces) are ideal, as are a growing number of jazz and rock recordings that, by virtue of their multiple tracking and editing, couldn't be duplicated in any live performance. Many discs of avant-garde "theater" pieces —*HPSCHD, Casta Bertram,* or *L's GA*—exist as unique entities in their recorded form, so removed from their visual or spatial counterparts in the "live" world that they may, in fact, qualify as distinct, specifically nonvisual *concrète* realizations. In any event, no one could mistake them for the originals. It also helps to know that the composer has most probably supervised the recording sessions, effectively adapting his creation to this particular medium; the *Nude Paper Sermon,* by Eric Salzman, to note one final illustration, is really two separate and distinct works—one created specifically for a Nonesuch recording, with brilliantly imaginative mixing of channels and juxtaposition of disparate styles, the other a live mixed-media piece intended for theatrical realization. (The composer, of course, assumes responsibility for both of them.) One could also admit disc recordings of opera, on the same basis —it's impossible to mistake *them* for the originals, either—but there might always be a nagging suspicion that the composer's absence is a telling factor here. Had Wagner or Verdi or Puccini worked with the recorded performance in mind, what changes might have been made for disc realization?

All other music would probably be *verboten*: We'd hear our string quartets, symphonies, and piano recitals "live" and hopefully listen in settings that come close to their composers' intentions. Let's experience the *B Minor Mass* only in church, Mendelssohn's *Midsummer Night's Dream* music only in a garden . . . and by now we begin to see how impractical all of this might be. Recordings and even concert halls have become important to our lives precisely because we don't have the time or the resources to search out cathedrals, hold salon parties (or be invited to any), engage chamber musicians to perform in our living rooms. By making performance "public" in the worst sense, we've also made it more accessible, in terms of both wider audiences and a greater variety of music. Recordings, in particular, have opened up a musical universe—from Navajo songs to sitar recitals to Monteverdi operas to virtuoso African drumming—that no direct experience short of a world tour could provide. In these and so many other cases, the recorded presentations are all we may ever have, and we're thankful for them.

And so the situation of "performance" is no less confusing now than it was at the beginning of this chapter. I must admit that this is partly intentional, and serves as my way of stressing, finally, that in this area no one has any firm answers; on the contrary, we're just beginning to discover some of the questions. It would be sufficient for our purposes, then, if we simply come to a closer realization of the changes in our perception effected by recording and of the wider implications of these for *new* music and the performance of *old* music.

9. Jazz, Rock, Pop, and Serious

Another important result of the "recording revolution" of the past two decades is that stylistic distinctions have begun to break down. With respect to the newly composed music of our own time, it's difficult to say in many cases where the line between "serious" and "pop" really is—or whether it even exists at all. Even in the case of older music we encounter a similarly eclectic response by the listener; it's not uncommon for an individual to mix records of Varèse, Brahms, Palestrina, Ravi Shankar, and the Beatles in the pile on his phonograph changer. Perhaps this indicates a heightening of discrimination—we relish stylistic differences because we have become acutely aware of them—and a broadening of discrete, refined "tastes." I would suggest, rather, that the phenomenon reveals a *lessening* of discrimination in the traditional sense, a sweeping reclassification of musical experience in terms of function ("background" music, music for dancing, music for attentive listening) and performance mode ("live" and "recorded") instead of the geographical-historical criteria that other generations have applied. The *formula* for discrimination has changed.

The relaxation of the line between "pop" and "art" music is particularly important, and I should stress at the outset that it's not entirely unique to our own era. Composers of the Middle Ages and Renaissance used folk and popular material in their music for the church or court; Austro-German folk music crops up in the work of Haydn, Beethoven, Schubert, Mahler, in fact, the bulk of the standard "concert" repertory, all the time. The twentieth century has produced a remarkable body of "art" music founded in folk or ethnic style, from Bartók and Kodály to Bloch, Vaughan Williams, Sibelius, Copland, Prokofiev, Stravinsky. And the popular elements, whether American jazz, ragtime, French cabaret songs, nursery and circus tunes, or whatever, have figured prominently in the work of more composers of our century than I can name in a short paragraph; Ives, Satie, Virgil Thomson, Poulenc, Milhaud, and Gershwin would do for a starter. With the possible exception of Ives, all of the above are "neoclassical" in that their attempt is to fuse popular-folk elements into the traditional concert language prevalent before 1945: It's significant, perhaps, that the major works of these composers predate World War II. A blending of pop style with that of the postwar "avant-garde"—the new wave stemming from the influence of Webern, Cage, and Varèse—was less prevalent, certainly not the all-pervasive preoccupation of the 1910–40 period; the most important achievements in this area were those of Gunther Schuller, working in a style he designated as "Third Stream Music," and such isolated compositions as Milton Babbitt's *All Set* for jazz ensemble in a quasi-serial twelve-tone idiom (available in a Columbia Records album devoted to various aspects of the "Third Stream").

The interaction between jazzmen and "serious" experimental composers worked both ways, of course: John Lewis of the Modern Jazz Quartet worked closely with Schuller, and Charlie Parker approached Varèse for composition lessons shortly before his (Parker's) tragic death. (Again, this is hardly new; Brubeck's relation to Milhaud and Bartók, in an earlier decade, could be cited in the same vein.) As disc recordings began to be made from tapes, rather than "cut" directly in studio sessions, some jazz-pop performers saw the advantages of tape technique and, in effect, used a number of *musique concrète* ideas for their own purposes. A pop group of the late 1950's called the Chipmunks was literally created via speed-change in playback, and pianist Bill Evans used multitrack overlays of his own playing to create elaborate ensemble effects.

We can see, then, that "pop" and "serious" have had a long collaborative history together. On the other hand, there has always been a rather thin line dividing them: What *is* unique at present, then, is the apparent erosion of even this thin line. A number of factors mentioned earlier are of importance here. For one thing, the special nature of the recording as a performance mode—plus the facts of record manufacture, advertising, marketing sales, and listening situation—can only lead the buyer (or listener) to the conclusion that the "record" is itself a special category of music, separate and distinct from other categories. The recording of Mozart's *Don Giovanni* has more in common with *Gesang der Jünglinge* or the *Jimi Hendrix Experience*—in terms of our experiences, perceptions, and responses—than it has with a live performance of it or of any other opera. And, if we restrict ourselves to the "classical" repertoire—well, what is "classical?" As Eric Salzman writes,

> The category "classical" itself is a meaningless catch-all. Is new and relevant non-pop that grows out of and interacts with the new culture to be considered "classical" music at all? This is more than a technical problem. To the record rack jobber and distributor, my own *Nude Paper Sermon,* as well as Gregorian Chant, Vivaldi, Schubert string quartets, Von Suppé Overtures, and Cliburn's Greatest Hits are all in the same category.

Secondly, the wide availability of records has produced an unparalleled situation in which anyone can hear (or, if he cares enough about music, has already heard) compositions from every conceivable culture, period, and geographical area. This has undoubtedly influenced listeners, and, of even greater importance, it has influenced the younger generation of composers and performers. Our present rock stars, and their young audiences, represent the first generation to have grown up with the long-playing record and the tape recorder; one result of this is that a surprising percentage of the people actively involved with the rock-pop-folk world (when compared with their counterparts a few decades ago) are intimately familiar with "classical" music—not only the Great Masters, either, but non-Western music, so-called primitive music, and the most experimental works of the avant-garde. The Beatles learned a great deal from Stockhausen and *musique concrète,* while Joseph Byrd (leader of the now defunct group The United States of America) remains an ardent Cage disciple and electronic synthesizer designer. Frank Zappa, of The Mothers of Invention, is perhaps the most eclectically learned of all; his devotion to the music of Varèse is well known and stems from the chance purchase of an early Varèse recording as a teen-ager in the mid-1950's. Recordings played a major role in Zappa's musical maturing, as he notes: "You see, when I was a kid I used to save up for a month, so I could get an R & B album and, the same day, the completed works of Anton Webern"—and they have influenced other rock performers in similar ways.

Thirdly, rock-pop-jazz music and experimental "serious" music have converged in their mode of performance. It's entirely possible for a pop singer or ensemble to appear on the stage of Carnegie Hall, just as it's equally likely that avant-garde theater pieces will take place (as did Larry Austin's *The Maze*) in a university gymnasium or (Morton Subotnick's *Ritual Game Room*) a student union. Amplification and distortion often figure heavily in live performances of both "categories"; similarly, in the studio recording situation, both may rely upon sophisticated *concrète* techniques, making use of tape delay, speed changes, tape reversal, reverberation, multichannel mixing, and the like. (I hesitate to mention tape-editing, since this is now integral to *all* recording, whether Mozart, Stockhausen, or The Rolling Stones.) Emphases do change, of course, and it's interesting to note that, whereas, in the 1950's, the more experimental jazz work took place in live performance and the "serious" avant-garde in the electronic studio, the 1960's witnessed a mild reversal of form, with the rock groups discovering the wonders of elaborate studio technique and the avant-garde rediscovering the virtues of the live performance. In the 1970's, the extremes (on both sides) seem to be leveling out, and the close parallels in performance—whether live or recorded, pop or art—are more evident than ever before. It's obvious that the best of the rock records are highly sophisticated "electronic" ventures and that the "serious" composer's attempts to break down concert-hall formality are in one sense imitative of age-old "popular music" practices. Consider Henry Pleasants's description of "the places where jazz flourishes—or used to flourish: nightclubs, cabarets, musical bars and dance halls, all presumably disreputable. And the audience! Young people who chew gum, smoke, tap their feet, pop their fingers and applaud in the middle of a number, just as audiences used to do in Mozart's time." With a few minor changes in locale, the scene described might be that of the Cage-Hiller *HPSCHD* in performance or Terry Riley's *In C* or Cornelius Cardew's *Treatise*.

The mention of Riley's name brings up another perplexing question of the 1970's: Can we (or should we try to) determine whether a given composer is creating "art" music or "pop" music? Does it matter? Terry Riley is a "classically" trained composer, schooled in Oriental and African techniques as well as the Western tradition; his *In C* has had a remarkable reception by "serious" critics—one calling it the "symphony of the Global Village"—and is generally regarded as avant-garde "art" music. But, then, what are we to make of his *A Rainbow in Curved Air* or *Poppy No Good and the Phantom Band?* Both of these share the ostinato-drone-with-infinite-variations outlook of *In C* but have used the elements in a recording studio situation. In the Columbia recording, Riley himself becomes a vast ensemble of sound sources, playing one instrument and then another, the whole transmuted by echo devices, recurring loops, and an assortment of sound-on-sound techniques. As an avowedly "electronic" realization, the recording of the two pieces might be considered even more avant-garde, experimental, or whatever than *In C*, and yet the record is treated as a pop-rock issue. Riley's collaborative record with John Cale, *Church of Anthrax,* is equally innovative, the two performers creating a collage of piano, organ, viola, saxophone, harpsichord, guitar, and string bass. This is also regarded as a rock record; perhaps the existence of a vocal number automatically pushes it into that category, but one can't be sure. How do we "categorize" John Cale, incidentally, when he performs in this instance with "serious" musician Terry Riley and on other occasions with The Velvet Underground? It seems absurd to make distinctions here, but Columbia Records obviously does just that: In issuing all three Riley releases, Columbia has chosen to put *In C* on its "Masterworks" label (along with Mozart, Purcell, Varèse, Stockhausen, *et al.*) and the other two on the rock-pop shelf.

This confusion is just as apparent on the European side of the

Atlantic. Cornelius Cardew, for example, simply defies categorization; he has worked with Stockhausen in Cologne and Foss in the United States (as a member of the Creative Associates of Buffalo), teaches at the major conservatories of London, is often referred to as the "English Cage"—*and,* with his AMM Ensemble and Scratch Orchestra, produces concerts of improvisatory music that often verge on the extremes of far-out rock. Hugh Davies, another Englishman, worked at the ORTF Studios in Paris and compiled the massive *International Electronic Music Catalog* referred to in an earlier chapter. You can also hear Davies, though, on a German ECM disc, where he serves as live-electronics man for a highly imaginative group called The Music Improvisation Company. Such dual role-playing is hardly surprising in Britain, where many rock groups and avant-garde performers aim at the *same* audiences of youngsters, and where Boulez and Stockhausen are "stars" of the same magnitude as John Lennon; in that sort of situation, one activity would hardly diminish the validity or status of the other. Nor is Lorin Hollander's reputation as concert pianist tarnished by his performance on an electric Baldwin at New York's Fillmore East or his compositions, which seem to be part-pop, part-Prokofiev. It seems apparent, then, that all the barriers are down; performers, composers, audiences, and record-buyers are moving from one musical universe to the other with relative ease.

This is not to say that there are no differences between the two styles: The jazz-rock-folk-pop idiom still retains, in varying degrees, the notion of steady beat, rhythmic syncopation against it, regularly recurring melodic lines (with recognizable patterns), some sense of tonality or key, and harmonies built from traditional chord structures. The "serious" avant-garde rejects much or all of this, more or less, in favor of stylistic directions that we noted in earlier chapters. But I have to say "in varying degrees," "more or less," and so on, because the stylistic boundaries often merge as well—some rock music, like Zappa's, occasionally dispenses with tonality and metric stability, while a growing literature of experimental "art" music draws on the simple chords and regular beat of the pop world. This is inevitable, now that we have pop composer-performers with a thorough grounding in that "other" world of new music and "serious" composers with the stature of, say, William Bolcom—a creator of symphonic scores, teacher at major universities, respected member of the young "avant-garde," if that term means anything after all this—composer of off-Broadway musicals and a ragtime piano virtuoso. Even admitting that this kind of stylistic fusion is increasing all the time, though, doesn't deny the fact that the two musics have their differences. Audiences differ as well, of course: Traditional music-lovers may find rock too overwhelmingly loud; experimental "serious" composers may find its beat and harmony something of a bore; rock fans might have equally negative reactions to "classical" or "avant-garde" works. The point is *not* that all musics have become one, or that they all appeal to a universal audience, but that, with respect to new styles of all kinds, they are converging from different directions upon a common focal point and interacting as rarely before. Or, to state this from another viewpoint, we all continue to "categorize" the various musical works we experience, exercising our preferences and tastes as we see fit. The crucial change lies in the ever decreasing validity of phrases like "classical" and "popular" as avenues of categorization; such labels have lost their meaning and we must articulate our preferences in other ways.

Each of us approaches this new stylistic fusion from the vantage point of his own particular musical background. Mine is undeniably and exclusively "classical" in its origins; I've never performed in a jazz group, dance band, or rock ensemble, and my listening experience in this area is casual at best. I mention this—particularly in view of the comments I'm about to make on electronics in the rock-pop field—not to apologize for my credentials but simply to state them. Those readers who are either under thirty or acutely aware of developments in this field (or both) will probably just choose to ignore this section of the book; the only value, for them, in reading on might be in comparing their own reactions to those of a fusty "serious" musician whose training and experience traverse only the narrow road of "art" music from Gregorian chant through Babbitt and Cage. I suspect, though, that many readers will be in my own position, discovering for themselves—and on the basis of whatever experience they possess—those aspects of the new pop-rock scene that interest them most. If your main concern is with *electronic* music, you'll soon find that there are at least three major avenues of exploration:

1. Practically any instrument you can think of has been "electrified"—electric pianos, electric trumpets, electric violins, and so on down the line. Their primary purpose seems to be that of amplification—to a level of loudness that, for many ears, approaches the utterly deafening—with the added attractions of distortion and timbral alteration. The first such instrument to become a jazz staple was the vibraphone, popularized by Lionel Hampton in the 1930's; it quickly found acceptance with "serious" composers, and the lyric, sonorous qualities of the instrument (resonance and variable vibrato-tremolo are the rationale here, not sheer amplification) led to its use in many chamber works of the post-Webern era after 1945. The electric guitar is so well known a phenomenon that it hardly needs discussion here. I've particularly enjoyed hearing recordings by Joe Zawinul on electric piano and Tony Williams with a vividly coloristic electric drum set, both employing great imagination and sensitivity in the use of these instruments.

The Don Ellis Orchestra is virtually an all-electronic band, with the brasses and winds given added bite, strength, and timbral variety by electrical manipulations. Ellis's group also uses an electronic keyboard called a clavinette (capable of flatting pitches and producing microtones), and his own trumpet—with an extra valve—is similarly wired for amplification. Furthermore, Ellis uses tape loops extensively, building giant echo effects and canonic imitations. The delightful sonorities are interesting enough to compensate for the fact that the musical language is otherwise rather tame; melodically and harmonically, little happens that wasn't anticipated by the super-Big Bands (Stan Kenton, Sauter-Finnegan) of the 1950's, and the supposedly "experimental" rhythms and meters don't begin to match the asymmetrical drive of Dave Brubeck, let alone Stravinsky or Bartók.

2. Electric studio techniques are at least as sophisticated as they ever were in the Cologne, Paris, Illinois, or Columbia-

Princeton "serious" studios. I've mentioned tape-editing, the adroit use of microphones, and the mixing of separate channels often enough now, so it can be assumed that these go into the making of practically any record; the objective, of course, is that of creating the aura of a continuous live performance, artificially simulating "reality" very much as an average motion picture does. The listener is asked, in effect, to pretend that the medium itself does not exist or that its sole intent is to capture and preserve (rather than create) the performance. What's more interesting for our purposes, though, is the positive use of the medium in a thoroughly *concrète* manner, with no illusions advanced as to the performability of the selection "live." The best-known examples, perhaps, are those of The Beatles, particularly *"Revolution No. 9"* (from *The Beatles*) and *"A Day in the Life"* (from the *Sergeant Pepper* album). Here we have the splicing of unrelated scraps of tape, tape reversal, variable speed changes, sequential loops—in fact, just about all of the devices used by Schaeffer and Henry, Luening and Ussachevsky.

In the same vein, the recording of Joe Byrd's group The United States of America (for Columbia Records), using synthetic rather than natural sound sources, approaches the virtuosity of Subotnick or the Cologne period of *elektronische Musik;* before it disbanded, this group was perhaps the only rock ensemble to concentrate heavily on electronic sources, chiefly those supplied by the Byrd-Durrell synthesizer. I never saw the group in live performance and have no way of knowing to what degree the music—often haunting, occasionally bizarre or grotesque—relied upon tape technique in its creation. There is enormous creative vitality here, however, and the disc is definitely worth hearing.

This is by no means the sum total of works or groups using *musique concrète* devices or synthesized sound on records, but merely the few I found most interesting. On other records, you may hear snatches of Sousa marches, fragments of Gregorian chant, the voices of Churchill and Roosevelt, sounds that are filtered and ring-modulated, and the whole arsenal of effects that originated in the classic studio of the 1950's. For many groups, the recording studio has become their most important *instrument.* As Arnold Shaw notes in *The Rock Revolution,*

In 1966 the Beach Boys spent ninety hours in a studio to produce a single 45 r.p.m. disk. The Beatles' *Sgt. Pepper's Lonely Hearts Club Band* was four months in the making and cost over $56,000. Songs are no longer written and then recorded. They are most frequently conceived in the recording studio, with the process of recording entering actively into the shape and form and sound that the song ultimately takes. . . . Major studios are now equipped to cut as many as twenty-four separate tracks at a time. . . . Today's rock and pop scene is a reverberating cosmos of microphones, amplifiers and magnetic tape recorders.

3. Electronics has come to dominate the live performance field as well, not only through simple amplification but by the "processing" of vocal and instrumental material so as to alter its sound. There may be a number of units added to one's amplifier or separate boxes on stage (often activated by a foot pedal) that filter sound or ring-modulate it, the latter sound called "fuzz tone." Feedback, the screeching-squealing sound resulting from a mike being placed too close to a speaker, can be exploited effectively, to achieve a sense of terror or great delicacy of nuance. You might wish to hear, for example, a number called "Feedback" in The Grateful Dead's album *Live/Dead,* which runs the gamut of dynamics and texture. The Mothers of Invention use the device with great success as well. In live concerts by many groups the concept of "total theater," noted in earlier chapters with reference to the "serious" avant-garde, plays a crucial role: The audience experiences not only an array of sound, but dazzling strobe lights, blinking colored lights and projected images, motion pictures shown at odd angles, heated conversations between performers and listeners, movement and physical gesture about the performing space. It is another major illustration of the pop and art worlds converging together on a significant point. Various camps may attach different labels to the tendency—Frank Zappa, whose Mothers of Invention excelled in this area, termed it "freakout," while in more academic circles it's called "mixed media" or "intermedia"—but the parallels and analogies are too obvious to miss.

As with the nonpop examples of this movement, recordings (by eliminating the visual) only capture a fraction of the live experience. In any event, I'd still recommend records by The Mothers very highly; whatever you miss in the disc realization, you have, nonetheless, a wildly eclectic musical panorama, drawing upon many recent experimental directions (including electronic ones) as well as grotesque references to earlier "masterworks." For virtuosity of a more directly electronic sort, the art of Jimi Hendrix is unparalleled. Once again, the visual excitement is lost, but the staggering display of feedback, filter effects, "fuzz," echo, and the like more than compensates for the lack. In fact, *The Jimi Hendrix Experience* album impressed me more than any other single example of rock-electronics I've heard.

A number of performers have also turned to the use of electronic synthesizers, of the small voltage-controlled variety, in their live performances. These include The Electric Flag, Sun Ra, Paul Bley, and Annette Peacock. As with their counterparts in "serious" music, the synthesizers can generate their own tones or modify such external sources as voices or instruments; in performance, they're often used to do both. The results I've heard haven't been overly interesting, but, as we've seen, the synthesizer is infinitely adaptable to whatever style its user prefers, barring only the ultraserial, and any number of exciting developments can occur in this area in the future. I hope, for example, that there are more ventures like the one called *An Electric Christmas,* staged at Carnegie Hall in December, 1967. Organized by Morton Subotnick, the event demonstrated the mingling of seemingly disparate musical worlds by overlapping them in a monumental collage of forces. The combination of the New York Pro Musica (an ensemble specializing in medieval music), Circus Maximus (a rock group), Subotnick's own electronic performance—live and taped —on a Buchla system, and film and light projections produced a unique spectacle. After a succession of individual solos and collaborative mixings, the entire evening culminated in a semi-improvised performance by all of a fourteenth-century *chanson.*

This, of course, brings us back to our starting point: the coming together of various stylistic trends, creating a wholly new amalgam for the 1970's. *An Electric Christmas* is only one example; Eric Salzman's *The Nude Paper Sermon,* the Mozart-based *HPSCHD,* or Zappa's learned-rock creations, all noted previously, are equally prophetic for the future. The rock opera-oratorio *Jesus Christ Superstar* is in its best moments a magnificent grab-bag of stylistic juxtapositions, from Ligeti to Handel to Bartók to pure rock to far-out electronics. A group known as Ars Nova produces a record in which thoughtfully made instrumental parodies of Machaut and Monteverdi alternate with vocal numbers along the lines of the Italian and Spanish Renaissance. Serious music critics find in *Sergeant Pepper's Lonely Hearts Club Band* the first indications of extended "serious" form—in the words of one, "a popsong cycle, a Tin Pan Alley *Dichterliebe*"; another critic writes, in *The New York Times,* "The wedding of Bach and rock, of Purcell and Pop becomes not only permissible, but inevitable for the predictable future."

I hasten to add, once more, that stylistic differences, and their appeal to a variety of audience subgroups, will continue to exist; "pure" Bach will remain Bach, and the traditions of folk-country-ethnic music will, in the hands of some performers, stay unfussed and uncluttered. Nothing would be duller than the assimilation of all musical distinctions into a totally homogeneous blend, and what's encouraging about the present direction is that various strands manage to remain remarkably distinct even at the moments of their greatest interaction. An even more encouraging aspect of today's tendencies is that they are forcing us—finally, once and for all—to abandon our cultural baggage of overworked labels. "Classical" music (when not applied specifically to the works of Haydn, Mozart, and Beethoven) is the most meaningless phrase of all; "serious" music is hardly that in an age when so many composers branded with that label write witty, unashamedly funny, bitingly ironic pieces; "concert" music is a wholly misleading term in a period when performers and composers alike are moving away from the concert hall and into other musical environs; "art" music is hardly an improvement when so many serious composers are anti-"art" and so many pop entertainers have taken on the pretentious title of "artist." And, for that matter, what is "popular" music? The most uncompromisingly experimental rock and jazz groups will never be truly "popular" with the large mass audience, and, if the test-of-time criterion is to be applied, J. S. Bach may be the most popular composer who ever lived.

In short, the Age of Musical Pluralism is close at hand, altering the composer's creations and the audience's listening habits. Both facets are related, because composers are always listeners first. Harold Schoenberg of *The New York Times* has written, "All techniques are being synthesized. The Beatles had something to do with it, and John Cage and the Columbia-Princeton Electronic Music Studio, and the jazz boys, and some of the movie composers, and some television commercials, and Vietnam, and the psychedelics. Young composers today enthusiastically use everything within reach." And the debt is anything but one-sided. If rock-jazz performers have learned much from "serious" music, the boldest of the avant-garde "art" composers have absorbed an equally important set of values from the pop area. If serious scholars and critics have, by their pronouncements of "art," opened up an intellectual audience for rock, the rock records, in turn, have introduced an entire generation of listeners to Cage, Varèse, Ives, Vivaldi concerti, Beethoven quartets, not to mention Babbitt and Subotnick electronic efforts. As Frank Zappa once put it:

> Rock has made everything possible because it is capable of and willing to assimilate everything, . . . because a fantastic number of kids are willing to listen. . . . We mention lots of experimental composers on our album covers; and that could do more to get kids into the heavy stuff than all the preaching in the world. That's a hell of a lot more for culture than Babe Ruth ever offered!

10. New Approaches to Music Teaching

This consideration of the musical "future" would be incomplete without reference to the really significant changes taking place in the schools. These changes—new subjects in the curriculum, the introduction of electronic facilities, a more honest acceptance of the legitimacy of rock and jazz, and the use of "avant-garde" techniques to encourage creative work (both composition and performance) by all students—reflect the very diversity of musical life in the 1970's discussed in the preceding chapter. The teaching of the art relates, as it should, directly to the contemporary practices of that art. In the visual arts, this sort of interconnection has existed for many years, and there are few respectable art programs that haven't made use of collage techniques, photographic images, abstraction, and pseudo-cubist representation, chemical sprays and lacqueurs, and building materials from wire to plastic to concrete to foam rubber. It's also been assumed that such experimentation can be attempted by all age groups and at different levels of competence and talent—that is, the *creative* experience (using, perhaps in simplified form, the tools and aesthetic positions of the mid-twentieth century) is regarded as one valid form of "introduction" to art, a legitimate format for "art appreciation."

There hasn't been a parallel emphasis in music teaching until quite recently: In fact, if school music were as consistently innovative in dealing with contemporary activity as school art has been, there would be little need for me to discuss "new approaches to music teaching" in these pages. I don't propose to trace the

183

origins of this disparity between music and art, except to note that both fields of study have had to pass through various stages of acceptance by the academic community, the most painful of these being the transition from a solely historical-theoretic-aesthetic approach (substitute "appreciation" when dealing with the nongifted general student) to one that recognized the equal validity of practical experience. It is precisely at this point, I believe, that the traditional division of emphasis between the two school programs developed: The "making" of art was quite naturally regarded as the study of painting, drawing, sculpture, and (gradually) the newer experimental media, while the "making" of music—especially for the average student—came to mean the *performance* of music, and most often of highly traditional music. There are any number of reasons for this; for one, it reflects the widespread public image of art as an experimental, ongoing contemporary activity and music (with the possible exception of pop) as a field for "interpreters" preserving a time-tested literature. (Compare the music and art columns of your newspaper, for example, or the music and art sections of *Time* or *Newsweek,* and the disparity will become obvious.) Secondly, in all but the most enlightened schools the arts existed as an adornment for institutional ritual—commencement activities, wall displays, athletic contests, "pageants" relating to other academic interests, publications—rather than for their creative value *per se.* In this context, the school "public" of listeners and viewers reinforced the distorted analogy by encouraging and requesting examples of student art (often highly innovative), on the one hand, and ensemble performances of Tchaikovsky, Sousa, Bach gavottes, and Victor Herbert operettas, on the other. Furthermore, and again reflecting the lack of interest in really new music, "composition" was regarded by all—students, teachers, and parents—as a highly orthodox discipline, rigidly bound to the language of the tonal system. If this is so, we must admit in all fairness that you simply can't write music sounding like Handel or Gershwin without a great deal of specialized instruction: One must learn about chords and their sequences, melodic phrase construction, the tonal system itself, rhythm and accent, the ranges and capabilities of traditional instruments, and the notational symbols that have traditionally specified these factors on paper. Given this thoroughly conventional approach to student composition, its implementation would be impossible in a free-wheeling format analogous to that of the introductory design course offered by the average art department.

There are an equally large number of reasons for the change in this attitude in recent years. A few of these have been suggested in the earlier sections of this chapter and can be summarized by the simple statement that our musical awareness has broadened enormously within the past decade, thanks to our near total immersion in a world of electronics. It's also significant that the tape recorder is, after all, not an esoteric device found only in experimental studios, but a familiar object in many middle-class homes. It would be safe to say that the average student is surprisingly sophisticated in his understanding of tape technique and in many instances is more versed in the subtleties of editing, multitrack collage, reverberation, and the uses of feedback than his tradition-oriented teacher. The familiar electric guitar has also brought the potential for live-electronic experimentation into many households. Concern for "new music" is now, for the first time in this century, directly related to a wealth of experience shared by many amateurs.

And composers are taking note of the fact. For some composers the movement of school music in the direction of the avant-garde motivates them to further this direction, by writing pieces intended for classroom use—a new kind of *Gebrauchsmusik*, perhaps, whose twofold purpose is to stimulate student performance and to encourage student composition along similar lines. (I hope to note a few examples of this sort later on.) Other composers, while not specifically writing for classroom performance, make use of amateurs of all ages in their works, finding them enthusiastic and responsive performers. The word "amateur," in fact, may be meaningless here, at least as far as the traditional allusion to a limited "skill" is involved; some of the students I've worked with at Bowdoin College (in performances of pieces by Cage, Oliveros, Cardew, Bussotti, Erickson, and others) may not have much facility with conventional note-reading or performance upon the trumpet or clarinet, but their real skill in working with electronic equipment—revealing many years' worth of "performing" experience with the medium—is often remarkable. Composer Edwin London, from whom Bowdoin commissioned a work for student players, has remarked in this context (at a meeting of the American Society of University Composers),

> Is it any wonder that the recent availability and proliferation of such things in the home and school as tape recorders, movie projectors, slide projectors, and the electric circuit associated with rock and roll has not (as it has) uncovered a vast and unfilled need[?] . . . In many homes and garages all over the country where the expression "plagal cadence" has no meaning, the thing expressed by the term is in various states of amplification. . . . When we look at the performing media of the past, crystallizing over a long period of time—the string quartet, the piano, the orchestra, etc.—we know that they once had a relevant social usage and function. They were not always art objects. Violins were used at dances, and pianos were in many homes where people did not necessarily think of themselves as Rubinsteins; they simply enjoyed fooling around playing the piano. The fact that people have tape recorders, slide projectors, electric guitars and so forth in their homes today gives everyone the potential of becoming active creators, if not great ones. Most people, particularly young ones, like to fool around generally, and it's from this play with the new media, especially those having little continuity with or derivations from past "musical" materials, which is producing a fresh approach.

To this healthy student curiosity and generally broad level of student experience we can add a final factor of importance: the availability, at relatively low cost, of electronic equipment for heavy-duty school use. The quality and versatility may not be of "professional" caliber, but the advantages of easy portability and long wear under conditions of comparative strain make such machines invaluable for the classroom. There are many varieties of tape deck or tape recorder that meet these conditions, and the small, nonmodular voltage-controlled synthesizers—such as the Putney, ElectroComp, ARP 2600, Mini Moog—are ideal in school situations. With a minimum of this kind of apparatus, any school could, for example, initiate a program, or at least one course, in electronic music composition. Two such courses have been described in the special electronics issue (November, 1968) of

Music Educators Journal: a project at the Julia R. Masterman Junior High School in Philadelphia, which used the resources of studios in Philadelphia and nearby Princeton University, and a similar one conducted at Greenwich, Connecticut, High School. The Greenwich program was one of a large number instituted in Connecticut under the sponsorship of Project PEP (Pilot Electronic Project), funded by Title III of the Elementary and Secondary Education Act and the Connecticut State Department of Education. It's worth noting, also, that the sturdy, inexpensive ElectroComp synthesizer, manufactured in Connecticut, was designed to meet the needs of the PEP program—another instance of collaboration, in this case that of engineers, musicians, and school administrators. Anyone desiring further information about the program can write to the Connecticut State Department of Education, Box 2219, in Hartford.

As I've suggested, it's likely in many situations that the beginning teacher may possess less electronic sophistication than his students. In any event, the teacher will want to acquire the broadest possible background before embarking on a course of this type; for this reason, a variety of workshops and summer institutes have been set up in different sections of the United States, open to students, young composers, and (primarily) teachers of music —the summer institute directed by Jean Eichelberger Ivey at Baltimore's Peabody Conservatory, Robert Ceely's BEEP workshop in Boston, and the University of New Hampshire summer program directed by John Rogers and Hubert S. Howe are but a few of these. Will Gay Bottje heads a similar electronic workshop for teachers at Southern Illinois University in Carbondale; he has also written a series of articles entitled "Electronic Music —Creative Tool in the Classroom" for *The School Musician,* which may be of help to teachers considering work in this medium.

All of the above stress the need for experience with voltage-controlled equipment (and, in the New Hampshire program, the computer generation of sound as well). I would not want to deny the value of such experience for the teacher—and, eventually, his or her students—in the light of the technological advances of the past decade. But I'd also like to suggest that highly effective programs for the schools can be (and have been) achieved with much less sophisticated apparatus. Techniques of *musique concrète* can be introduced if a school can assemble two or three tape recorders, microphones, a phonograph, and suitable splicing-editing equipment. Even the very youngest of schoolchildren respond immediately to the creative potential of speed changes, tape reversal, and other practices that entail a bare minimum of expense or experience. I've tried this approach with groups of high school students and even once on a local educational television program—a sort of electronic Julia Child show, reversing tapes and adding channels rather than cooking a stew. The point is that, as interest in electronic music becomes more widespread, "economy" becomes less a factor in making its mysteries—or at least some of them—accessible to large numbers of people. Some impressive beginnings have already been made on the most limited of budgets.

Another important aspect of the avant-garde in the schools deals less overtly with electronic music, although it is related to it nonetheless: I am referring to the growing use of "experimental" music in courses designed for the average, initially uninvolved student, courses usually designated "Introduction to Music" or "Music Appreciation." Anyone who has ever suffered through a course of this sort in its most traditional format—whether as student or teacher—will recall the generally uninspired, unmotivating set of experiences it usually entails: listening to great quantities of records, supposedly to discover aspects of "form" or historical "style," attendance at concerts (either for the same purposes or to improve one's manners in polite society), and—at the precollege level—a minimum of class performance, usually unison singing of simple tunes to the drab accompaniment of a dutiful pianist. This is the situation at its worst, of course; in the hands of a skilled, musically gifted teacher even the most conservative of programs might reveal untold insights. But the exceptional moments of real worth don't disguise the fact that, of all facets of the music curriculum, the Introduction-Appreciation course was the most badly in need of overhauling. It was least successful, paradoxically, in realizing those aims that had initially called it into being: the building of an intelligent, alert lay audience and the encouragement and nurturing of whatever kernel of musical potential for performing or composing that resided in each individual.

The problem is hardly unique to our era, and teachers have been grappling with it in one form or another for generations. What interests me most is a relatively recent head-on attack, perhaps the most "revolutionary" solution of all, made by a scattered group of young composers with a keen interest in the development of young people. I hasten to add that "revolutionary" or "avant-garde" or "experimental" may be the *least* appropriate words to use in describing this new approach—that is, unless you regard utter simplicity as "revolutionary." The heart of the notion, in fact, is a return to the most fundamental concepts underlying our musical perceptions; it is a study of music not from the vantage point of a preordained body of "literature" but rather from the intrinsic values of the musical experience itself. For example, students in many "Introduction" courses today are being asked (or requested to ask themselves) the following questions:

1. What is the physical-acoustical basis of sound?
2. On a more "qualitative" level, what distinctions can be made between "musical" sound and noise? Sound and silence? High and low? Loud and soft?
3. In what ways does this sound (noise, silence) articulate the passage of time? How do durations, pulses, rhythms, tempi function in this regard?
4. What are the characteristics of various sound-producing bodies? Are all moving bodies potential "instruments"?
5. With what range of possibilities do sounds succeed one another? What are the possibilities when sounds occur simultaneously? Are these "forms" or "textures"?
6. To what degree does written notation specify musical actions, and which actions? Do different notations have different purposes?
7. What does it mean to "perform"? What is the relation of performance to notation, to composing, to listening?

By means of this kind of reasoning and probing, the class will most probably arrive at the point eventually where the rondo form is introduced, where they hear and discuss a Bach fugue or

Schubert song or Mozart symphony. Or, then again, perhaps not: The aim of a course like this would be to emphasize musical sensitivity as a *universal,* apart from considerations of any specific culture or history, and references to the "masterworks" might be peripheral at best. Most likely a large percentage of the music played would be the students' own creative work—either improvised or written out along the lines dictated by various unorthodox notational schemes—or brief exercises created by the composer-teacher.

The young Canadian composer R. Murray Schafer has followed this general philosophical approach in his appearances as guest lecturer before numerous groups of schoolchildren and "Introductory" university classes; he has summarized the most provocative points, drawn from these lectures, in a series of short books published by BMI Canada, Ltd. You might wish to examine *Words on Music* or *The Composer in the Classroom.* I particularly enjoy Schafer's *Ear Cleaning,* in which he directs the class into a series of confrontations with basic musical materials, often by means of ingenious exercises and assignments:

> Take a single tone. Appoint a student conductor. The conductor works out hand signals to indicate to the class the different dynamic qualities of tone he desires. By means of dynamic shading—loud, soft, slow or rapid growth and decay, rapid changes, echo effects, etc.—he shapes the tone.
>
> . . . So much for loudness. How soft can music be made to sound? Various students are called to the front of the class and asked to hum a note as softly as possible. The class closes their eyes. When they hear a note they put their hands up. The amplitude of the sound must now be progressively reduced until one by one the rows of hands stay down. . . .
>
> (Schafer:) Everybody take a sheet of paper and experiment with it as sound. How many different ways can you think of to make a sound with it? . . . [Now] as I point to you at random I want you to make a sound with your paper that is substantially different than that produced by the preceding person. This will tax your ingenuity and alertness more because you won't know what your predecessor is going to do until he does it. . . . By giving the paper a voice we have exposed its sound-soul. Every object on the earth has a sound-soul—or at least every object that moves, sounds.

You'll notice that, throughout all of this, the students themselves are performing, often conducting as well. Their musical experience is not only more speculative and aesthetically directed than that of the traditional "Appreciation" course, but—an ironic twist— infinitely more *practical,* too. The most well-intentioned philosophical conjecturing on earth would have lost its effectiveness without the correlating activity of live, immediate music-making.

A number of English composers have carried the practical aspects of this approach, as I've suggested before, to a new kind of classroom *Gebrauchsmusik,* creating short pieces (nontonal, often improvisational in part, exploring a variety of textures and notational devices) for student performances. One of these composers, George Self, has published a book entitled *New Sounds in Class* (Universal Editions, available in the United States through Theodore Presser), which maintains an attitude corresponding to that of the Schafer books but substitutes a number of compositions for Schafer's verbal play. Self, David Bedford, Bernard Rands, and other respectable figures of the English avant-garde have produced a series of compositions (again published by Universal/Presser) under the general heading "Music for Young Players"; these brief works are easy to perform (but challenging enough to make the students dig in), often brilliant in their effect in concert, and the most stimulating kind of educational adventure possible.

Another young Englishman, Brian Dennis, has written a valuable book called *Experimental Music in Schools* (Oxford University Press), complete with twenty short pieces of his own and a detailed accounting of the methods he's used to encourage similar student works. He composes within a notational scheme similar to that of the "Music for Young Players" series—in fact, he, Bedford, Self, and Rands are said to have conferred on a more or less standardized notation before embarking on their individual projects. Dennis's choice of instruments for performance also agrees generally with that set by the other series: an imaginative use of voices, hands, feet, and such simple percussion instruments as milk bottles, pencils, oil drums, glass bowls, flower pots, clocks, and the like. He differs from his colleagues most markedly in his use of electronic tape both in conjunction with student performances (planned or improvised) and in the creation of actual tape pieces. He begins with relatively simple experiments, mostly with volume control and speed change in playback.

> If a given material is recorded at 1⅞ i.p.s. and played back at 7½ i.p.s. the pitch or relative pitch will have risen two octaves and any basic pulses or rhythms will appear four times as fast. If pressure is applied to the left hand spool during the recording process, both the speed and the pitch will appear to rise when the material is played back. . . . Sounds recorded within inches of the microphone naturally sound very striking particularly if the instrument in question resonates in a particularly subtle way, like a cymbal. If for instance one records a single cymbal stroke, one can make a superb "electronic" effect by having the volume control on zero for the attack (i.e. at the moment the cymbal is struck) then subsequently turning the volume up and down to catch the resonance.

Dennis then proceeds to an increasingly complex series of instructions for the composition of self-contained *concrète* pieces, outlining in detail the choices in splicing and multitrack mixing that would lead to various formal arrangements, assuming that the student has a number of source tapes made from improvisations or natural sounds. He also discusses the possibilities of the live-plus-electronic situation, using a prerecorded student-created magnetic tape against a soloist or ensemble in a variety of ways.

If all of this sounds dreadfully naïve—or, worse yet, dull musically—I˙can only state that I've witnessed performances by school groups that kept me totally engrossed: I recall, in particular, a Dutch performance by a strictly amateur teen-aged ensemble from Amsterdam (using their voices, hands, and a single harmonica) and two different presentations in London of groups of youngsters (ages ranging from about seven to twelve) coached by Bedford and Dennis. On all three occasions the experience was as musically *commanding,* the playing as forceful and as sensitive as that of many "professional" avant-garde ensembles.

I don't want to give the impression that Europe (or the British Commonwealth) holds the monopoly on this kind of educational approach. Parallel activity is taking place throughout the United States, on all levels from grade school through college. It would seem only natural, given the western proclivity for experimentation in the arts, that California should be in the vanguard, and two instances there are worthy of particular mention. One is the recently founded California Institute of the Arts, a professional school that stresses, perhaps more than any school has dared before, a thorough all-pervasive interaction among the arts, a unique concern for "intermedia" that encourages the collaboration of composers, sculptors, dancers, poets, film-makers, and the like. "Specialists" are asked to work together in this way, not simply from the vantage point of their expertise but in the unexplored territory that exists *between* their respective arts, discovering parallels and analogies (and perhaps incompatibilities) as they go along. Study ranges from the traditionally "academic," to a wide range of non-Western approaches, to the use of the latest materials and media—lights, film, plastics, lasers, computers, electronics. The presence on the faculty of Mel Powell, Morton Subotnick, and James Tenney gives a fair indication of the level of electronic music evidenced there.

But Cal Arts, is, after all, a preprofessional institution, and you might expect this sort of wide-open experimentation in an atmosphere highly charged with young talent and strong motivation. The music program on the La Jolla campus of the University of California, San Diego, is, by contrast, even more remarkable in that it operates within a *non*-professional undergraduate context; certainly the most "radical" aspects of the UCSD musical curriculum are to be found in the introductory course, rather than in the more predictable upper-level and graduate areas. Music 1— the equivalent of the standard "Appreciation" course, open to all undergraduates—is built around a core of imaginative game-playing, improvisation, and intensive practice in student composition. The official catalogue listing and description for the UCSD Music 1 and a slightly more "advanced" (although still nonprofessional) alternative course are as follows:

Music 1. The Nature of Music. Development of music perception and discrimination through participation projects in tape music composition and small group improvisation, and through critical observation of the preparation and performance of selected ensemble literature by experienced musicians. . . .

Music 10. Projects and Studies in Music. A study of the nature of music, how it is made, how to listen for it. Projects include improvising in groups, tape music composition, and invention of music notation. Old, new, and newest music will be listened to and studied. . . .

What we have, then, is a speculative probing—not an obsession with Great Works of the past, although these may serve as illustrative examples—akin to that advanced by Schafer, the stress on creative student work that we saw emphasized by Dennis, and a heavy reliance on tape as an integral tool in the entire process. The catalogue description does not reveal the final ingredient, the real catalyst, that enables the program to function successfully: the high-powered music faculty of UCSD, each member involved professionally in some aspect of the new music scene of the 1970's. Kenneth Gaburo, Pauline Oliveros, Roger Reynolds, Robert Erickson, Bertram Turetzky, and Harry Partch, among others, have exerted a strong influence on the student activity. The music department has published a report on the program (as of 1969), including examples of the improvisatory "sound games," tape composition assignments, student compositions, and notational experiments; it is highly recommended reading for anyone seriously interested in this fresh way of looking at music education. A tape of student works complements and illuminates the text of the printed report. This is particularly valuable in dealing with the innovative notations of many student scores, and (for me, at least) brings the true nature of the UCSD program, in all its multiplicity and diversity, into the sharpest possible focus.

The use of the tape recorder dominates the UCSD approach, and references to tape run, like a recurring *leitmotif,* through the entire project report. Student improvisations, for example, are taped for immediate playback and discussion; these tapes themselves may later be used as sources for *concrète* compositions. In notational experiments, fully written-out pieces are performed and taped for later comparison of the notation with the actual sonic object. Portable tape recorders are used to collect environmental sounds for eventual use in compositions: Pauline Oliveros's "Zoofari"—a class excursion to the famed San Diego Zoo—is a by now legendary example, exploiting what is perhaps the best animal-sound resource in the nation. The tape lab exercises, designed to maximize the creative potential of editing, splicing, mixing—the whole arsenal of the 1950's classic studio—offer a challenge of an entirely different nature. It's significant that electronic synthesis *per se* is somewhat underplayed, although the campus houses Buchla and Moog units; the voltage-controlled equipment seems to be used most often for the modification of external signals (environmental or "musical"), rather than as sole sound source for prerecorded magnetic tape composition.

If I appear to be dwelling on the San Diego project, it is because I find it of enormous interest—and because its implications for the future are so vast. This is not to slight other, equally provocative, developments; the growth of study in areas of jazz and pop, for example, bears watching, as well as the movement toward new (or the return to old) performance environments on many campuses noted earlier in this chapter. "Ethnic" music and the study of non-Western traditions have already had great impact on the college level—UCLA, the University of Washington, and Wesleyan University of Connecticut are among the major centers—and are beginning to capture the curiosity of younger students as well.

Where does this all lead? Any guesses at this point would be all too obviously premature; the most that can be said is that the future of music in the schools—*all* music, very new and very old, Western and ethnic, folk, rock, and "serious"—appears to be more hopeful than at any time in recent memory. The fact that we live in an era inundated by phonograph records, tape, amplifiers, contact mikes, performance options galore, and a stylistic pluralism without parallel has had its effects in the classroom. Music teaching, too, has been obliged—inevitably—to become pluralistic, moving from a parochial absorption in "literature"—the Great Works—to a recognition of the total diversity (actual and potential) surrounding us. It can no longer be a case of "Here are the Masterworks." There are too many other questions begging to be answered and—with the guidance of a perceptive teacher—capable of being recognized and analyzed by students themselves. The UCSD report has stated the direction of the future most succinctly:

> . . . . we purposefully took an unstructured position—a position which said that music was an open-ended affair of sound, time, intuition, the senses and human imagination . . . to let the student know at the very outset the commitment to new ideas and technology, to invention and exploration, to the need to think freshly. The student was not to be just a reflective analogue of his present musical understanding or culture; he was to create, to invent, to rethink, to realize.

If enough of the next generation's composers, performers, and listeners develop and extend their awareness in this way, recognizing and using the full gamut of their faculties, the musical future will indeed be in good hands.

Part IV
Observations by Composers

Introduction

In bringing this volume to its conclusion, I'm obliged to admit that no single viewpoint—mine or anyone else's—can ever present a true picture of electronic music in all of its bewildering, fascinating diversity. The phenomenon we've been discussing is, above all, "current," thriving, still growing, and being reshaped by the talents and energies of many individuals; ideally, then, the last word should be *theirs*. Although a survey of techniques, historic moments, and major works can be eminently helpful, it's also true that nothing is as revealing about the present state of an art as the concerns, observations, and reflections of its practitioners. These people, whose creative efforts *are* the substance of electronic music, are best equipped to articulate, each in his or her own way, the individual, highly personal directions that collectively comprise the over-all scene.

With this in mind, I wrote to a number of composers actively engaged in electronics, representing, I hope, a cross-section of generations and aesthetic positions, and asked them to write short statements that could be used in this section of the book. Without wanting to limit the kinds of commentary I might receive, I did suggest three possible points of departure:

1. A historic, perhaps even "nostalgic" reference to some moment in the past that had been of importance to the composer: apprentice work in one of the great studios of the 1950's, or composition study with major figures, or some other form of reminiscence

2. Comments directed specifically to a work (or a number of works) by the composer, available on commercial recording or otherwise accessible to the general reading public, akin to "aesthetic" or "technical"-procedural program notes
3. Any hopes, fears, predictions, or planned projects for the future that the composer might wish to write about

As might be expected, the responses have taken many forms. Some composers answered in all categories—a few even labeling them (1), (2), and (3)—while others limited themselves to a single area. Quite a few managed to combine all of my suggested topics into a unified, extended essay. And one or two iconoclastic souls discarded my format of possibilities entirely, producing instead essays that were entirely unexpected (therefore doubly welcome). In publishing them all here, every effort has been made to preserve the style, punctuation, grammar, and general format of the originals—that is, "editing" has been limited to the most trivial of spelling corrections. The impact of each composer's message comes across best, I believe, in his or her own style.

Given a representative sampling of composers whose interests range from computer sound generation to *concrète* collage to totally live mixed-media, it's hardly surprising that many of these commentaries differ markedly from each other. The fact that one composer may advance positions and value judgments sharply at odds with those of his colleagues is something to be thankful for —not only good for the purposes of this book, but good for the state of music. On the other hand, you may notice that many of the composers agree (without prior prodding, I should add) on a number of ideas: The relation of tape technique to film-making, for example, is noted in several essays. Perhaps the point in question might have been made only once, and the similar, although subtly different, restatements deleted from other articles. But, then, in whose essay do I retain the comment, and from whose should it be edited? Every point raised in each composer's essay is of significance to that composer! Furthermore, the very fact that a position or analogy or technique is shared by many says something about *it*—not necessarily that it is "true" or valid, but that it is certainly influential. For whatever they are worth, then, the occasional redundancies stand.

Although most of the essays were written specifically for this book, a number have appeared in print elsewhere; these few are either extracted or reprinted in their entirety, and acknowledgments are noted in the individual texts where this is the case.

The various commentaries speak well for themselves and require no further introduction from me. If you find the collection as stimulating and enjoyable as I have, the composers and I will be more than satisfied.

Jon H. Appleton

(Jon H. Appleton is the director of the Dartmouth College Electronic Music Studio and has recorded many of his works for Flying Dutchman Records.)

Ever since I began composing music I have struggled with the problem of expressing affective states. It has occurred to me that theatre and motion pictures are the most obvious medium for an artist with this as a primary concern. As Charles Keil points out in his book *Urban Blues*, "In Max Weber's analysis of Western musical evolution, emergent rationality seems also to entail disenchantment, demystification, and a corresponding diminution of expressiveness for the sake of order."

But, like so many musicians, I came to music first through the works of nineteenth century composers where affect and order are not contradictory. This is not to say that serialism or other forms of twentieth century musical syntax prohibit inclusion of affective goals. However, I have come to believe that these goals are of secondary importance in most twentieth century "art" music, and this realization has forced me to abandon conventional contemporary approaches to musical composition.

As a trained listener I can enjoy the music of, say, Milton Babbitt because it intrigues that aspect of my musical intelligence which seeks order and intricate structure. But, it took me some time to realize that this kind of music was not the kind I wanted to compose. It did not take long to discover that composing music in the nineteenth century tonal idiom greatly restricted my originality. I firmly believe that the vocabulary *has* been exhausted as so many critics have contended. Yet, my first composition teachers were unable to help me find a new music equally rich in expressive possibilities because they themselves worked in those twentieth century traditions in which affect was of minimal importance.

My first mature works were instrumental and vocal ones which were well made and as affective as possible considering the acoustic and structural limitations I imposed on myself. The composer, like the listener, brings a set of expectations to a non-tonal piano piece, for example, which restrict the affective possibilities. For many reasons these works have never pleased me First of all, they represent a compromise between compositional goals which weaken the works because I am conscious of them. Most important, I am dissatisfied with these pieces because I don't know for whom they are intended. I have begun to feel like Keil's urban blues singer who occupies "a unique and intermediate position between West and non-West: unlike that of his Western contemporaries, his first obligation is to his public rather than to a private muse."

It was not until I began composing my own kind of electronic music that I finally felt a firm commitment to musical composition as an expressive form of communication. My first important piece, *Infantasy* (*Appleton Syntonic Menagerie,* Flying Dutchman, FDS 103) was composed at the Columbia-Princeton Electronic Music Center in 1965. It was not well received by the other composers working there with the exception of Vladimir Ussachevsky, but I knew that I had discovered a way of working with sound which I felt to be affective and at the same time musical in the traditional sense.

Electronic music is only a convenient label for this kind of music. I have become concerned solely with the affective properties of sound, and whether they are of natural or synthetic origin is unimportant. What I have discovered is that certain sounds have affective properties which can be isolated and developed in a musical context. My work is most similar to *musique concrète* without the interest in the *objets sonores* as something to classify but rather to be used in building more complex, affective structures.

My more recent music has become a kind of aural theatre and yet, it operates on a traditional musical level as well in the way sound situations are chosen, modified and intercut. For example, in the concluding section of *Times Square Times Ten* (*Appleton Syntonic Menagerie*, Flying Dutchman, FDS 103) I started with the ominous sound of a subway train idling. It is ominous partly because in the earlier sections of the piece that use trains, the suddenness of their arrival and departure is surprising and consequently, their idling creates tension and expectation. Instead of having the doors slam shut and having the train roll out of the station, I took the rhythm of the idle and applied it to a similar, complex electronic source which rises in pitch until it becomes the sound of hundreds of "spring peepers," small tree frogs, chirping in the quiet of the night.

Because listeners have understood this "musical" progression and because I can state it here with such clarity, I must conclude that affective communication has been achieved. *Times Square Times Ten* was composed in 1969, and at that time I had not yet developed a working method, thus having to spend many hours listening to different sounds I had collected and trying to project them into new musical-theatrical contexts.

My most recent piece, *Dr. Quisling in Stockholm,* commissioned by the Swedish Radio, was coldly calculated by comparison to my previous pieces. I knew the "subject" of the piece and the affective states I was after, and I simply went out and recorded the source material. The location of each source in the piece and its electronic transformation could be mapped out on paper, and the piece took one six-hour mixing session to put together. When the parts were assembled it matched my intentions exactly. It suddenly occurred to me that I had been able to duplicate the process used in composing instrumental music. The conception and working out of ideas could be accomplished independently of the studio: I knew my sources as well as I know the orchestra.

Larry Austin

(*Larry Austin was one of the founders of* Source *magazine, a member of the New Music Ensemble at Davis, and a member of the University of California, Davis, faculty. He is currently writing a book on electronic music.*)

Electronically, I grew up with solid state synthesizers. My first tape piece, *Roma,* was completed on Paul Ketoff's prototype "Synket," shortly after its installation in early 1965 in the basement studio of the American Academy in Rome. To my knowledge, *Roma* was the first composition completed on the Synket. Returning to the U.S. next fall, I began work at the San Francisco Tape Music Center, again finding myself "on the spot" in early 1966 when yet another prototype synthesizer was being installed, this time the "Buchla Electronic Music System." I was among the first to compose music on Don Buchla's new synthesizer (others were Don himself, Charles McDermed, Morton Subotnick, and Ramon Sender). By fall, 1966, Buchla had installed a similar system in our UC Davis studio (which also has a Moog). In the summer of 1969 I was able to purchase my own portable Buchla system, especially designed for my private studio. It has, of course, been in constant use since then in my studio as well as in live performances on tours in North and South America. During this period of work with synthesizers (and computers), I have been fortunate also to have been associated with distinguished practitioners of electronic music, notably: Karlheinz Stockhausen, during his 1966–67 tenure at Davis; David Tudor, here in Davis for the winter of 1967; and John Cage, in residence at Davis for the fall of 1969. I believe these close musical associations had a lasting impact on my music. Since 1965 I have composed over twenty compositions utilizing electronic music.

The increasing availability of electronic music instruments is helping to bring about a new understanding of the nature of the medium. The resulting fluency with such sonic materials and sensitivity to their flow have freed younger composers to concentrate on the important problems of content, expression, and context, necessary to solve for an emerging aesthetic for electronic music: *new romanticism*. Music made by machines would seem to preclude what we normally think of as "romantic"—passion, sensibility, emotive power—but the paradoxical is the case: an expressive, warm, human quality is revealing itself in new electronic music.

Young electronic virtuosi are exploring and developing viable techniques in fascinating areas: the phenomena of movement and placement of sound in space; psychological and physiological effects of sound on man (psychoacoustics); the synthesis of speech with computer-generated sound; the control of sound (and eventually music) directly with brain waves; and, concurrently, the development of new theories of perception, so necessary for the creation of value systems for electronic music. Born at the beginning of this age of electronic and computer music, they know these instruments as an integral part—not just a curious appendage—of their immediate musical heritage. They are actively engaged in creating music for these instruments in the same way that the piano has gained the status of a repertory instrument since its invention by Cristofori in 1709. The difference is that, what took over two hundred years to nurture for the piano, is being accomplished for electronic instruments in a much shorter span of time today It is a fact that, because of such rapid advances in the technology of electronic music instruments over the past few years, techniques and concepts of much importance to music are being developed, not in ways we formerly understood, but as complexes of events—non-linear, overlapping, layered, turned back on themselves and tautly inter-related—like the electronic music compositions which are themselves created from this maze of new information. As late as twenty years ago it was still reasonably possible to understand, through conventional methods of analysis and consequent assimilation, even the most complicated compositional techniques and aesthetics which had to that time evolved; mass communication and rapid travel plus electronic technology have, since then, complicated the process exponentially, multiplying information by itself. Contrast this situation to the simple additive process of handing one piece of information to the next person, his analyzing it and, in turn, handing it to another. This difference has important implications for the new "young musicians": in the electronic and computer-generated music medium, the time-honored master-apprentice learning processes may be too slow and almost non-functional. Thus, in the face of the amount of information required to be creative with our present and future electronic music machines, our learning must be modernized.

New composers of electronic music are expressing a newfound romanticism, not unlike their nineteenth century counterparts. The important difference is, however, that the visions of a Berlioz, a Liszt, a Wagner, or a Busoni are not just idle dreams of creating magic musics; "sonic visions," the "sounding space," the "sounding mass" . . . all such dreams are realizable today. In a 1967 conversation recorded in the first issue of the magazine *Source* (devoted to the publication of avant-garde music), German composer Karlheinz Stockhausen and California composer Robert Ashley discussed with me their feelings about new music. At one point in the conversation, expounding about deeply moving music, Ashley said "It's beautiful because it's really aural magic." I added "It happens with ecstasy," as Stockhausen responded, "It's just incredible. You get goose skin and everything. And you cry. You fall in love." Compare our reactions to the music of our time with Liszt's comment that, "Music embodies feeling without forcing it . . ." or Hegel's 19th century book on aesthetics saying that, "The special task of music is that . . . it becomes alive in the sphere of subjective inwardness . . . the musical art work absorbing us completely and carrying us along with it . . . exerting an elemental power lying wholly in the element of *sound.*" The new romantic movement in electronic music exhibits these same qualities of feeling, subjective inwardness, love of sound, and complete emotional absorption.

Finally, one of the most hopeful signs for electronic music is that a great many more people have developed appreciation for and even critical acuity in the medium. Discriminate tastes and higher standards are being developed, because electronic music has taken on value. Music lovers hear and appreciate beauty in this music. It's here to stay.

Robert Ceely

(Robert Ceely is director of Boston Experimental Electronic-music Projects [BEEP] in Brookline, Massachusetts. In 1963–64, he worked in the RAI Electronic Music Studio in Milano, Italy. Currently, he gives workshops in electronic music and is on the composition and theory faculty of the New England Conservatory of Music.)

EXCERPTS FROM "THOUGHTS ABOUT (ELECTRONIC) MUSIC"

I have been composing electronic music since 1963 when I walked into the RAI studio in Milano, Italy, and began a composition called *Stratti*. Today I have my own studio (BEEP) and am a teacher as well as a composer of electronic music. The comments that follow represent my present state of mind about electronic music; perhaps eight years hence my experience will lead me to different conclusions. . . .

As a teacher of electronic music I have tried to take the most basic and practical approach possible. It seems to me that the effectiveness of a course or workshop in electronic music is directly proportional to how quickly the participant gets his hands on the equipment. Beware of esthetics, listening assignments, and the historical approach. . . .

Rather than counting up the sequencers or the number of Scullys a more reliable guide as to how good an electronic music studio is is to listen to the music made there. It is most helpful to listen to the music of the director of the studio if in fact he has composed any. . . .

For the past year or so I have thought of what I do when I work in my studio as sculpting sound. I suggested "Sculpting Sound" as the title of a talk I proposed giving under the auspices of Harvard Project Zero. My proposal was accepted and on March 8, 1971 I gave a lecture demonstration with the title "Sculpting Sound." . . .

Not long ago I found some long sheets of white drawing paper. There were eleven sheets and each had a heading as follows:

low sounds	sequencer
flute like	good sounds (short)
slow bubbles	woodpecker
violin-like wail	woodwind airplane flutters
whip like vocal sounds	drums
bass ostinato	

For a section of a recent composition I placed the sheets on the floor. I had collected many versions of eleven sounds I liked and had them on a quantity of five inch reels. I walked around the room placing each small reel on the corresponding sheet of paper. Eleven beads strung in about thirty different ways. Hardly material for *Perspectives of New Music*. The piece is called *MITSYN* and some of it was done on a PDP-9, though very little in comparison to the whole. Nevertheless, most in the audience knew it had been at least partly done on a computer. Mr. "Super Ears" remarked how refreshing it was to hear stable pitches. This about a section done in my studio. . . .

Robert Frost said writing a poem in blank verse is like playing tennis without a net. Perhaps computer music is like winning without a game. It is certain that computers will be used like a sophisticated sonic metronome. A conductor must prepare a particularly difficult composition; he delivers the score to an MIT freshman who does a computer synthesis of the most difficult sections; the conductor then uses this as an aid in rehearsing the instrumentalists. The Rhythmicon constructed by Theremin for Henry Cowell is now gathering dust in the Smithsonian.

Ives has been accused of so much. Nevertheless, I think he composed the first computer music. His second piano sonata—

the "Concord"—is certainly composed for a more exact inter-preter than a mere pianist. It is true "density music" and it is a music which is not restricted to any one timbre; Ives was hearing so many timbres that he had to limit himself to one. The prose directions are as computerly as the music: *"slightly slower; almost a 3; (quite slowly and as a song) but not too evenly; (climbing up with rush and action); Viola part (ad lib) pp—if played—but bringing out accent; to be heard as a kind of an overtone; scarcely audible; very fast—heavily, or in a kind of reckless way; from here on as fast as possible, faster if possible; small notes in piano to be played only if flute is not used."*

Electronic music will no more rid the world of performers than medicare will rid the world of doctors. The symphony orchestra which is the AMA of music will surely die and with it the performer who is overpaid for merely being more or less com-petent in performing one hundred and fifty years of music. The Paul Zukofskys and Buell Neidlingers are too good to be content to play in symphonies and their versatility will ensure their survival. I have not turned away from the symphony; they have turned away from me. Let a major symphony commission a work from me; I will compose a work that will stand their ears on end. . . .

Joel Chadabe

(Joel Chadabe of the State University of New York, Albany, faculty has recently supervised the construction of an experimental multisequencer studio at the campus.)

. . . Electronic music is understood, at the present time, in two ways: first, as a means of enriching the materials of music by extending the world of sound possibilities and, second, as a technological art medium wherein the sounds produced are the result of an electronic logic that could as easily generate activity in another medium, such as light. Needless to say, these categories are not mutually exclusive, and they are continually merging, but for the moment they seem useful differentiations.

The exploration-of-sound approach is a traditional extension of music history. Synthesizers, for example, are thought of as "instruments" and are treated as if they were instruments. It seems natural that they should be designed and used to play traditional music with new sounds, as has happened so often in the past when new instruments have been invented.

There are, however, crucial differences between previous new instruments and synthesizers. Traditional instruments make only one sound. A piano, for example, makes only a piano sound, and it is, in that sense, a *specialized* instrument. Synthesizers, because they offer a selection of basic waveforms which can be processed and combined in many ways, like a musical erector set, produce many different sounds and are, consequently, *multi-use.* . . .

We can note that there is today, in all fields, a definite trend away from specialized tools and materials towards multi-use tools and materials.

And it might be interesting to consider the use of traditional instruments in light of this trend and with reference to electronic music. They are thought of as specialized sound producers which can be made more general by means of electronic modification. There is a growing interest in sound modifiers in all kinds of music. And this interest has a particular importance because it expresses, in part, a widespread feeling that electronic music must be brought into live contact with an audience through performance. Modifying instrument sounds is one interesting way of performing with electronics. . . .

Understood as a technological art medium, electronic music makes no demands on traditional musical skills or history. Synthesizers are conceptualized as "systems" of electronic functions rather than as instruments, and are meant to produce sounds that are not at all reminiscent of traditional music. The continuity of a composition is derived from some automated electronic process, rather than decided by a composer according to historical models, and each sound is only the manifestation of that process at a particular moment.

A clear example of one type of process is the sensing system. You walk into a room and see a center pedestal on which there is the sound production equipment and several lights. Depending upon how you walk through the room, photocells sense your passage and turn on lights or sound sources. From your point of view, you see lights go on and off and you hear sounds from different loudspeakers around the room. Clearly, this is a different musical situation from the concert hall where each sound is individually produced and placed within some previously determined musical form.

There is great appeal in experimentation with this use of technology in art, not the least aspect of which is that it requires little or no previous education to appreciate it. At its worst it may seem like a trivial game, at its best it may seem like magic. . . .

To say that the new age is come is facile effect. History does not replace, it supplements. The most remarkable aspect of today's artistic environment is the coexistence of so many centuries at the same moment. Yet even if old art is appreciated because of the refinement of its language, new art, even when the new artwork is not refined, is always a model of the world of the present. That is worth attention. And as we explore in every direction, so we explore in sound. . . . As the results of these explorations become common knowledge the technology will become more available and accessible to everyone. In the near future we will see more interesting systems, more understanding educators, more interested students, more accessible machines. As we feel more comfortable with the machines and their logic of operation, . . . and as we develop a feeling for the unexpected event as a part of a larger process, our perceptions will change. . . .

David Cope

(David Cope teaches at the Cleveland Institute of Music. He is the founder and editor of The Composer *magazine and author of* New Directions in Music.*)*

In one sense, the outlook for electronic music is no brighter or dimmer than music for string quartet, in that both forms still offer the composer an opportunity to create good music. In another sense, however, the electronic medium furnishes a larger timbre and rhythmic vocabulary nearly unknown prior to the mid-twentieth century, providing the composer with a vast new realm of freedom and exploration. It also offers the composer the possibility of being both performer and composer (a luxury at a time in history when good performances of contemporary music are exceedingly rare) and the ability to work in "real time" (that is, like Haydn: having an orchestra available on call for immediate "playback" of materials just composed) as opposed to "abstract time" (the time it takes a composer to notate: far exceeding actual performance time).

In analyzing the outlook for the future, however, these advantages can equally be disadvantages. A composer can very well be a *bad* performer; "real time" can become a tiring agent (as one constantly hears his work immediately played back or "performed" during composition); new sounds can become just that and not much more (composers tend to develop preoccupations with how sounds are produced, finding complicated ones somehow more appealing than uncomplicated ones, rather than considering "is it musical?": new sounds do not in themselves give any more opportunity for the composer to create good music than do old ones). The initial intrigue with electronic sounds seems somewhat exhausted at this writing, and the future of the medium (and that future is guaranteed) should lie less with exploration and more with creation of good music. . . .

The major advantage to working with electronic equipment and sounds which seem undiminished by overdone "exploration" is rhythmic freedom. No other ensemble of instruments is equally capable of fractioning time into controllable particles as the components of a well-equipped electronic music studio. While some listeners may feel that the opportunity to free rhythm from any immediately recognizable meters is removing some inalienable musical basic, it must be pointed out that to a large degree meter was introduced and continued only to keep performers together in ensembles; while necessary, [it was] certainly not particularly musical in itself. The disposition of time is much more controllable in the electronic studio.

Both *Krap* and *Weeds* (available on Discant Recordings, Los Angeles) were composed with this in mind. *Krap* (somewhat based on the idea of Beckett's *Krapp's Last Tape* in that the sound sources are earlier tapes; in this instance, tapes of some of my earlier works, altered through a Moog Synthesizer) develops an "attack schedule" totally unavailable by any other means. It is not *what* will come but *when* that serves as a basis of the work. The metrical and notational restrictions necessary for an accurate performance by a "live" ensemble would surely negate the very basis of this work.

Weeds presents a continuous world of many sounds within which very minute rhythmic alterations occur. The variation of the relatively stationary set of materials is very subtle, so subtle in fact that many have commented that minutes went by before they noticed that the entire sonic environment had slowly but nearly completely changed.

Neither work develops a wide range of timbres. Neither pretends at "new" sounds. Both, however, do invest much of their worth in "when" a change comes about, a change which could not have been conceivably controllable by any other vehicle than electronic sound production and control.

For this composer, unusual sounds offered by electronic means hold no special appeal. Electronic music has, however, opened an infinitely free realm of dramatic choice of when, in time, sound can occur.

Lukas Foss

(Lukas Foss is one of the leading figures of the music scene as a composer, conductor, and pianist. He was also the founder of one of the first improvisatory "groups," organized at UCLA during the mid-1950's. His work utilizes electronic amplification and distortion in live situations; he has encouraged and sponsored experimental work by younger composers in his capacity as founder and codirector, with Lejaren Hiller, of the Creative Associates of Buffalo.)

LIVE MUSIC IN AN ELECTRONIC CLIMATE
(LETTERS AND MEMOS)

Dear Joel [Chadabe]:   *March 22, 1971*
    Your Supersynthesizer sounds like the right erector set for me. I am arriving Sunday night ready to turn myself in. I have a plan for a piece involving the musicians playing from tape instead of playing from music.

    April 4. Four days in the campus studio and little progress. Joel is right. One must understand electricity for electronic composition.
    Today he explained:
    "A voltage control oscillator varies its frequency output proportional to the value of an applied control voltage. Please repeat."
    "A voltage control oscillator varies its frequency output proportional to the value of an applied control voltage."
    "And again."
    "A voltage control oscillator . . ."

"And again."

"A voltage control oscillator . . ."

"All right. Now, *what does it mean?*"

"Joel, I am a poor student."

"You are doing relatively . . ."

"No—I cannot think electricity. Maybe I am not willing to accept new information. That's what C. thinks."

"Suppose I stopped teaching and turned myself into a technical assistant: You tell me the sounds you need, I plug the cords in, and you listen critically."

I was putting 13 patch cords back on their respective hooks as I answered his generous offer: "Joel, your patience is . . ."

"For heaven's sake, Lukas, that cord goes on that hook. Thanks —studio routine, you know. Very important."

April 27. Today we had the first live rehearsal of *Today* (my title will insure that the piece stops at midnight). The tapes are endless in their permutations. What I like is that they cannot be imitated by instruments. So I asked the instrumentalists to imitate them and got something else. Much better than improvisation which is always so predictable. Avoid improvisation by asking for imitation and avoid imitation by giving them sounds that cannot be imitated.

April 29. The most interesting moment at today's rehearsal happened when the musicians abandoned their tapes and connected their instruments, physically (the bells of two wind instruments touching, one blows into a hose connected to a trombone resulting in a composite sound). I must concentrate less on the tapes and more on discovering an arsenal of instrumental connection possibilities.

April 31. Not solved. The musicians move around, megaphone, superball mallets, and tubes connecting sounds but the music does not happen. It remains so much fishing for sounds.

May 2. The answer perhaps: a game. Invent a game the rules of which will *make* the music happen. A game which insures the consistent grouping and regrouping of the musicians. Solos, duos, trios happen of their own accord and in different corners of the stage, like invasions of territories (the Japanese game "Go?"). The traditional gamesmanship of musicians: to play the right note at the right time, is replaced by plain gamesmanship: how to come out ahead.

May 5. *Today* is not a game name. Changed it to *M.A.P.—Men at Play.*

May 7. Jesse suggested light signals. If I cannot make my signals "musical," I wind up with another mixed media thing in which the composer hopes that the sum total will cure the poverty of the single ingredient (it never does). I should like *M.A.P.* to be a game without the usual props, extraneous non-musical elements. No dice, no cards, no numbers, no scorekeeping. Therefore also: no need for the audience to follow the game in terms of who is winning or losing. Let them watch all this movement on stage, all this tension without the knowledge of the game, like watching a strange people at work.

Tanglewood, August 2. This morning at the Curtis Hotel the waitress asked me if I was M.A.P.? (Had I heard right?)
"On what?"
"M.A.P., Modified American Plan," she elucidated.
I think I will have to change my title, or at least remove the dots between the letters: *MAP.*

Kenneth Gaburo

(Kenneth Gaburo spent a number of years working at the experimental studio of the University of Illinois, where he also directed a choral group specializing in avant-garde works. He has continued both interests in his present position at the University of California, San Diego.)

MURMUR (herein defined as a quality) ONE: The apparent infinity of sophisticated electronic music-making instruments designed for an infinity of music(s) especially hoped for in the late fifties and seen then by many as some kind of liberation from the contraints of conventional electronic instruments
which in turn was some kind of liberation from conventional-conventional instruments
e.g. orchestras
both states being liberations as well from musical sound-structures and cultured positions closely associated with those conventional instruments
has merely resulted in a new set of cultured positions
but significant constraints remain
for
if one accepts the proposition that the sound-generating-processing system contains the composition within itself
then the constraint is a function of the instrument's potential
if
contrarily
one accepts the position that the sound-generating-processing system is at best only the potential source for a composition
then the constraint is a function of the composer's head
but when the hoped-for infinity was promulgated it was so in the absence of machines as we now know them excluding the RCA Electronic Sound Synthesizer and embryogenic computer systems.

MURMUR TWO: The infinity, therefore, existed largely in the creative imagination of the composer who once again believed himself to have found a new region possibly sufficient, but clearly necessary, to further express his intuitive and intellectual desires. What he in fact found was a collection of (more properly an assemblage of) electronic hardware, most of which were not designed for compositional purposes (to say nothing of the infinity). That environment is now generally referred to as the "classic"—frequently expressed as a pejorative, in the light of the new instrumentation —studio. To the extent that the term "classic" is used to force some kind of distinction between the state of the art then and what it has become, it is clearly inappropriate. Almost no studio was of the first rank, or standard, or coherent as a system, or fully-developed, or even yet of acknowledged excellence sufficient to satisfy the composer well enough. Only potential existed. From the technological point of view, that potential is now seen to have been very low, while the current music-machine's potential is seen to be very high. From the creative-qualitative point of view these associations can easily be reversed because the search for the instrument became as important as the search for the composition. There was beauty in that search.

TRANSIENT ONE: The question of where the music was/is—in the machine, in the head, or neither one exclusively—often had/ has to be temporarily arrested as one faced/faces the problems of impedance mis-matching, channel noise, audio fatigue, recalcitrant engineers who refused/refuse to take us seriously, or electrical shock due to improper grounding. The search, rather than "classicism" or "dehumanization" was/is clearly there even in the far more elegant RCA Columbia-Princeton Electronic Sound Synthesizer which, although designed for more trivial purposes, quickly became/becomes an instrument when placed in the hands of creative people. But not just search. For music came/comes. To be sure, earlier works simply have to be regarded as backbreaking feats when measured against the machine's resistance and the composer's own lack of technical knowledge. Even more back-breaking now, because electronic composition is often confused with technology or temporarily aborted because of the emphasis on learning what the latest gadget does that the previous one did not do, resulting directly from earlier primitive first-associations with the machine-instrument which was expected to respond in more than a utilitarian manner and which caused immediate outcries for more efficient instruments, thereby installing for the first time to my knowledge the collusion/collision between efficiency and the creative act. The devaluation of the splice was inevitably a high-priority item in any cultivated discussion although in my opinion it became/becomes one of the supreme moments of decision-making in the compositional process second only to the eraser and deserves special mention as a measure of the importance of second thoughts/thoughts.

ELABORATION OF MURMUR TWO: There is a strange parallel between the glorious junkshop referred to as the "classic" studio and the current rage for personal, home-made instruments, bypassing rather significantly the wide range of sophisticated instruments now available.

Bypass, because as electronic instrumentation becomes more refined technically and its generating-processing components become more precise, the machine becomes, paradoxically enough, more, not less, closed as a viable system. It is true that this criticism was leveled against the assemblage studio as well. Now, however, one clearly runs the risk that the inherent technical perfection of the machine (a distinct advantage) designed to serve precise musical functions, will cause it to maintain its own sound-identity no matter what (a distinct disadvantage). In the earlier circumstance the sound-identity of a given instrument, say an audio oscillator, was too un-interesting in itself to be maintained compositionally (a distinct advantage) and the if-at-all-available processing devices were frequently unpredictable (a distinct disadvantage).

Bypass, because with more refined equipment composers become readily caught up in the fascinating *means* by which sound-complexes, emanating *directly* from the instrument, may be produced. To some, the process becomes as important as the result. To others, this condition is quite unacceptable. At the same time, the "natural" beauty of these sound-complexes is often so compelling that the composer's intellectual capacity is frequently obfuscated by the machine's sensual capacity. To some composers this is a value. To others, first sounds, no matter how elegant, are to be distrusted. Furthermore, these sound-complexes, which are a function of an instrument's peculiar qualities, generally hold for *n* instruments of a kind. This characteristic militates rather strongly against individual uniqueness when such uniform instrumentation is utilized by *m* composers. To some this form of "group" association is consoling. To others, the only reasonable answer is to move elsewhere. Therefore, the parallel to earlier activity with respect to the current bypass condition is again, the search. The difference lies partially in the fact that earlier, many composers *faced* black boxes, while now many try to *make* them. Crucially, the search for the instrument on the way to the composition has become the search for the composition on the way to the instrument. And, one learns quickly that not all unijunction transistors classified technically as substitute-equivalents produce, qualitatively, the same sound at all.

Bypass, because the efficiency and directness of the new instrumentation has caused it to be quickly absorbed by commercial culture, or relegated to the position of being used as teaching instruments; or because its sophistication comes too late for some who have moved elsewhere; or because of computers; or because the desire to probe *into* the machine itself, instead of *in front* of it, is so compelling; or because electronic music and its concepts have in turn influenced the way we think about conventional non-electronic instruments, resulting in a return to them in fascinating new ways. But return is not altogether proper here. For, since the late fifties, some of us have been interested in the structured synchrony-potential of music-machines, concrete sources, and live performers. The intrinsic beauty of concrete sources and live performers (in my case weighted in favor of the voice, each sample of which carries its own special nuance), seemed less a reaction to the machine in order to keep the music "human" than it was to *raise* the properties of the machine (never sufficient) to a level of respectability. Those components are still necessary in my opinion, only now so in order to *reduce* the level of the sophisticated machine to the point where it is not omnipresent.

EXPLICATION OF MURMUR ONE:

> Will I recognize the sound I want when I have heard it?
> Will I want the sound I have heard when I recognize it?
> Will I recognize the sound I have heard when I want it?
> Will I have heard the sound I want when I recognize it?
> Will I want the sound I recognize when I have heard it?
> Will I have heard the sound I recognize when I want it?

This set of charges to myself has served me well. Moreover, if one substitutes, say,
"the structure", or
"the identity", e.g., my compositional identity, or
"the music-machine", for
"the sound" in the above set,
the logic of the set is unchanged,
although the *sense* in which the so-charged set of charges exists is clearly transformed in each case.

A PARTIAL DISSOLUTION OF THE TRANSIENT: In the interim I have developed a gentle respect for the machine, although I do not know any more than I did about whether it is I who have a resistance to it or the other way around. (Is it a peace treaty we have?) Without wishing to establish an equivalence statement, I believe it to possess human-like qualities. It is not infallible, nor is it infinite in its musical attributes. It is as temperamental as I and frequently much clearer. (You either conduct or you don't.) A given module, moreover, is unquestionably idiosyncratic. The trick is to treat the music-machine *as if* it were human in order to maintain its uniqueness. (It is interesting to note that among other criteria, your component specifications are frequently given in terms of their life-span.) By getting into its guts, either through changing components *via* home-made circuit fabrication, or deeply investigating the properties of a commercial product, the music-machine becomes variable, possibly even flexible. And if not infinite, then abundantly resourceful. (I'll try not to kick you anymore.) There develops in the compositional process a sensual *and* intellectual interplay between us, and ultimately we come to some agreement, the machine and I, for the completed work has never been as much as I wanted, nor as little as I could find acceptable. (Feedback works!) Still, we lack technology in the area of controls, especially in real-time performance. The current thinking by some engineers is that we may have to give up that fantasy. Question: When will it be possible for one individual to manage all of the controls necessary in order to produce a structured, real-time composition? (Perhaps we should enter into a conspiracy?)

William Hellermann

(William Hellermann, born 1939 in Milwaukee, Wisconsin, is presently living in New York City. Works for tape alone include Ariel *(1967) (recorded in "Electronic Music," vol. IV, Turnabout —TV34301) and* Ek-Stasis *(1968). Works for tape and instrument are* Ek-Stasis I *(1970) for timpani, amplified piano, and tape and* Passages 13-The Fire *for trumpet and tape, using a poem by Robert Duncan of the same title. Works employing instruments with electronic extensions are* Round and About *(1970),* Columbus Circle *(1971),* Circle Musics 1, 2, *and* 3. *All tape portions were realized at the Columbia-Princeton Electronic Music Center.)*

Electronics in music means a change beyond, even larger than, the technical, and has created, and will continue to create, a new poetics for music. There is a new norm, that of electronic sound, created by the daily use of radios and phonographs and, to the extent that the normal becomes natural, a new nature of sound.

Most important and most overlooked is what mere amplification means to a sound. What comes out of a loudspeaker, we know, is not the real thing. But, on the other hand, it is more than something artificial or distorted. These associations arise only because electronic means have so often been applied to musics intended for another mode of presentation. If, however, electronic sound is taken on its own terms and used as an integral part of the total musical idea, one finds that it has a special character belonging to itself alone. Just like the violin, which in the past was originally heard as the imperfect imitation of the human voice before becoming accepted as an independent musical sound, electronic sound now has its own identity.

Its special characteristic quality is that, as a sound, it is more public and yet more personal at the same time. This is accomplished by the amplifier and the loudspeaker working together to boost the volume and blend all the different parts into one homogeneous core, while taking this and aiming it directly at the listener. The result is a sound, which, because of its loudness and lack of rough edges, can't be confused with a normal speaking voice. And yet, because of the presence and tactile qualities that come from being able to hear each detail, the sound can't be confused with an inanimate, dead thing, either. These are the things I think people are talking about when they say electronic music is "scary," "otherworldly," or "gets inside your head."

In addition to a new sound quality, electronic amplification has also meant that all kinds of sounds, too soft to be usable in the past, are now available. This is of special interest in live performance where a whole new world of instrumental micro-sounds can be employed, and, more importantly, controlled. Of special interest to me is the new instrument that is created by simply connecting a traditional instrument to an amplifier-reverberation unit with foot pedals to control volume and amount of echo. This primitive arrangement, which, after all, is only the electric guitar setup applied to all instruments, takes on a new life when it is used in music built around unusual means of sound production. Knocking, blowing, or scraping sounds, for example, generally didn't work out too well before, because they stood out too much in the context of traditionally played passages (not to mention the fact that they often sounded like mistakes), unless they were very judiciously employed. Also, since there was little room for variation on any given sound, they were usually employed for punctuation or special effects. Now, when amplified, these sounds can be made to blend in successfully with all kinds of playing, and, best of all, developed and extended in many subtle ways not possible before. This means that a music which is purely electronic can be created, without sacrificing the immediacy of live performance.

This new range of possibilities for electronics in live situations shouldn't be taken to imply that either unamplified instruments or tape music are now obsolete. What happens is that the special character of both comes into sharper focus. The tape medium in particular can now be understood more objectively for what it is, and not as a threat to the live performer. For me the tape recorder used as a means of sound production has never suggested the use of musical materials or structures that belong to live performance. Its special nature is to serve the composer in creating sound *objects*. (Things that are finished in every detail and are built up by the application of techniques appropriate to a workshop.) (The composer as a constructor or assembler of music, somewhat like a sculptor, who uses his hands and fancy new tools to carve out or weld up a piece of music.) What results is an object to be contemplated, preferably in the leisure of one's home, rather than a social event to be participated in.

The social basis for live performance music, on the other hand, can now be more clearly recognized than it has been in the recent past. The knowledge that the tape studio is the best place to make objects has made the idea of doing the same thing in the concert hall less attractive. Consequently, it seems unlikely that the inherited notions that musical quality is synonymous with exactitude of notational detail, and that a good performance is only a question of not making a mistake, will continue to prevail. Performance music should be concerned more with processes and people than with finished products.

My own music, at present, is very concerned with electronics in ways implied by these views. In *Round and About* (1970), for example, I invented new notations for unusual means of sound production to be performed with amplification-reverberation units. The point here is that these new sounds are then developed within a very detailed framework involving a great deal of imagination on the part of the performer. In my more recent scores, *Columbus Circle* (1971) and *Circle Musics 1, 2,* and *3,* I have become increasingly concerned with the score as a starting point for performers, using symbols that indicate definite relationships and formal objectives, while still remaining open to personal interpretation. . . . In any event, electronic sound, either on tape or as an extension used to enhance the role of the performer, will continue to be central to my musical ideas for some time. I find electronics so important as the determining background for all twentieth-century music, that I have begun to think of all new music as basically electronic. Some pieces just don't happen to actually use amplification, that's all.

Lejaren A. Hiller, Jr.

(*Lejaren A. Hiller, Jr., a pioneer in computer music research, was the director of the University of Illinois Studio for Experimental Music. He is now at the State University of New York, Buffalo, and codirector, with Lukas Foss, of Creative Associates of Buffalo.*)

In writing my *Machine Music for Piano, Percussion and Tape,* I decided to use the electronic tape medium as an integral part of a performed concert piece. Although compositions of this sort were not a novelty even then, it was not so usual to make the tape part as closely related to the instrumental parts as is done here. In fact, the tape recorder part throughout exchanges musical materials with the other two instruments. *Machine Music* is also very rhythmic and metrically laid out. I wrote it this way specifically because I had become frustrated with so seldom hearing any sense of forward propulsion in most tape compositions whatever virtues they might otherwise possess. Rhythmic interest and variety, I suggest, is substantially a function directly proportional to the zeal and patience the composer is willing to bring to the task of splicing together many tiny bits of tape. This problem is not avoided, by the way, by building up long passages of redundant ostinati with tape loops and sequencers. Sophisticated computer programing, perhaps, would work, but that is another story.

Machine Music possesses the following symmetrical plan:

> I. Trio I
> II. Solo I (Piano)
> Duo I (Tape and Percussion)
> Solo II (Piano)

  III. Solo III (Tape)
    Duo II (Percussion and Piano)
    Solo IV (Tape) ˏ
  IV. Solo V (Percussion)
    Duo III (Piano and Tape)
    Solo VI (Percussion)
  V. Trio II

Trio I is a compact sonata form movement laid out as follows with the main section set at a tempo of *Furioso* (♪= 216). (The bar numbers refer to the published score):

Bars		Number of Beats at ♪ = 216
1–2	Introduction (grave; marcato)	—
3–16	Exposition (first subject and transition)	60
17–22	Exposition (second subject and close)	30
23–35	Development	60
36–49	Recapitulation (first subject and transition)	60
50–55	Recapitulation (second subject and close)	30
56–57	Coda (grave, marcato)	—

Each *Duo* and each *Solo* lasts precisely one minute. The three *Duos* are closely related musically, as are *Solo I* and *Solo VI* and *Solo II* and *Solo V*. *Solo III* and *Solo IV* are derived in turn from these. The instrumentation is so arranged that each performer has the opportunity to play a given basic musical structure once and just once. Moreover, the tape recorder enters in every other section throughout the composition, thus permitting its operator each time to cue up and get set for his next entry. Incidently, the tape part is fully notated in the score, not only for documentation, but also for the benefit of the performers, since they must precisely co-ordinate themselves to it as well as to one another.

The three *Duos* are identical melodically and rhythmically but differ from one another not only in terms of instrumentation and hence tone color but also "tonally" by successive transpositions by a major third (G#-C-E). The music itself, in 5/4 meter (really

10/8) and most simply laid out in *Duo II*, consists of four basic "lines." Line 1, reading from the bottom up, consists of four notes, assigned durations of 4, 5, 6 and 7 beats respectively. This guarantees a non-repeating accompaniment for 420 beats, so I set 210 beats as the total length for each *Duo*, since the next 210 beats would be the same except for the four-beat note. The "tune" of line 3, played on the piano strings in *Duo II*, uses only the other 8 notes of the chromatic scale. Line 3 also contains rhythmic interpolations to fill in beats not supplied elsewhere. Line 2 is a 3-bar ostinato based on three notes repeated 4 times on beats 1, 4, 7 and 10 of each bar. This pattern repeats every 15 beats. Line 1 consists first of a repeated note on beats 2 and 6 of every bar and second of note pattern that chromatically expands outwards (in the bells in *Duo II* from A♭ up to F and down to C).

Solo I is simply a chord played on the piano *pp* according to the metric plan $(1+2+3+ \ldots +10)$. *Solo VI* is the retrograde of this played *ff* by the percussion. *Solo III* is the combination of these on tape played *mf*. The duration of each sound event on this tape cue is exactly 0.5 second as notated. The contents of these sound events are random cuttings from all the work tapes used to make the other five cues.

Solo II, for solo piano, is much more complex. It consists of four contrasting ideas presented in bars 1 through 4. Each idea is developed independently in successive bars by transportation, inversion, retrogradation, systematic shifting of material within the bar, and so on. The details of all these changes are easily perceived in the published score. Then, since there are 24 bars in all, each item occurs 6 times and occurs according to the following symmetrical system:

/1234/4123/3412/2143/3214/4321/

Solo V is essentially the same music, this time, however, reconceived for percussion. I have been told by several percussionists that this is the most difficult piece they know of in the percussion literature. Finally, *Solo IV*, is more or less generally related to these two virtuosic soli in that it is dense and aggressive in texture.

The sounds on the tape here are also reminiscent of the two *Trios*.

Trio II, of course, serves as a traditional finale and climax. Remember that this is a piece meant to go somewhere dramatically and not just be a chunk of soundscape. *Trio II* not only contains many elements derived from *Trio I* in particular but also the bulk of the more theatrical elements in the work—the use of a roller toy, the title of the composition spoken backwards on the tape and the close terminated by an alarm clock. The coda, however, recalls *Solo II* and *VI* its metrical plan.

Some people, because of its title, think *Machine Music* is computer music. It is not. The title is meant perhaps to evoke images of machinery because of the motoristic flavor of the piece, but that is about all. I have discovered to my chagrin that once my name became associated with computer composition, it has been utterly impossible since to convince many people, including some critics, that I am capable of doing anything else musically. *Machine Music* is also meant to be humorous and rather satirical. I have also discovered that this too often baffles and even infuriates. One introduces humor into the concert hall at one's peril.

Hubert S. Howe, Jr.

(Hubert Howe, Jr., is known for his extensive research in computer generation of sound. He teaches at Queens College, New York, has written manuals for various synthesizer systems, and codirects the annual summer institute in electronic music at the University of New Hampshire.)

ELECTRONIC MUSIC AND THE FUTURE

Electronic music has been ushered in with sweeping statements about the obsolescence of live music and the eventual supplanting

of human performers by electronic instruments, even controlled
by robots and computers. I do not believe that these fears will be
borne out by the future. For while electronic musical instruments
are in many ways more versatile than live instruments, in general
the kinds of sounds produced by each media are in no way comparable. The future of live music is not dependent upon its "competition" with electronic music, but upon the way in which composers and performers of the future respond to its own unique
characteristics and capabilities.

While I have no reason to be certain what kind of direction live
music will take in the future, I am certain that electronic music
faces a very exciting and growing future. Already many composers,
including myself, are involved with electronic music to the extent
that it is virtually the only medium they compose in. New discoveries in instrumentation and equipment design have greatly increased the pace of development. Composers have begun to explore new dimensions of sound which cannot even be controlled
in live music. Electronic music is currently experiencing a period
of exploration and experimentation which is truly unparalleled in
the history of music. I look forward to a continuous development
and refinement of the medium, which will grow in harmony with
other forms of music.

Jean Eichelberger Ivey

*(Jean Eichelberger Ivey directs the electronic studio at Baltimore's
Peabody Conservatory and has founded an annual summer workshop there for teachers. Her* Pinball, *recorded for Folkways, has
been mentioned earlier in this volume.)*

After considerable experience in composing for live performers
and in tape composition, and with every intention of continuing
both, I find myself at present most interested in works which
combine the two. My first finished works of this kind, *Terminus*

for mezzo-soprano and tape, and *3 Songs of Night* for soprano, five instruments, and tape, were premièred at Peabody in the spring of 1971, and a recording of them is now in preparation. (The score and tape of *Terminus* are available from Carl Fischer, Inc., publishers.) For some years I have entertained the notion of a series of pieces for various solo performers plus tape, partly because so many performers ask for such additions to their repertoire; and I have also done some work on a large monodrama for voice, orchestra and tape.

In some ways, writing for live performers plus tape seems to me the most difficult of all types of composition. It combines all the problems of composing for live performers and the problems of pure tape composition, with some special problems caused by their interaction. The challenge of coping with all these problems simultaneously may be one of its principal attractions for the composer.

A pure tape composition is like a painting—one puts it together alone in the studio, drawing on all one's resources of equipment, imagination, and taste. Unlike traditional composition, where the composer hears his work only in his mind until, often much later, performers bring it to life, the tape studio offers ready access to sound. The composer can test out his ideas on the spot, rearrange, manipulate, and structure, under the constant stimulus of hearing each successive step. Like the painter, he beholds his work taking shape before him. His finished tape, like the painting, needs no interpreting performer but embodies its creator's ideas alone. The composer's control over the final results, as well as his responsibility for them, are at a maximum.

Composing for live performers, on the other hand, involves a kind of forecasting of probable reactions. It requires an intimate knowledge of how voices and instruments behave, how performers react to each other, to notation, and to the whole performing situation including the audience. Whether the composer intends aleatory results or great precision, some unpredictability is inevitable; each performance differs, grossly or subtly, from every other. The appeal of this quality of change in live performance has, I think, been overrated. We do not expect of a painting, a literary work, or a film that it change each time we experience it.

If such a work draws us back to it again and again, it is because it offers such complexity, subtlety, and multiplicity of interpretations that it seems impossible ever to experience it completely. The same can certainly be true of a tape piece. Nevertheless, the possibility of the unpredictable is one of the special features which live performers provide.

A more serious lack felt by many in tape music is the lack of visual interest. One thing we have learned from tape concerts is the importance of visual aspects in concerts as a whole. Seeing the conductor raise his baton, watching the performers make their characteristic gestures, even the rearrangement of the stage between pieces, all contribute an interest of which we were scarcely aware until it was no longer there. It is quite a different experience to sit in a concert hall where nothing happens visually, where without warning sounds suddenly emerge from loudspeakers. A visual focus for attention can of course be supplied in many ways—by lighting or darkness, by the use of film, pantomime, or kinetic art objects. But the visual experience of watching a live performer is perhaps more directly appealing, more natural and unforced, and more integrated with the unfolding musical situation, than any other.

Linked with the unpredictable and the visual, as well as with less easily defined components, there are complex human interactions between audience and player to which both respond. The hearer delights in a virtuosity which he could never imitate but with which he imaginatively identifies. The player feels himself inspired, perhaps, to outdo himself, to bring off effects he would never think of in rehearsal.

The combination of live performers with tape seems to offer all the wealth of both worlds, plus a dimension which neither can reach alone. It also presents special problems. Synchronization between performer and tape, if it is to be more than haphazard, needs careful planning by the composer. The tape will not adjust to the performer, and the performer cannot adjust to the tape unless he has adequate information. To make a score of the tape part in all its details, including many which are not easily reduced to visual symbols, is usually impractical; fortunately, it seems unnecessary to the performer, and might even be confusing. A simplified score with clear cues only where the performer needs them, plus timing information through metronome marks or a time-scale in seconds or both, seems to work quite well. In some cases, clear sound cues must be deliberately incorporated in the tape part for the performer's benefit, perhaps to establish pitch or durations, or prepare for an important synchronized event. I find it advisable to allow at least some leeway. Aiming at précise synchronization at every point will probably result in a tape part that is over-simplified and/or a performance that is unduly strained, mechanical, and lacking in spontaneity. . . .

Certain other problems arise from the variability and limitations of playback equipment. When sending a tape out for a performance he will not supervise, the composer runs the risk that it will, after all, sound quite different from what he intended. I have heard, at tape concerts in eminent institutions, tapes played backwards or at the wrong speed! Aside from such gross errors, which the composer can only hope to avert by clear, conspicuous labeling, some directions are extremely difficult to give with precision. One of the most problematical is the loudness level of the tape. Indicators and their meaning differ from machine to machine, even on tape recorders of the same make and model. The balance between channels of a stereo tape may be affected. Other amplifiers, other speakers, all impose their special characteristics. Even if identical equipment is moved from place to place, the changed room acoustics will necessitate testing and adjustment. Rather than prescribe a certain setting of the controls, which can have meaning only in one situation, it seems preferable at present simply to give the operator some cues in the form of conventional dynamics and verbal directions. He can be told that a piece begins *f* or *pp*, or that a certain sound five seconds in must be overwhelmingly loud. This whole question of prescribing levels is one to which sound engineers might profitably direct their attention. Perhaps a simple portable "loudness meter," like a light meter for cameras, could be devised. Problems of loudness and balance are multiplied, of course, where in addition to the tape the balance with live performers has to be considered.

In any case, if the composer cares how his piece will sound, he cannot overlook the importance of explicit directions about equipment and its operation. These are as important as his dynamic markings and other performance indications in the performer's part.

Gottfried Michael Koenig

(Gottfried Michael Koenig was one of the original participants in the early Cologne Radio studio experiments and now directs the elaborate studio at the University of Utrecht, Netherlands. His works are recorded for Deutsche Grammophon and other European labels.)

One of my most unforgettable experiences occurred at the outset of my occupation with electronic music in 1955 in the Cologne studio. Heinz Schütz, the studio technician, had developed a method of synchronizing a great number of sound-layers in succession on a single tape-loop. For this purpose he had changed the order of the heads so that they were, in the tape-run direction: playback head, erasing head, recording head. At each pass of the tape-loop the existing contents were copied (and at the same time shifted by the distance of playback head/ recording head in the direction of the tape), and also mixed with a new sound. All the sounds were first stuck together in such a way that the distance, always the same, between two sounds corresponded to the length of the tape-loop, and then played back on a second tape recorder, resulting in a gradual synchronisation of the prepared sounds on the loop. The loop had of course to be long enough to provide space for the shifting of the sounds at each subsequent copy. I used this technique to make my first electronic piece; I was able to observe how new sounds were added at each pass of the loop until the entire composition was finished.

This reminiscence can vouch for my relationship to electronic music. I have always tried, though under different technical circumstances each time, not only to exploit the "mechanical" facilities of an electronic studio but to make them the basis of the realization process too. In my *Klangfiguren II* I did this with the ring modulator, in *Essay* with the transformation by machine of pre-composed sound structures. In *Terminus* an existing sound structure was transformed, the result becoming in its turn the basis for further alterations with the intention of using all intermediary and final results in the composition. In this manner the work is a report on the realization technique, which for me is inseparable from compositional activity.

I was able to take a further step in production technique in the Utrecht studio after a voltage control system had been designed and installed there. For the eight versions of the series of *Functions,* all the basic sounds and all control signals for ring modulation, filtering, amplitude modulation and reverberation were first recorded on tape—the control signals were first frequency modulated. For the sound production I worked out 36 different combinations of the equipment which I used to transform the basic sounds with the help of voltage-controlled equipment. In order to economize on work, all the sounds based on one and the same combination of equipment were produced in turn, to be distributed in the appropriate places according to the score later. After I had prepared the respective circuit, the basic sounds and control signals were run on up to four tape recorders and (after frequency demodulation of the control signals) fed to the circuit.

In the spring of 1971 a computer was installed in the Utrecht studio. In future it will extend the work with voltage control. My idea is that a series of library programmes will be prepared, to be available to the composer in the same way as studio apparatus and into which he merely has to insert his special data. The Utrecht computer can at present deliver up to eight control signals, and will certainly be able to deliver more in future.

In connection with the computer, whose functions incidentally can be simulated to a great extent by a good voltage control system, I must certainly refer to the theoretical benefit which composers and musicologists can obtain from the highly developed technique of sound control. My own personal interest is mainly in the "etiquette" that will develop between the composer and the production technique. Up to now most composers in the electronic studio had previous orchestral experience, and it was not always easy for them to translate the musician's professional routine, which is taken for granted in instrumental scores, into technical instructions to the studio equipment. Not until recently have I been seeing an increasing number of composers at our courses in the Institute of Sonology who have already learnt to think in new terms of the musical material and language during their previous musical studies. I could imagine that besides the strong urge towards improvisation on the stage which still remains in the tradition of interpreted music even when electronic equipment and synthesizers are used, a science of the musical sound could develop, not proceeding from the performability but from the producibility, even from the conceivability of a world which can only be perceived by the ear.

Daniel Lentz

(Daniel Lentz has taught at the University of California, Santa Barbara, and presently directs the activities of The California Time Machine.)

Since little of what I've written in the last five or six years would lend itself to audio discs, I have recorded on one of the alternatives, video tape. *Rice, Wax, and Narrative* is available on 2 inch, high band color tape from NOS Television, Hilversum, Holland. *CONCERT: Canon & Fugle* is available on 1 inch and ½ inch color tape from Universal Video Systems, Miramonte Drive, Santa Barbara, California. Both were recorded on 2-track stereo.

A few years ago I began indulging in music of the imagination, or of the mind, or music without sound, or whatever one might choose to name it. This music, like any music before it, begins with an idea. It differs from this other music, however, because it *ends* with the idea. There is no elaboration, sonically or otherwise. It remains in its simple state, going nowhere, doing nothing clever, or noble, or beautiful, or sad or happy. In this sense it is pure. You cannot whistle its essence any more than you can talk about it.

Before I found a way to package the concepts involved in this music (a difficult task since they called for neither notation nor realization) I arranged and participated in a number of "in absentia" performances along with other members of The California Time Machine, a group I formed in 1968. These performances were accomplished without performers in any way present with audiences. Performance material reached the (usually surprised) audiences via FM-AM radio broadcasts, Citizen Band radios, airline communications, police and hospital communications, newspaper ads, reviews, restaurant menus, and miscellaneous messengers.

In the midst of The California Time Machine's last European tour I was trying desperately to devise a way in which to get out of a performance commitment we had made in Paris, and still get paid. (There was no way in which the group could make it to Paris on the same day. If there was, we could have worked out a displacement within the city limits.) The idea finally occurred to send/mail them a "Do-It-Yourself" concert package. The PARIS PACKAGE (as it is known by the members of the group) contained all the necessary ingredients for a successful concert performance: program notes, descriptions of the planned activities, performance materials, kits, and so forth. None of the enclosed materials encouraged acoustic or sonic events; ideas or concepts only. The package was mailed, and we have not heard from the sponsors since. We did hear that the performance was canceled however. No "music," no money. Still, the experience opened the door to new and interesting ways of packaging concept music. A *Pennsylvania Package,* an *Oklahoma Package,* a *California Package* and others have been put on the market variously priced from $5 to $100 each (all composers attempt to sell their music in one way or another; this way is just a little less subtle than most), the specific price being determined by the amount of concerts enclosed and the manner in which they are enclosed (various plastics), as well as the amount of supplementary materials enclosed.

While producing these conceptual concert packages, I have

continued to compose in the more traditional mediums of instrumental, electronic, and theater music, or sound pieces as they will soon be called. Like most composers of my generation, I have had the "classical" training of my elders. The temptation is to use this training, thus indulging in the comforts and glories of neoclassicism. The rampant neoclassicism of today (as evidenced in the cataphonic gyrations of certain clics on one hand and the quotations from the dead on the other), of which most of us are guilty, will most likely go the way of all the backward-looking music of the past.

Alvin Lucier

(Alvin Lucier, a member of the Sonic Arts Group, was well-known as composer and conductor of the Brandeis University Chorus—which commissioned and premièred many experimental live-electronic works—before he assumed his present position at Wesleyan University.)

VESPERS (1968)

The idea for *Vespers* came to me in a dream I had in 1967 in which I saw a group of beings moving slowly through dark rooms carrying small objects that beamed sounds out into the environment for the purpose of guidance, as in sonar, and for the collection of data. I had the feeling that these beings—non-human or humans of an advanced mutation—were embarked upon a long exploratory mission or a slow migration through space and time and were telepathically relaying information concerning the physical and spiritual characteristics of the rooms through which they moved to an authoritative intelligence very far away.

Inspired by the imagery of this dream, I began reading Donald R. Griffin's book on acoustic orientation, *Listening in the Dark*. By means of echolocation—sounds used as messengers which, when sent out into the environment, return as echoes carrying information as to the shape, size and substance of that environment and the objects in it—bats as well as other creatures that inhabit dark places maneuver freely, hunt food and survive exquisitely in a world without light. I became envious of the prodigious sound-sending-and-receiving acuity of these creatures and began searching for ways to enable myself and other human beings to participate in it. I soon came upon the existence of small, hand-held echolocation devices called Sondols (*sonardol*phin) that were similar in appearance and function to those sound-beaming objects I saw in my dream. These devices, designed by Listening Incorporated for use by boat owners, acoustic architects, and the blind, emit fast, sharp, narrow-beamed clicks whose repetition rate can be varied manually. With enough practice and discriminating hearing, human beings can learn to use the echoes of the Sondol-generated pulsed sounds to measure distances, avoid obstacles and make acoustical signatures of reverberant environments.

When the ONCE Group in Ann Arbor invited me to present a work on their festival in 1968, I decided to make a composition in which performers, having learned the basic principles of echolocation and using Sondols as navigational instruments, would accept the task of moving to a pre-chosen point in a dark space without the help of visual information. During the rehearsals it became clear that any personal preferences as to speed, duration, texture, improvization—any musical ideas based on past experience—served only to interfere with the task of echolocating and made coherent movement difficult or impossible. It became necessary, therefore, to avoid all conventional musical gestures and to surrender one's personality to the environment, that is, to read its physical characteristics as a score that yields directions for physical movement and sound-production with reference to space and time. All sound situations that developed—the speeding-up or slowing-down of outgoing clicks for the purpose of measuring distances, silences made to avoid masking the echoes of other players by one's own clicks and their multiple echoes, shifting sound-spaces caused by changing scanning patterns—became events in a musical process that could be thought of as a kind of dance music or slow sound-photography.

I have participated in many subsequent performances of this work, making changes in the choreographic design depending on the physical properties of the performance space. On several occasions, I have given toy crickets to members of the audience so that they could participate in the articulation of the sound-image of the environment. Once in Helsinki, several hours after an evening concert, I heard members of the audience moving through the city playing their crickets. I regarded that situation as a particularly beautiful use of the idea. For the purposes of publication I wrote a detailed prose score in which I introduced several other means of sound-production including footsteps, finger-snaps, foghorns and portable generators of thermal noise or 10,000 hz. pure tones in order to make the performance of this work more accessible. I envisioned the future possibility of diving with whales, flying with bats or seeking the help of other experts in the field and also suggested that mechanical analogues such as billiards, squash and water-skimming could be considered kindred performances of this work. The title *Vespers* was chosen for the dual purpose of suggesting the dark ceremony and sanctifying atmosphere of the evening service of the Catholic religion and to pay homage to the common bat of North America of the family Vespertilionidae. It has been recorded for Main-stream Records by the Sonic Arts Union and is being used as accompaniment for *Objects,* a new dance work of the Merce Cunningham Dance Company.

Otto Luening

(Otto Luening pioneered in the development of tape music in the United States, composing with Vladimir Ussachevsky the first major American works for the medium and cofounding 'the earliest American studio at Columbia University.)

McClure's Magazine, in July 1906 published an article entitled:

"New Music for an Old World
Dr. Thaddeus Cahill's Dynamophone
An Extraordinary Electrical Invention
For Producing Scientifically Perfect Music . . .

. . . Electricity Used to Produce Music . . . the workmen in the shop speak of Electric Music. In the end the public will probably choose its own name . . . we welcome the new with eagerness; it has a great place to fill; it may revolutionize our musical art, but, in accepting the new, we will not give up the old . . ."

Dr. Cahill's demonstration came to the attention of the Italian pianist and composer Ferruccio Busoni who wrote in his "Sketch of a New Aesthetic of Music" (1907) that Twentieth Century Music must find new paths because the scales and intervals that had served music well in the past were no longer adequate for the needs of contemporary composers. He wrote: ". . . I received from America direct and authentic intelligence which solves the problem in a simple manner. I refer to an invention by Dr. Thaddeus Cahill. . . . Only a long and careful series of experiments, and a continued training of the ear can make this unfamiliar material approachable and plastic for the coming generation and for Art."

Robert Moran

(Robert Moran is based in San Francisco, but his adventurous work in live "media" presentation has become internationally known.)

Primal Source Catalogue

Chapter I

Electronic Music

electronics (-tron'iks), n., possible v.; Refer:
(Greek Choric) Farnsworthy translation of Sophocles *Electra,*

Scene III, "She's the smallest known particle, but dear Zeus, what power"

2. as in "an electrical unit," (-tron'icks) (ancient Christian Gnostic term), as in: "Tronics (icks) is the way you do it, not say it!"

music (mu-zik), n., pre-Syrian. Said aloud, this noun is self-explanatory.

medium (as in media), n., v., prep. (Tri-State English term)
Refer: Minerva Stone's book   *My Miasmic Media*   (1938); Chapter I., "The finest way to make electronic music is to send empty tapes through the Air Mail. Lovely radar and radio signals are picked up and 'notated' on the tapes. Send them back and forth many times, then sit back and listen."

academicism (ak-a-de-mism or ak-a-dem-a-sizm), n. (Roman) pertaining to pedantic spirit; Example: "Overloading the switches." Location of academicism: Refer: all colleges, universities, conservatories, institutes where pre-establishment composers now have secure positions. Example: "Of course degrees are foolish if one is a composer . . . in fact I don't have one! However, concerning a Masters Degree in Electronic Music, I firmly believe that we must require the following courses. . . ."

composition (kom-poz-i-shun), Ur-German nominal noun; pertaining to putting it all together, EX: "I'm going to compose something"; 2. Pertaining to taking it all apart, EX: "I'm going to compose something"; 3. mutual settlement or agreement (Refer: academicism) as in: (from *Primal Source Catalogue* on Education) "My teachers say that I am doing it well. My teachers like me. I will become a teacher-composer. My degrees will help me I am told. This is how I compose. I am putting it all together."

Composition Lesson No. 1

Reflect upon any electronic device, used in producing electric music; study it with care; take notes; notate it; put all notes, bits of information upon your grand piano; put a new tape on your tape machine; have the tape machine record the environment of the room; burn down your complete apartment, including piano, machine, notes, etc. . . .

humor (hew-more), Balkan; state of being. Almost unheard of commodity in most electronic music and electronic music departments. EX: from Benjamin Farnsworthy's play, "Laughter Among the Doorbells" (1965)—

Man: I love to see Nam June Paik's "one for violin." It's really fantastic.

Friend: What's it about?

Man: Well, a violin gets totally destroyed!

Friend: Wow!

Man: Then there's his wonderful "one for piano" in which a grand piano gets whacked to pieces with an ax.

Friend: That's great. God, I'd love to see it.

Man: Then there's his "one for radio" in which a transistorized radio is lowered into a fish tank, and drowns itself to death.

Friend: That's really something else. Say, why not do a composition called "one for electronic synthesizer," in which the equipment is dropped from the top of the stage proscenium into the orchestra pit?

Man: Jesus Christ! Are you some type of pervert, or somethin'?

* * *

EQUATIONS for any Electronic Music Process
(Primal Source Entertainment)

a. write compositions in which everyone on the globe can participate simultaneously

Question: what do we need?

Answer: we have all we need, that is technologically . . . it's all possible.

Question: what don't we need?

Answer: politicians, capitalism, and (in general) governments

b. Instant notation: Vladimir Francheski's essay, "Sinus Waves Above and Beyond": "The actual recording of a sound(s) is the notation itself."

c. concerning record and tape companies: make citizen's

arrests upon all presidents of these companies; Refer (PSC)
—Sound Pollution Problems.

d. electronic compositions should be arrived at via the electricity
innate within each performer's body; consider pressures of
all sorts.

*   *   *

Gordon Mumma

*(Gordon Mumma, one of the original members of the ONCE
Group, has pioneered in the use of live electronics in a theatrical
and mixed-media context.)*

HOME CANNING: GUERRILLA FACILITY

The recording is a different medium than the concert hall. The
differences were apparent in the beginning, in the making of
"acoustical" recordings, when musicians sacrificed the com-
modious concert hall to cluster in small studios and play into
the stuffy entrances of wooden horns.

Technological advances—electronics, long playing recordings,
high fidelity, stereo and multi-channel sound, magnetic tape, and
electronic noise-reduction—have made the difference seem even
more significant. Besides technology, the artistic and sociological
differences are increasingly apparent.

The composer who makes music directly on tape by electronic
means works more realistically with the recording medium.
Acknowledging the serious limitation of dynamic range, the
composer can explore new realms of timbre, rhythm, and continuity. If the result still tastes of the canning process, at least
it seems more relevant, having been born and raised in the can.

An aspect of electronic music has developed which is performed
live. It includes entirely new music-making devices, as well as
the electronic extension of traditional musical instruments. Live-
electronic music has nourished a virtual renaissance of creative

activity, in which the social delineations of "popular" and "serious" music have disintegrated. Soloists and ensembles of live performers of electronic instruments abound: Pink Floyd, David Tudor, Rolling Stones, Sonic Arts Union, Terry Riley, AMM, David Rosenboom, MEV, and the Beatles, to name but a few. Establishing new extremes of dynamic range in live performance, they have achieved a popularity which requires their attention to making recordings. . . .

The Sonic Arts Union works in both media. Primarily a live-performance electronic ensemble (with extensions from music into theatre, cinema, television, and dance), the Sonic Arts Union made a guerrilla facility to accommodate four fundamentally different live-performance situations on one record. The four works are Robert Ashley's *Purposeful Lady Slow Afternoon,* David Behrman's *Runthrough,* Alvin Lucier's *Vespers,* and Gordon Mumma's *Hornpipe,* issued on a Mainstream record.

When it was necessary to adapt from the live to the recorded medium, the procedure was to try and adapt the facility rather than the music. A guerrilla facility should allow adaptibility, though it wasn't always easy.

Robert Ashley jammed his singers into a public restroom, the bells were placed at the far side of an indoor reflecting pool. David Behrman spread his *Runthrough* apparatus across two marble floors. *Vespers* required special binaural microphones, complete with earlobes, with the specific intention that the recording be heard with headphones.

Vespers presented the recording industry with a perplexing dynamic range problem. The VU [volume unit] meters, indolent averaging devices that they are, indicated only a moderate level of loudness. But the unique wavefronts of Lucier's echolocators, which make the sounds of *Vespers,* shattered the record grooves even at recording levels low enough to hear the surface noise. A solution was found only after experiments with the best lathes of two major recording companies.

In *Hornpipe* the sounds of the cybersonic horn occur along various points from close proximity to extreme distance, and with greater dynamic range than is possible on a record. The solution was to increase the distance of the points so as to decrease the dynamic range by acoustical means. Thus, the use of electronic compressors, annoyingly audible in most present day recordings, was avoided. This approach was also used on the WERGO recording of Christian Wolff's live-electronic ensemble piece *Burdocks*.

These were artistic decisions achieved by new social circumstances in recording. Guerrilla facility for recording implies that composer-performers extend their creative responsibilities to the entire recording process. It is a promising approach to better accommodate live-music in the recording medium, and encourage useful innovation in recording techniques.

Pauline Oliveros

(Pauline Oliveros teaches at the University of California, San Diego, La Jolla, where she pioneered in the development of the Introductory course mentioned earlier. Her interest in environmental "theater" music, often stressing live electronics, is well-known.)

VALENTINE

Sometime during the mid 1930's I used to listen to my grandfather's crystal radio over earphones. I loved the crackling static. The same grandfather used to try to teach me the Morse Code with telegraph keys. I wasn't interested in the messages but I loved the dit da dit dit rhythms. I used to spend a lot of time tuning my father's radio, especially to the whistles and white noise between the stations. I loved the peculiar acoustical phenomena which involved my parents' voices on long rides in the car. I would lie in the back seat listening intently to the modulation resultants produced by voices interacting with engine vibration. I didn't care what they were saying. I also loved our wind-up Victrola, especially when the mechanism was running down with a record playing. I loved all the negative operant phenomena of systems.

Later in the 1940's, my family spent evenings and Sundays

together listening to favorite radio programs. My favorite programs always had the most accomplished sound effects man;
i.e.: "Fibber McGee and Molly" (the hall closet), "Inner
Sanctum" (the squeaking door), and others. The recurring scene
of just sitting in a familiar living room with familiar folks,
oftentimes playing parlor games such as dominoes, parcheesi,
cards, etc., while listening to the provocative radio medium,
tempered by each person responding with his own imaginative
flight or associations, made a cumulative experience of great
power in my memory. We got excited! Sometimes from the games,
sometimes from the programs or from the whole combination
of conditions.

Valentine for SAG, a live performance composition, comes
directly from this experience, although it also contains the seeds
of my present and future interests. *Valentine* was commissioned
by the Sonic Arts Group (now Sonic Arts Union) and composed in 1968. SAG represented a family relationship to me
since half of its members, Mary and Bob Ashley and Gordon
Mumma, had been part of the ONCE Group of Ann Arbor.
The ONCE Group and The San Francisco Tape Music Center,
of which I was a member (another music family with electronics
and theater as special interests), developed in parallel with similar
aims and interests during the late 1950's through the 1960's. Our
groups corresponded and shared music, ideas and interests
regarding studio development, tours and concerts. On tour we
finally met in person and discovered, among other things, the
family-like character of our groups. This interchange led to some
strong continuing relationships and ultimately to associations
regarding my own personal family. The other members of SAG,
Mary and Alvin Lucier, David and Shigeko Behrman were close
to both ONCE and myself through mutual friends.

Valentine consists of a game of Hearts with the four players'
hearts amplified. The card table is also amplified. The player's
voices, picked up by the heart microphones through the chest
cavity, resemble that far away filtered character of listening to
the sound of voices from another room in childhood. Naturally
there is a complex of interests presented by this situation which
also includes an amplified reader or narrator who reads an

historical text on the making of playing cards, a projected image of the Queen of Hearts which finally changes to the Queen of Spades, a lone croquet player who hits the ball occasionally in search of missing wickets, while two men in carpenter's attire build a picket fence.

The interest of this piece depends greatly on the players' real involvement in the game of Hearts and their peripheral interest in the hearing of their own heartbeat bio-feedback loop while the game is in progress. If the players' interest is real, audience sensitivity should increase, and the players' heart rates should change significantly with various events during the game. Of course with practice and repeat performances, players might learn subtle ways of controlling heart rates which might protect their interest in the game (who has the Queen of Spades?) or increase the rhythmic activity of the amplified heart ensemble. The range might be from apparently no significant change to the threshold of apoplexy. The narrator is an irritant or complement to the parlor scene, much like the radio was in my home. Sometimes the heat of the parlor game was more interesting than the radio program, sometimes vice versa, or sometimes a synthesis of the whole situation could be felt. Always there was a shifting, transforming complex of mood or atmosphere and relationship to and through the events, people and environment.

The imagery of the card players, the Queen of Hearts, the croquet player, the carpenters, the picket fence are apparently static, associations extended in time. No goals of interaction develop. The audience may play with these images without knowledge of my associations. For instance the card players might suggest musicians passing time in the basement before returning to the orchestra pit. Individual mental interaction may change or complement this apparently irrational collection of images resulting in a lively scene. If no relationship develops between audience member and the performance scene, then the audience member is a closed system waiting for a pulse of some different intensity and quality to act upon him and change his motionless state.

Beyond the sentiment embodied in *Valentine* is the technical problem of gaining access to the autonomic nervous system for musical purposes. The development of such an idea depends greatly, of course, on a technology which can supply equipment sensitive enough to amplify myriad tiny differences. It also depends on the realization that each single heartbeat of any living organism is unique and that the differences are of qualitative value. I hope to live long enough to have access to the proper technology in a sympathetic environment in order to become aware of the range of these differences and to utilize this microsphere in many other modes of artistic expression.

Steve Reich

(Steve Reich is an active free-lance composer living in New York City, whose works have been recorded on Odyssey and Columbia.)

SOME OPTIMISTIC PREDICTIONS (1970) ABOUT THE FUTURE OF MUSIC

Electronic music as such will gradually die and be absorbed into the ongoing music of people singing and playing instruments.

Non-Western music in general and African, Balinese, and Indian music in particular will serve as new structural models for Western musicians. Not as new models of sound. (That's the old exoticism trip.) Those of us who love the sounds will hopefully just go and learn how to play these musics.

Music schools will be resurrected through offering instruction in the practice and theory of all the world's music.

Many symphony orchestras will gradually disappear leaving only a select few regional music museums similar to the dedicated Pro Musica medieval ensembles we have now. Instead of symphony orchestras young composer/performers will form all sorts of new ensembles growing out of one or several of the world's musical traditions.

Serious dancers who now perform with pulseless music or with no sound but that of their own movement will be replaced by young musicians and dancers who will re-unite rhythmic music and dance as a high art form.

The pulse and the concept of fundamental tone will re-emerge as basic sources of new music.

Gerald Shapiro

(Gerald Shapiro is the director of the Brown University studio, and a consultant to Tonus, Incorporated, manufacturer of the ARP. The excerpts below are drawn from the program accompanying a performance of his works at Automation House, New York, in 1970.)

I. FROM THE YELLOW CASTLE

I have come to conceive of music as a way of listening—rather than the sound which is listened to, and of a piece of music as a process of interaction resulting in that special kind of listening we call music. In its present form, the event which is called *From the Yellow Castle* consists of three such pieces. All three are participant-activated, there are neither performers nor audience. Neither is there any performance in the usual sense of the word, for what is composed is the listening process itself. In each of these pieces, the participants are involved in an intensely communicative relationship with one another and with the technology of the piece. The medium and the end result of that relationship is sound and the experience for myself and for those who have participated in these pieces is one of total involvement in that sound and in the complex interrelationship that it, and we, are a part of.

II. THE SECOND PIECE

THE ONE ABOUT FINDING YOUR WAY IN THE DARK
THE PIECE FOR ROS AND HARRIS

Score
    Close your eyes and leave them closed.
    Each participant is a sound source.

Each sound source is different.

You are free to move toward or away from any other participant.

Take your time; listen; find your own way.

INFORMATION FOR PERFORMANCE

Each participant is equipped with a headset and the necessary electronic apparatus for the piece. This apparatus contains circuitry which continually transmits a unique, complex audio signal, detects these signals from other participants and routes them to the headset. Because of the highly directional, short range characteristics of the transmission system, participants will be able to "look" around the performance space and understand the distance and placement of the other participants relying solely on auditory cues from their headsets. It is also possible for two or more participants to move toward one another until they are within touching distance, again relying completely on auditory information. These two actions form the first phase of the piece and lead to the second.

Each participant has, in addition to the circuitry mentioned before, a high frequency (approx. 2 MHz) oscillator whose output makes a direct electrical connection to his skin and to one input of a beat frequency detector. Phase two begins when two, or more, participants touch. At that moment, all transmission and detection is turned off for the participants involved and they hear instead a sound whose frequency represents the difference between their individual high frequency oscillators. It is possible to slightly alter this sound by touching more or less firmly. A different sound will result for each pair, or group, of participants touching one another due to differences in skin characteristics and different oscillator frequencies. Participants are free to move at will between phase one and phase two as often as they like.

A performance of *The Second Piece* begins with a group of participants being given the helmets and initiated into the possible actions of the piece by means of the score. They are then escorted into the darkened performance space and left to explore the permutations of listening and interaction inherent in the piece.

When any participant is finished, he simply opens his eyes, leaves the performance space and is replaced by a new participant. The piece continues until everyone present has had the opportunity to participate.

Barry Vercoe

(Barry Vercoe was born in 1937 in Wellington, New Zealand. He was educated at the University of Auckland, where he studied with the New Zealand composer Ronald Tremain, and at the University of Michigan, where he worked under Ross Lee Finney. He has taught at Oberlin College Conservatory and has also been a Ford-sponsored composer for the Music Educators National Conference—MENC. Since 1968, he has been engaged in extensive research in digital sound synthesis and is currently Assistant Professor of Music at MIT and Director of the Studio for Experimental Music.)

Musicians employing electronic devices have always been the scavengers of engineering and industrial technology. Industry in turn, while providing the means for research and development, has also been quick to make innovative use of finished products that have found their way to the market place. In the utilization of digital computers an immense number of commercial and scientific applications were discovered when manufacturers finally moved away from experimental specially-designed equipment towards standardization and the development of general-purpose machines and general-purpose languages. However, this important stage has probably already reached its zenith: the most ambitious project to date in multi-purpose programming languages (PL/I) seems not to have caught on due to its complex all-inclusiveness: also, recent technological advances have caused a new flurry in the minicomputer market. Although it is too early to predict this with certainty, I suspect there will now follow an extensive period of reorganization while manufacturers begin to focus on particular needs and learn how to meet these special demands at competitive prices.

A parallel to all of this can be seen in the micro world of digital sound synthesis. Once past its initial period of research and development—carried out primarily at Bell Telephone Labs and two or three university music departments—the concepts and procedures of sound synthesis were most easily disseminated in the form of pre-packaged programs written in general-purpose languages for general-purpose machines. However, these had still not solved some of the earliest problems of computer-generated sound, namely its high cost and its lack of real-time or interactive operation. Even the advent of larger and faster computers has brought little improvement, since these machines are usually multi-programmed to make more efficient use of costly peripheral equipment; thus the composer is not likely to find himself alone with this new computing power. Improvements will likely come in two stages: (1) a more widespread use of special-purpose languages for use on general-purpose machines, and (2) the development of special-purpose "hardware" that will more easily be adapted to the composer's needs. The first stage is already in progress with the current dissemination of specially-developed languages such as MUSIC 360, MUSIC 7, and TEMPO. The second stage is not yet in sight, requiring as it does a somewhat revolutionary change in the form of commonly marketed components, but, as mentioned above, signs of its coming can already be observed in the nature and direction of present-day industrial research. When it finally does come about it will signal a welcome end to the enforced estrangement between the studio-dependent and the computer-oriented composer.

Raymond Wilding-White

(Raymond Wilding-White founded and directed the studio at Case Institute (Cleveland), and now teaches at De Paul University, where he has formed a company called The Loop Group.)

There is a basic similarity between *film* and *tape* that separates them from their supposed relatives *theatre* and *music*, relatives and ancestors included, and this is their ability to capture reality, that is to produce physical analogs of actual visual and audial events. Both film and tape take from the environment a record which is then altered and combined, after which a playback system returns it to the environment. This differs fundamentally from the method of the traditional composers—a term that must include Boulez *et al.*—who work with a conventionalized symbolic system based on abstract pitch and time relationships; an art which is an art of syntax and whose results must be made tangible by some sound-producing machine, from synthesizer to orchestra; note that "orchestration," the closest that traditional method gets to the handling of actual sounds, has always been an untheoretical, acquired art that has held a secondary position to the syntactical disciplines of pitch and time. Thus the basic aesthetics of a Milton Babbitt and of a Pierre Henry are irreconcilable, for in the first the syntax dominates the sound and in the second the sound dominates the syntax. Look at it another way. Though they are all called by the same name, are the score, performance, and a recording of a Mozart symphony the same thing? No; and, although the last two produce a very similar sound and the first produces no sound, it is the first two that are related and the last that is not; it is frozen sound, sound become physical matter and, as such, as much source material to the concrete composer as stone is source material to the sculptor. Thus the paradox of recorded chance music which stops being chance the moment it is recorded, just as a series of random numbers stops being random the moment it is printed.

In his earlier writings, Cage declared that electrical instruments would "make available for musical purposes any and all sounds." This is still tied to a traditional dogma shared alike by Webern, Beethoven, and the sound effects man: an oboe and a gunshot must always and only be an oboe and a gunshot, and the meaning of the oboe will be revealed by the score, the meaning of the gunshot by the script. Sound is a function of the present and "all sounds" will have occurred only when the universe comes to an end and thus Cage now sees the nature of sound as less important than its existence and has generated a view of form that puts the composer in the role of a temporal traffic cop. All sounds are, to one extent or another, loaded sounds—loaded with a network of associations as complex and as variable as there are places, times, and people, and this loading is as much a part of the recording as it is of the original. The formalist minimizes this fact and builds his creed on syntax, the pragmatic composer recognizes it; but both consider a musical work as largely invariable, and the fact that listening is an intensely creative act has been largely ignored before the advent of Cage and tape.

In the world of tape and film, process is an integral part of method; you hear or see the source through the hardware, and where the traditional composer or playwright moves from abstraction to reality the concrete composer and the cinematographer moves from reality to abstraction. In a tape and live composition—*Whatzit No. 2* for tape and bass—the tape is merely a mechanized instrument. Better is the use of tape as an extension of the performer—*Whatzits No. 3 & 5* for piano and pre-recorded piano. Best is where performer and tape are mutually extensions of each other—*Whatzit No. 4* for tape and orchestra. Principles of unity, variation, contrast, balance, and climax are as applicable as ever and my early 60's tapes, based on the structuring of highly loaded sounds—*Ecce Homo, Don't Call Us We'll Call You, Pavanne*—were almost neo-classic in this respect. But in all of these I felt that tape was not entirely tape—form still took precedence over sound and process. Hence the Monochromes Series: *Fanfare for Jasper Johns, Gurú, Time Motion Study, Crusade, Of Time and the River, Rothko, Campaign, The Blues, Concerto Grosso, The Natives Are Restless, Slinky, Folksong, The Wedding—Parts 1, 2, & 3.*

One texture resulting from one basic source, one basic process and one simple formal scheme. *Gurú:* Broken crockery —variable speed—canon. *Fanfare:* National anthem—montage— symmetrical proportions (from Johns's "Three Flags"). Similar as these two works are in concept, the audience reaction was vastly different, for the first reaction of all audiences, from Bunker to Bernstein, is the same: Spot what is recognizable, then classify by type and judge accordingly.

By thinking visually along parallel lines, multi-media works using these tapes have worked well and have avoided those two great banes of mixing sight and sound, the meaningless wallpaper of projected light or the pointless chatter of background music.

Finally the integration of live theatre with playback and projector, in my case The Loop Group. By returning to simple sectional form, each with its own devices, balance between the media is obtained within each section, contrast and balance are achieved between the sections. *Monochromes I* (1969); *Tribute to Society, History, Industry and Technology* (1970); *Bad News* (1971); *De Profundis* (1972).

Charles Wuorinen

(Charles Wuorinen was one of the original members of the Columbia-Princeton Center, and cofounded The Group for Contemporary Music. His Pulitzer-Prize-winning Time's Encomium *was recorded by Nonesuch.)*

EXCERPTS FROM "TOWARD GOOD VIBRATIONS" *

. . . For some years I have been trying to draw attention to what I think is the important distinction between music performed and music reproduced, and I have suggested that music which is conceived for electronic realization without the agency of performers must partake of a profoundly different nature from that destined for performers' interpretation and projection; or rather, that however conceived a work, electronic realization will cause it to acquire that different nature. Further, that up to now even the least aware composer is conditioned to assume the presence *in music itself* of what is in fact only an external contribution by the performer—clarifying violations of the text—and that this assumption raises problems when applied to the electronic medium. I mean by "clarifying violations of the text"

* Published originally in the journal *Prose*.

that even in those areas where it seems most exact (pitch and time) musical notation actually presents the cultivated performer with a mere set of generalities. He cannot "just" play what's "there"—he must decide what it means first, and then adjust its notational crudity to the real sonic world, until he —and we—can hear through the notational suggestions to what the composer intends by them. The way a composer's score *sounds* when performed is the result of these contributions by performers (and they may not always be the right ones!); ignoring their existence or assuming their availability when there are no performers present is a fatal error.

When I composed *Time's Encomium,* I tried to face this issue. It seemed to me that many workers in the electronic medium had ignored it, and that their failure to see it resulted most spectacularly in gross structural defects: I had heard almost no electronic works which seemed formally satisfactory. I thought I had detected two reasons for these flaws. In the first place, the events which make up much electronic music are vastly more general in their individual natures (*e.g.,* noises versus pitches) than those in traditional music (hence difficult to relate precisely one to another and hence of low power in defining that complex network of relations which is large form). In the second, traditional music has always depended on its performers to stress those of its aspects they judge necessary to clarify its forward unfolding; this resource (as I said) is assumed unthinkingly by most electronic composers to exist in the electronic medium, but since it does not, the forward unfolding of even the simplest forms is seriously impeded. . . .

What appears musically precise or specific is in fact not. The seeming exactitude of many aspects of musical notation makes many composers think that if only a reliable means can be found consistently to represent this "exactitude" synthetically in sound, human misrepresentations of compositions will be no more. But when one comes to commit oneself electronically to a "precise" event, never after its realization again to be inflected by interpretation, it develops that what one thought was precisely specified in conception was really only generally outlined. It is gratuitous to speak of creating circumstances in which composers can realize every musical event "exactly" as they want, since no composer ever *has* known exactly how he wants it, and since even the most exact vision of the event at the moment of realization will alter with time.

Write a note for flute: no matter how well you know the note, a player can vary it within what you thought were minima. Write a short note: no matter how exact its length may seem in your mind, when you come to perform it, you will find a range of easily perceived variations that lies within acceptable limits. These are the lessons and resources of live performance. They point to the fact that even the most detailed and exact score is actually a set of generalities. They reveal the staggering size of the musical universe, the capacity to perceive which is one of man's rarest treasures. Even the smallest event in a musical fabric, an event of which there will be thousands of similar others in a single work, contains within it an infinity of variation and capacity for interpretation. This variation is not merely at the margins of the perceivable but contributes to the central range of meanings borne by the work.

The imprecision of the seemingly precise, the generality of the seemingly limited, the lesson that composition consists of ordering generalities whose interrelations are virtually infinite, all imply revision of two current notions. One is that an electronic work is more securely what the composer meant than is one realized by performers. It is not; rather but one freezing of the relations that were originally asserted as the composition. And since no one has ever really specified a musical event "precisely" during the act of composition, the precision of what he specifies "precisely" during the act of electronic realization must remain mostly self-deception.

The other notion is that aleatoric approaches allow "freedom" to composer, performer, or listener. But since all composition asserts only generalities, the relation of the aleatoric to the fully composed is really that of unfinished to finished; inversely, as much freedom of variation exists for the realization of traditionally specified music as is said to exist in the aleatoric. It is just that with the latter, the area of allowable deviation is on a vastly grosser scale, the events are huge things, and the range of meaningful relations among them is therefore enormously reduced in scope and power. A work employing such means can utter only the most childish structural sentiments. It can assert only the most trivial simplicities, since it lacks the capacity for discrimination to define the more subtle.

It seems that many composers are unaware of how general the musical structures they set up really are. They often, fail to appreciate the number of different meanings such structures can acquire; hence they are not sensitive to the dangers of freezing such relations electronically, without first meditating on the problems I have tried to outline. Perhaps it is because so many musicians (and listeners) concentrate on *substance* within music rather than relation, that so much obvious is overlooked. We have a way of feeling that if we can but know the *things,* their interrelations will somehow come along with them in the rumbleseat. But this attitude is disastrously overconfident: it is the relations that enable us to identify the things, and things themselves are merely convenient ways of designating bundles of relations. Notes and other noises are the things in music, but notes themselves are just arrays of vibratory relations. Music itself can never be said to exist; it has either just happened, or is about to. And at that instant when music is sounding, it is merely using acoustic actuality to assert and define a set of related intervals of time and pitch, intervals that are themselves only "empty space." This is why one may say that music is the "nothing between the notes."

All music, live or electronic, has its origin in these measures defining and delimiting "empty space." That the "space" is a metaphor does not alter the case. It is here, in the realization that the external differences of the live and electronic result from different ways of defining and filling these relations, not from different basic goals, that we understand the interdependence of the two and can glimpse a possibility of union between them. This interest in unification by penetrating to the common source of two phenomena is not the same as the current penchant for homogenization, which merely seeks to erase the infinity of surface differences amongst things by force without ever trying to understand what brings them together. It is a notion which therefore can be extended to other, broader, polarities. I think of the differences between twentieth-century music and its ancestry, which have been greatly overdrawn, or between Western music generally and that of other high musical cultures.

Such generalization is strenuous and dangerous, but we are fortunate to live in an age which witnesses the formation of broad ideas. We should not be blinded to their emergence by the pettiness and ineptitude of so much around us.

Part V
Do-It-Yourself:
Tape Composition at Home

No musical style has ever flourished for long as the exclusive property of "professionals." On the contrary, much of the standard literature of the past—such as concert pieces, chamber music, opera, ballet, sacred works—was created in an atmosphere of vigorously healthy amateurism; aristocrats and, in later generations, middle-class families played instruments, kept them and used them often in their homes, enjoyed singing, and occasionally dabbled in composition. The survival of this tradition into the present owes much to the fact that so many of us, while not highly trained in the subtleties of the art, continue our own active music-making in one way or another. Music is, aside from its intellectual and expressive dimensions, one of the great spectator sports: Ritual and pageantry dominate most of its history, and in this respect music, dance, theater, and athletic contest—the public expressions of any culture—have much in common. They are all built on a broad base of amateurism: the professional stage linked inevitably to the flimsiest grade school play, and sand-lot baseball to the big leagues. Not that this should be surprising; the very word "culture" implies pervasive activity within an entire community, and the class-conscious use of the term to denote the isolated efforts of a very few reveals a misreading of history.

Electronic music is no different from other important artistic developments, in that it, too, proceeds from a commonly available *home* resource—not the family parlor piano or the amateur string quartet, but the tape recorder. In the past two decades an ever growing number of students, tape hobbyists, rock performers, and hi-fi enthusiasts have discovered the joys of experimenting with their equipment. Many are already quite familiar with the finer points of tape-splicing, feedback, ways of creating echo, speed changes in playback—in short, the basic means of creating *musique concrète* from everyday prerecorded sound sources. When *High Fidelity* magazine initiated its Electronic Music Contest in 1969, the editors anticipated the submission of a mere handful of amateur tapes; to their surprise they received well over 100 tapes from all parts of the United States, composed by salesmen, mathematicians, students, accountants, performing musicians, teen-agers, housewives, at a consistently high level of technique and musical inventiveness. It's a fact, then, that such people do exist, and in greater numbers than we might have imagined.

Musique concrète is the easiest kind of electronic music to attempt in the home, since the most delicate procedures are those of manipulating the sounds, and this can be done with relatively limited apparatus—in fact, as a minimum, one tape recorder (with microphone) and splicing equipment. True "electronic music"—creating the sources themselves as well—would probably entail some further degree of expense and time, and I will comment on this aspect only briefly later on. Let's assume that you have no particular desire to synthesize your own sounds and that, in any event, your chances of using audio generators or a voltage-controlled system are limited; there's still no reason why you can't utilize the resources of your tape recorder to produce some really interesting compositions, within the limitations of the *concrète* technique. A variety of distortions, multichannel combinations and unusual rearrangements of material is possible; as you'll see, even more can be done if you have two or three tape recorders. If what you care about, on the other hand, is a precise, ordered structuring of pitches and rhythms—something like Babbitt's *Composition for Synthesizer,* or an electronic rendition of *Dixie*—you will need rather sophisticated equipment (not to mention a thorough background in the traditional skills of composition, such as harmony and counterpoint) and the patience to make literally hundreds of splices in your tape. We'll have to assume that what you have in mind creatively is more compatible with the equipment at hand.

First of all, examine your tape recorder (and I'll assume, for the moment, that you have only one). As the tape passes from reel to reel it comes into contact with erase-record-playback "heads" that will become visible if you unscrew the protective covering usually placed over these. If there are three heads, they're in the order I've just named; if only two, playback and record heads have been combined in a single unit. It's preferable to have a machine with three separate heads, both for "monitoring" during the recording or copying process (a comparison of the signal being recorded with that of the playback) and the easy execution of echo effects. For the time being, it's important to realize that you can locate the position of a sound on tape, with a high degree of precision, by seeing where it lies with respect to the heads; this will be of enormous help when you wish to splice or edit bits of tape.

You also need to know how much of the tape is being recorded (or played back) by the tape recorder—that is, whether the machine is designated full-track mono (the entire width of the tape serving for one channel or loud-speaker), two-track or half-track stereo (capable of dealing with two channels in the same direction), or quarter-track stereo (four tracks can be recorded, but only two at a time, and playback is limited to two channels in either direction). Virtually all of the home units being manufactured today are quarter-track stereo, the chief advantage of this to the average listener being one of economy: The arrangement makes it possible to record twice as much material as on a half-track machine (by recording in stereo, then turning the tape over and recording in stereo again). The quarter-track's greatest disadvantage, however, is a serious one for people interested in tape composition; playing your tape in reverse, so that the succession of sounds and the articulation of each sound are backward, is extremely difficult if not literally impossible. That device would be terribly easy, though, with a full-track or half-track machine: After recording, you simply turn the tape reel over and play back. A simple illustration may explain why this is so:

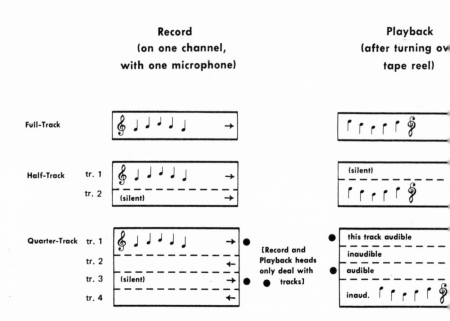

In short, a half-track or full-track recorder is preferable if reversal effects are desired, and there are additional advantages in using a machine with three, rather than two, heads. The average home quarter-track unit will very likely be one with three heads, so this latter need may be satisfied automatically. As for locating full- and half-track recorders, these can be found among professional studio equipment, machines for business or school use, earlier models dating from the mid-1960's or before; you may find it worthwhile to search one out. Other devices are found on specific makes or models of recorder—an echo setting, a "Cue" or "Edit" button, sound-on-sound and sound-with-sound, to name the most valuable for tape composition—and these will be discussed as their usefulness arises.

Secondly, you may want to consider the kind of tape you're

using. As the standard home recorder will take nothing larger than a 7-inch reel, the choice usually narrows down to three tape lengths (or, more importantly, tape thicknesses): 1.5 mil tape, when wound on a 7-inch reel, yields 1,200 feet of tape, while 1 mil gives you 1,800 feet and 0.5 mil a bountiful 2,400 feet. Translated into recording/playback time, these are, respectively, about 30 minutes, 45 minutes, and a full hour. Individuals who simply want to record great quantities of material without changing reels are naturally attracted to the thin 0.5 mil (as they are to the quarter-track recorder), but anyone planning to *edit* tapes would prefer the thickest of all, the 1.5 mil. Splicing the very thin tape is quite difficult, as you'll discover if you ever have to deal with it. Moreover, the thicker tape is stronger, more stable, and less likely to break. As for the type of material used for the tape backing, there is a choice between acetate and polyester, with some differences of opinion as to the relative merits of each; most composers prefer polyester.

So now, assuming that you have your tape and your single recorder, let's consider a number of procedures that can be used to advantage in creating a tape composition, beginning with the "source" tape itself.

1. *Sound sources and initial recording.* I'm assuming that you will begin with a blank tape—silence—and then record your source material on it. There's no reason why you have to, though, as any prerecorded tapes of music or speech can be effectively used for *concrète* composition; Yoko Ono is said to have made her first tape piece by splicing together innumerable scraps of Beatles out-takes, literally saving them from the cutting-room floor. My assumption that you're starting from silence doesn't imply that this is the best or only way. But, from a pedagogical stance if for no other reason, let's treat the act of composition as though proceeding from a position of utter purity, a sonic *tabula rasa*.

Use your imagination and don't be afraid to try sounds that may seem initially absurd to you: an electric appliance, Ping Pong balls on various surfaces, water sounds, a crackling fire on the hearth, the crying of an infant. If you desire artistic (or other) "limits" you might want to restrict yourself to sounds made in a particular room of your home, or associated with a specific individual, or representative of a selected time of day. I hardly need to mention traditional sources (those produced by instruments and the singing voice), as these suggest themselves immediately: single notes, scales, rapid improvisational passagework, unorthodox "avant-garde" sounds on your instrument— all of these are potentially useful. Whatever your sound source, try recording it at various volume levels and distances from the microphone, and you'll notice a great difference in the resultant playbacks. For example, very quiet sounds at high amplification and close miking may be of particular interest to you; you won't know, though, unless you're willing to experiment.

Don't limit your sources to those captured by the microphone; your tape recorder can also receive signals from a radio or phonograph, expanding your stylistic outlook in the direction of "collage" if you wish. That is, you can now include among your sources fragments from great symphonies, familiar pop songs and radio commercials, voices of statesmen and celebrities, and snatches of quiz shows, news releases, and soap operas, to be combined later in varying degrees of distortion and juxtaposition. The signals can be transferred directly from phonograph (or radio) to tape recorder by jacks connecting the output of the former to the input of the latter; if you want an undistorted recording, this is preferable to picking up the sound via microphones and then rerouting it into your recorder. On the other hand, if it suits your purpose, you may *want* a distorted quality in your "commercial" signal, and the use of a microphone directed at your loud-speaker may be just what you desire. Similarly, an "antique" effect that can be particularly evocative might be best realized by using an old scratchy record, a short-wave broadcast with some static, a transistor radio of only fair quality, or a tuning of your radio dial somewhere between stations. The most important factor to remember is that, short of contradicting the written instructions for the use of your equipment (which might conceivably injure it or you!), no idea is "wrong" *per se*. In making experiments, your own taste and judgment will determine which results are most suitable for your composition and which results go well together in combination; fortunately, the very fact that you can splice tape with ease means that unwanted material can be edited out at any stage of composition. Always assume that you'll be making more sound-source material than you'll ever need—an entire 1,200-foot reel of tape, perhaps, for a 5- to 7-minute composition—and then act on this knowledge with a certain security, healthy lack of caution, even bravado, in attempting as broad a spectrum of effects as you desire.

2. *Change of speed.* The average home tape machine usually runs at two speeds, 3¾ inches per second (ips) and 7½ ips, and some machines add a third—even slower—speed of 1⅞ ips (a higher speed, 15 ips, is available only on professional studio apparatus). You'll note that these speeds are all related by a factor of doubling or halving: when you play the same taped material first at 1⅞ and then at 3¾ the speed has been doubled, while an increase from 1⅞ to 7½ moves the tape at four times the speed.

Test your sound-source tapes (or any tapes, for that matter) by playing them at every speed your machine permits. It should be obvious that playback at a faster speed (faster than that of recording) increases the *tempo* of the material; the sounds seem to rush by at a much faster rate of succession. The *pitch* has changed as well, everything now appearing in a higher register, and there is a noticeable alteration of *timbre*. Reverse phenomena take place when the tape is slowed down in playback: Slower tempo, a lowering of register, and considerable changes in timbre can be heard immediately. Distortions in timbre may be the most interesting—and the most useful—of all. For example, a sound played at one-fourth of its original recorded speed (that is, much more slowly) takes on unusual vibrations and "beats"; that sound could be isolated and used for its sonic quality alone, discarding the rest of the slowed-down passage and thus ignoring its pitch-durational references. Or you could arrange to make a tape that retains conventional characteristics of register and tempo while shifting attention to the timbre. Record your own singing (or instrumental playing) of a familiar tune at a high tape speed, but performing about twice as *fast* and an octave *higher* than you might ordinarily; play the tape at a slower speed and see if you find the effect interesting. Conversely, record at a low speed, with your material lower in register and slower in tempo than usual and then set the tape playback for a higher speed. In each case, the actual "notes" of the music will be in their proper place and at the traditional tempo, but the sound quality will have changed—often in astonishing ways.

Experiments in speed change are more easily accomplished —and infinitely more variable—if you have two or more recorders to work with (and I'll suggest some of these procedures later on). With only one machine, you may have problems in combining many different speeds in a single composition if you've recorded all of your material at a single speed. (It's assumed that playback would be a continuous "unfolding" of tape at a single speed—that is, an entirely prerecorded *concrète* composition—rather than a live-performance manipulation of speeds during playback.) You can play the tape at a speed different from the one used in recording, of course, but then *all* the material is sounding at that new speed. I'd suggest, instead, that you change speeds periodically during the recording process, so that different effects will emerge during the continuous, uninterrupted playback. With a three-speed machine you may want to decide beforehand on 3¾ ips as the constant rate of playback; in that case you'll have to remember that any passages recorded at 1⅞ will produce high-speed "performance," material recorded at 7½ resulting in a low-speed playback.

In using the phonograph record as a sound source, an even greater variety of speed change is possible, particularly if your turntable offers the options of 33⅓ rpm, 45 rpm, and 78 rpm. (Some turntables can be slowed down to 16⅔ rpm, one-half the speed of the conventional long-playing record, affording a still wider range of alternatives.) Because the progression from 33⅓ to 45 to 78 is *not* a simple doubling, while the increase in tape speeds is just that, various speed alterations (by a factor other than 2) can be arrived at if you change disc and tape speeds in different combinations. Numerous higher-priced phonographs also feature a device to alter speed by a small factor— usually just enough to "tune" it to a live instrument—and this

can be used to introduce subtle waverings of pitch while recording from disc to tape. When I first became interested in tape
music—initially a fascination with *concrète* collage—I was
fortunate to have access to a totally variable speed turntable,
one that could run the gamut from virtually zero to a speed much
higher than 78 rpm in a single sweep: Bent tones, distorted
waverings, and impressive glissando effects were, in essence,
child's play. Glissandi, while not quite as monumental as those,
are possible if you manually "brake" the continuous speed of
the tape reel (or reels) during the recording process. Touch
the side of the reel with your finger, and vary the pressure; each
time you release your finger, the tape resumes its normal speed
of progress. As with many of the procedures noted here, the
effect would not be audible until playback.

3. *Volume controls.* I won't say much about this but simply
suggest that you consider the possibiilty of experimentation in
volume level. Again, this should be done during *recording*, so
that no manual adjustments are needed during the playback
period. Try a gradual crescendo—a slow building up of sound
—from silence to the loudest level you desire, or a diminuendo,
a fading out to silence. Abrupt volume changes are worth exploring; place a familiar work—like the Beethoven *Ninth Symphony*
—on your phonograph turntable, and record it on tape so that
it emerges as a series of asymmetrical punctuations from silence.
You'll discover that you have to flick your wrist quickly to move
from the lowest (silence) reading on the volume dial to whatever degree of loudness you desire without affecting any gradual
transition. Random changes of volume level would be particularly interesting in dealing with a sustained sound, and especially
one that undergoes obvious timbral change during its life (such as
a struck cymbal or piano tone); as I've already noted, Brian
Dennis discusses this procedure in some detail in his *Experimental Music in Schools.*

4. *Stereo tape recorders.* The most evident asset of a stereo
machine is that you can record two entirely different channels'
worth of material. First record on track 1 and then rewind the
tape back to its beginnings and record again on track 2. In
playback, the resultant sound will be heard, in stereo separation,

over two loud-speakers. Experimentation with speed changes and volume level can be done independently for each channel, so that the composite tape might contain a great variety of simultaneous juxtapositions. If you have a half-track machine, you can arrange your recording so that one channel appears *reversed* in playback; simply record your material on track 1, then turn the reel over (no need to rewind) and record *again* on track 1. (This will be track 2 of the actual tape, since it has been turned over.) In playing the finished tape, you notice that one channel presents the material as you recorded it, while the other loud-speaker produces the reversal of your original. When you're through playing the tape, turn it over once more and play again: Sound that you've just heard "backward" will now appear in its recorded original, while the material that was forward will now be reversed!

As you can see from our earlier diagram of tape trackings, this procedure will not work successfully with a quarter-track machine. It is possible to record all four tracks of a quarter-track unit, of course, but only two of them (those in the same direction) can be heard. You might wish to take your tape made on a quarter-track unit, all four tracks recorded, and play it on a half-track stereo machine; in that event you'll now hear all four channels (coming from two loud-speakers), with two of them reversed.

5. *Echo, sound-on-sound, sound-with-sound.* Reverberation or "echo" is easily achieved on any machine with three heads, as a continuous cycle can be set up between the record head and the playback head—that is, a recording, playback, rerecording of the playback, replayback of the rerecording, and so on, *ad infinitum.* As you've observed, the two heads are inches apart, while the duration represented by that space is related to the tape speed; the factors of tape speed and volume level thereby determine the quality, "tempo," and duration of the echo. It's possible to activate this interaction between heads by means of a single input-output patching in the back of your machine, and many tape recorders now have an "Echo" switch that performs this service automatically.

A number of stereo tape recorders also offer switches labeled

"Sound-on-Sound" and/or "Sound-with-Sound." These can be of great help in making two-channel stereo passages when you want some real synchronization (or, at least, controlled inter-relationship) of the two channels. I should note in this respect that the earlier suggestions I had made for stereo recording did *not* provide for such control; those were more or less "chance" assemblages of material, first on one track and then on the other, with no opportunity to hear the simultaneous result—that is, the counterpoint produced by the way in which the two sources lined up together—until playback of the whole. If your unit has these two switches, you will be able to hear the material previously recorded on track 1 while you add track 2 to it; you can also build up multiple-track effects by transferring your previously recorded tracks 1 *and* 2 to track 2 while you add a new track 1 to the composite mixture.

6. *Editing.* This is perhaps the most important technique of all: No matter what you've done in making interesting sounds, a lack of facility in editing will severely limit your freedom in making these into an effective piece. Conversely, really adroit splicing can turn even the most pedestrian of tapes—a "straight" Haydn string quartet, or dictations to your secretary—into a magical, wondrous, adventuresome composition. Invest in a splicing block, razor blades, a good deal of splice tape (of the sort specifically intended for sound recording, not the kind ordinarily used for wrapping packages or making repairs on torn paper), and begin editing—as often as possible, in fact, to gain practice in the technique. For most musical purposes, a diagonal, rather than vertical, splice is best, as it produces a smoother transition between the events you're joining together; secondly, be sure to affix the splice tape to the "outside" (the shiny side) of the recording tape—that is, the side not containing the magnetizations that produce sound, hence the side not in contact with the heads.

The many uses of editing—discarding unwanted material, rearranging segments in an order other than that of recording, producing unusual timbres by eliminating attack and/or decay elements, fragmenting material into tiny bits, and juxtaposing contrasted ideas in rapid succession—are too obvious to discuss in any detail here. I should remind you of three important factors, however, that might be overlooked:

First of all, in splicing a tape recording in stereo, you're inevitably splicing the entire width of the tape—that is, *both* tracks at once. It's impossible to eliminate, fragment, or otherwise operate on one channel of tape without altering the other as well. If something must be done with one track and not the other, the only solution is to separate the two channels by rerecording them onto new reels of tape, recombining them into a single stereo tape (by further copying) after the editing is done; this, of course, necessitates two tape recorders.

Secondly, don't forget that one of the chief advantages of tape composition is its sure control over *time*. Once you've decided upon the proper tape speed for playback, you can be assured that so many inches of tape will represent—exactly— so many seconds' worth of duration. By splicing precisely measured bits of tape, therefore, you can create rhythmic patterns of all kinds, as regular (or as fanciful) as your aesthetic aims, arithmetic-measuring skills, and splicing techniques permit. If you plan to compose a fair amount of tape music, you might wish to set aside a special desk or work table for editing, and mark (on the surface of this table) the most often used measurements. A strong vertical line every 3¾ inches would be sufficient; this will represent either 2 seconds, 1 second, or 0.5 second, depending upon the tape speed of the passage in question.

Thirdly, the importance of *blank* tape in the editing process is often ignored by beginners. This tape, of course, is silent and can be taken from a complete reel of blank tape kept handy for this sole purpose. One use of blank tape should be obvious: Almost any piece of music, particularly one in the Western tradition of "drama" and "narrative," needs silence to punctuate and articulate its unfolding. If you doubt this, listen to any music other than non-Western or certain areas of the avant-garde— certainly anything from Hadyn through Stravinsky—and listen especially for the *silences*. They are integral to the structure and to the drama; they help thicken the plot. A more subtle use of blank tape, though, is found in its alternation with tape fragments

of a continous sound. Take a taped segment of some length—
about 10 seconds or so—containing one sound or a continuous
unbroken pattern, and splice it into, say, 10 equal 1-second fragments; if each of these is alternated with a 0.5 second fragment
of blank tape, you'll now have a repeated-note pattern in a
regular rhythm. By varying the lengths of the individual fragments
(sound and/or silence), irregular rhythms will be produced just as easily.

I should note again, though, that any interspersions of silent
tape will cut equally into both tracks of a stereo recording. For
really interesting effects and the fullest use of the techniques
you've developed, it should be apparent by now that you really
need . . .

7. *Two or more tape recorders.* You now have the full capabilities of multichannel mixing, especially if both machines are
stereo units. Furthermore, each layer of sound—if made on
its own separate tape—can be edited individually before that
mixing takes place. Two different tapes, for example, can be
placed (in succession) on recorder A and copied onto channels
1 and 2, respectively, of recorder B. The composite stereo tape
may, in turn, be recopied from the recorder B onto channel 1 of A,
leaving room for more material to be added to channel 2, and so
on.

Speed changes are also made infinitely more variable—and
more immediately usable—when you can copy material from
one machine to the other. Our limitations are no longer those of
1⅞, 3¾, and 7½ ips. A low tuba or bassoon passage recorded
at 7½ ips may be played back at that speed but copied at a
lower speed; when the copy is played at 7½ ips, it has become
a "high-speed" variant, and, when the copy is *itself* copied at a
lower speed and that second copy played at 7½ ips, the resultant sound is higher still—a process that can continue until
the initially low-register material has ascended into the musical
stratosphere, perhaps to the threshold of audibility. As you
know, the sounds will also become progressively shorter and
shorter in duration. (One particularly mischievous composer is
said to have "reduced" Wagner's monumental *Ring* cycle of four
music dramas in this manner, eventually compressing—or dis-

tilling—it to four rapid, high-pitched clicks on his tape recorder.) The opposite effect—of forcing the material ever and ever lower in register and greater in duration—is, of course, equally possible. The ease of copying in this way means that you can record all of your sources at a single speed, if you wish, and affect as many speed changes as you wish later on. (Bear in mind, though, that your final tape will most likely be played at a single constant speed, and calculate all copying in terms of the eventual sound at that speed.)

Copying is also a blessing if you are particularly fond of a sound or passage (either directly on your source tape or one that has resulted from editing) and find that it may be useful if repeated a number of times in the composition. Simply make as many copies as you wish, and edit them into your final tape at the appropriate moments. I should add, since the discussion is now centered about tape copying, that—as with recording from the radio or disc—it's advisable to do this by internal jack connections, the output of one unit directly to the input of the other, rather than using an external microphone to pick up the signal. The microphone will add room sound, loud-speaker sound, and a greater degree of distortion with each copy. Not that distortion is always a drawback: it can be turned to your advantage if used creatively, as in Alvin Lucier's tape piece *I Am Sitting in a Room.* Truly amazing in its simplicity and stunning effect, the Lucier is made by a speaker recording his reading of a brief passage (beginning with the words of the title and, in essence, explaining the composition), then copying the recording, and recopying each copy, using the room distortion, until only the rhythms and inflections of the original statement remain. The point is that, with this as with any other electronic procedure, there is no dogmatic "right" or "wrong"—merely suitability, consistency, feasibility, and inventiveness. In any event, though, the direct transfer of signals from one tape machine to another is for most purposes preferable to any external rerouting through external microphones.

Still another advantage of two machines is that certain manual operations—those that would entail "live" playing if attempted with a single unit—can be performed on one tape recorder and copied onto another. A simple illustration is the use of the tape loop. Any segment of tape—a running pattern, or melodic sequence, or spliced alternation of sound and silence that produces a rhythm—can be joined to itself in a continuous circle or band and this band run through the heads of the tape machine. An ever repeating *ostinato* results, which can exist in as many alterations of tempo as there are tape speeds on your recorder. Incorporating a loop into a prerecorded *concrète* composition is all but impossible with a single machine, and in any case live performance with loops is notoriously precarious, as the loop is liable to break or become entangled in the tape mechanism at any time. Playing the loop on one unit and recording it on the other allows the composer to explore gradual changes in volume level (fading in and out of the recurring pattern), and to place the *ostinato* on one channel of his final tape against contrasting material on another channel. Entire multiple-track pieces can be built out of assorted loops, overlapping and intersecting at different speeds and gradations of volume. A second live operation—of great value for special effects—is possible if your machine has a "Cue" or "Edit" button that stops the tape drive (the reels remaining stationary) but keeps the tape itself in contact with the playback head. By manually rocking the tape back and forth, moving it forward or backward with your hand, you can create sharp bursts of sound—at the slowest or fastest speeds your fingers can control—that are quite unearthly. Record these on a second tape machine, adding echo if you wish, perhaps on only one channel (reserving the second channel for different material).

If you have two machines, see to it if you possibly can that one of them is a half-track stereo unit; thus, you'll be assured—whether the other machine is full or quarter-track—that you have *both* the potential of stereo recording and tape reversal effects (a dual advantage). After this much discussion of two machines, I hardly need elaborate on the advantages of three or more: greater efficiency and time-saving, further possibilities for special effects, simplicity in mixing, and so on. In fact, I believe I've stated enough about the *technical* aspects of tape music to satisfy the purposes of this chapter—enough, at least, to get any interested reader started on his own. If your preoccupations with the medium carry you still further, you'll certainly want to have access to three tape recorders; you may also wish to explore the possibilities of contact mikes and their use and perhaps purchase an inexpensive filter to alter the timbres of your material in ways that can't be done otherwise. Purely *electronic* sources may interest you, rather than "concrete" ones, and you'll find that, aside from using a synthesizer, a few simple options are available. For one, you can purchase an audio sine/square wave generator at a relatively inexpensive price. Or, at no expense whatsoever, try using the feedback from your own recorder as an "electronic" sound source; the hiss between radio stations similarly functions well as white noise.

An aspect of all this experimentation that still hasn't been discussed—and one that perhaps *shouldn't* be discussed—is what you *do* with all this material when assembling it into a "finished" piece. I tend to the belief that a composer's working methods (whether intuitive or learned) ought to be his own business, ruled by his own imagination and experience—in short, his preferences. Although one person may sharpen another's perceptions, one can't dictate preferences to another; in this respect, at least, composition can never really be taught. I don't intend to teach it, or make the attempt, here. The most that can be done within the scope of this book lies in the area of "general information" that might be put to compositional use—either by proceeding on the basis of the information or by ignoring it completely! For whatever it's worth, then, let's move into a brief discussion of . . .

8. *Composing.* It's difficult at any time to define this term, and even more precarious with respect to tape music. For many individuals "composing" represents the act of fitting the tape together—editing, copying, splicing out—into a finished product: The most important creative procedures are those of sorting, comparing, choosing, altering. In a similar vein, others would refer to the actual making of the source tape as "composing," because their imaginations are most fired when they're engaged in devising unusual sound sources, playing with volume levels, recording material at different speeds; like the editing composers,

the recording composers often perform best on an instinctive level, making on-the-spot decisions based on the sonic evidence at hand. The practices of both groups reflect the belief that, while *invention* certainly plays a role in the process, the primary task of "composing" is *selection*—and, most significantly, selection from alternatives that already exist. It's just as possible, though, to choose from the options offered by your imagination; many composers, selecting from alternatives that do not yet exist, plan their entire work before they ever deal with it concretely as sound. This is the way most traditional, nonelectronic music is created, of course; "composing" is the selection—mentally—from one's private set of experiences and memories, predetermined, before the fact of performance.

We've gone into this distinction before, in earlier chapters. It's now of practical concern to you, however, in making your own choices. Perhaps you need to try your hand at both, to see which suits you best. Compose one piece with no preconceptions at all, by walking into your home "studio" unencumbered by any ground plan, *then* attacking problems as they arise out of the immediate "feel" of the material. Alternatively, work out as much of the detail of your composition as you can—the determination of sources, their treatment, the succession of events to be shaped by your editing—in advance and then realize them in your "studio" with a maximum of efficiency. Different compositional needs and different temperaments may dictate one working procedure or the other without any conscious choice on your part; in that case, so much the better.

In any event, the finished work will have a "form." It can hardly help having one, since any chunk of time with sound and silence distributed within it takes on a particular shape. The traditional view of form is usually that of one stylized model or another—the rondo, the sonata allegro—representing the practices indigenous to a particular civilization and musical language; this is, unfortunately, a limited, pedantic approach, because, even with respect to the familiar models, no two pieces are ever really alike, and in any case "form" exists whether stylized model-building is present or not. In other words, don't *worry* very much about the form of your tape composition:

Whether it is "right" or "wrong" by established standards, it will at least be unique, which, in the last analysis, is the best thing anyone could say about it. On the other hand, a few general principles might be useful, since (1) you're probably following one basic model or another anyway without knowing it, and (2) it's always more satisfying to rebel against tradition if you know what that tradition is.

We could begin by making the simplest distinctions between two large categories of musical form: (1) those pieces during the course of which a good number of perceptible changes occur, and (2) pieces in which no real changes are noticeable— that is, pieces in which *nothing happens.* I would include in the latter category John Cage's *4'33"* (four minutes and thirty-three seconds of silence) and certain "drone" or recurring-pattern works—often lasting for hours—of the avant-garde and of some non-Western cultures, even though I'm well aware of the fact that there are a great many subtle changes taking place (in the music and in our consciousness) all the time; this concept of change within stasis is, in fact, one important rationale behind such music. To stretch a point still further, I would also enter into category 2 works that deal with one change only, a single aspect of the music being altered on a gradually sliding continuum. Ninety-nine per cent of the Ravel *Bolero,* or the opening few minutes of "Mars," from Holst's *The Planets,* can be described in this way as music that simply grows louder and louder (if I'm permitted to ignore conveniently the changes in orchestration); a single tone or cluster that rises in pitch, or a pattern that grows continually slower in tempo, ever more quiet, would also fall into category 2 if it constituted the entire piece and not merely one section of it. It shouldn't be too difficult to envision electronic applications of formal scheme 2, and I leave these to your own creative imagination.

If we return to category 1—representing the overwhelming majority of compositions in the Western tradition—we can begin to subdivide *it* into a number of "general" (but I hope not stylized) models. You can approach music that deals with obvious contrasts and changes in a number of ways, of course, and no single method of categorization applies to all pieces. Let me present two different, although related, methods. One is the statement that all traditional forms are comprised of pieces in which either the end is like the beginning, or the end is *not* like the beginning. This may sound facetious, but it points up the real distinction between music that is basically "symmetrical" —"patterned" along artificial lines that are culturally accepted —and music that derives its impetus from a dramatic, "narrative" thrust. On the one hand, the composer builds a musical sort of architecture (like a house, braced on all sides) or a musical sandwich with identical outer layers balancing a multitude of contrasts within; on the other hand, the creator functions much as a novelist might, introducing ideas and characters, engaging them in dramatic situations and moving them to an outcome that, while perhaps inevitable, is entirely unforeseen.

Another statement dealing with essentially the same distinction, but from a less Romantic point of view, is that all forms contain within them the elements of *unity* and *variety,* areas of stability and of contrast. These can be presented either successively or simultaneously. If these areas are presented in succession (that is, in alternation), we have the situation of the symmetrical musical building-sandwich I suggested earlier: a series of ideas that a music student would probably analyze as ABA (A the initial motive that returns at the end, B the contrasting section) or, to introduce still more contrast, ABACA, ABACADA, ABACABA, and so on. If, in your own tape piece, you are using a reprise of earlier material as your conclusion, you'll be happy to know that you're following one of the standard "classic" procedures. Category 2 is equally traditional; by suggesting the simultaneous presentation of the familiar and unfamiliar, I mean something akin to $AA^1A^2A^3A^4A^5A^6$ and so on—that is, the age-old model of "theme and variations." Each of the superscripts indicates a recognizable alteration—sometimes a drastic one— in the music's fabric; the underlying basic material (A) is always present. As *concrète* tape composition relies so heavily on the alteration and "variation" of source material, the applications of this principle to your own work are too obvious to mention.

I've purposely eliminated any mention of the relationship that traditional form has to tonality and the key system—particularly the elaborate sonata-allegro form, which hinges on this relationship—because I must assume that you're not equipped to deal with complex pitch relationships in your work. (Without a thorough musical training and extensive electronic apparatus, you'll be quickly discouraged if you try.) In any event the "sonata principle"—as Wilfrid Mellers dubbed it—is a highly delicate organism and an amazing hybrid that evolved from the relatively simple two-part structure of Bach's time (digression from the tonality, return to the tonality) into an enormous edifice overladen with influences of the "symmetrical," the "narrative," and the "variation." It was ideally suited for the language and aesthetic of the late eighteenth and early nineteenth centuries. The form and the material parted company some hundred years or so ago, however, and the signs of disintegration were apparent by the time of World War I; in the 1970's, "sonata" thinking is not really very useful, particularly in *musique concrète,* where the difficulties of putting it into practice are just not worth the effort.

One final query may remain: "chance" or "control"? Even though I've made much of the schism between the two positions in earlier chapters, I must confess that the division becomes less distinct in actual practice. Do you refer to the two in relation to the *composition* of a work or the *performance* of a work? A "totally controlled" piece (one by Babbitt) is ideally controlled at both ends of the process, and a "total chance" composition (perhaps a John Cage example) is similarly random with reference to both. In making a tape composition, then, you can bring as much enthusiasm for the accidental-random-indeterminate as you wish and even make your tape in ways that minimize your willful control over it—but, as long as your final product is a single prerecorded magnetic tape to be played over loud-speakers, you have permanently "fixed," and thus controlled, the performance. Once the tape is made, there is no "chance" in *musique concrète.* If you want to embark upon really randomized ventures, consider the possibilities of live-electronic performance: a number of tapes played on various machines (with free instructions to the "players"), experimental duos for prerecorded tape and live improvisation, the many ways of altering the live performance itself. From the opposite point of view, real "control" over your material may be difficult to achieve without recourse to a computer or sophisticated synthesizer. A relative approximation of control—the degree to which the sound sources you made match those of your preconception, the level of skill in your editing of rhythms and synchronization of channels, the quality of your tape recorder, amplifier, and loud-speakers in playback—is the best you can hope for. Whatever your goals, you're bound to encounter minor frustrations. But these only add challenge and a further stimulus; they should in no way diminish the real enjoyment of witnessing a composition come to life, both when you make it and when you hear it.

Good luck!

Selected Bibliography and Discography

The term "selected" is an understatement, a fact that will be obvious to anyone familiar with the field of electronic music. I have not attempted to offer a comprehensive list of available material, or even anything remotely approaching one. In a subject still in its infancy and already burgeoning with creative activity, there are simply too many new books, articles, and recordings of music continually appearing to make any sort of comprehensive list possible.

If anyone desires a more detailed survey of the field than the one I've offered here, a number of references can be consulted: Lowell Cross's compilation *A Bibliography of Electronic Music* for books and articles and Hugh Davies's *International Electronic Music Catalog* for a listing of works and information on studios. Both of these volumes are in need of updating as of 1973, and it's hoped that new editions will appear in time. The Schwann catalogue, of course, is always complete and up to date with respect to available records; on the other hand, it will delete references to records that are no longer on the market, and for information on these you might have to consult back issues. In recent months, Schwann has become exclusively oriented to stereo, at least in its "standard" edition, and reference to special issues would be necessary in searching out any monaural discs still commercially available.

The Bibliography and Discography that follow here reflect my personal choice of material that I found helpful in writing this volume, that I mention specifically in the text, and that I cite in my quotations. General books and articles on twentieth-century music (not always or exclusively "electronic") that might be of value to laymen or students are also included. In the same vein, I have added to the Discography recordings that are not "electronic" in any of the accepted senses, but that I felt would aid in presenting a more balanced picture of the avant-garde scene: instrumental music by which to measure the electronic music, so to speak. These records have been marked with an asterisk.

It should be assumed that records are stereophonic unless a monaural indication is specifically given for an entry. When a number of works by the same composer are included on a single record, they are all listed as part of the single entry; if two or more composers share a record, their respective contributions are listed separately under each composer's name.

Bibliography

ADLER, MARVIN. "What Next?" *Music Educators Journal,* LVI, 8 (April, 1970).

AHLSTROM, DAVID. "The Electrocution of Rock," *Music Journal,* XXVI (October, 1968).

APPLETON, JON. "Additive vs. Subtractive Synthesis," *Electronic Music Review,* 5 (January, 1968).

——. "Aesthetic Direction in Electronic Music," *Western Humanities Review,* XVIII, 4 (Autumn, 1964).

——. "New Role for the Composer," *Music Journal,* XXVII (March, 1969).

——. "Tone-Relation, Time Displacement and Timbre: An Approach to Twentieth-Century Music," *The Music Review,* XXVIII, 1 (February, 1966).

ASHLEY, ROBERT. *"The Wolfman"* (score, recording, commentary), *Source,* II, 2 (July, 1968).

——, LARRY AUSTIN, and KARLHEINZ STOCKHAUSEN. "Conversation," *Source,* I, 1 (January, 1967).

AUSTIN, LARRY. *"Accidents"* (score, recording, commentary), *Source,* II, 2 (July, 1968).

BABBITT, MILTON. "An Introduction to the RCA Synthesizer," *Journal of Music Theory,* VIII, 2 (1964).

——. "The Revolution in Sound: Electronic Music," *Music Journal,* XVIII, 7 (October, 1960).

——. "Twelve-Tone Rhythmic Structure and the Electronic Medium," *Perspectives of New Music,* I, 1 (Fall, 1962).

——. "Who Cares If You Listen?" *High Fidelity,* VIII, 2 (February, 1958).

BARLOW, WAYNE. "Electronic Music: Challenge to Music Education," *Music Educators Journal,* LV, 3 (November, 1968).

——. "Electronic Music and Music Education," *Electronic Music Review,* 6 (April, 1968).

BECKWITH, JOHN, and UDO KASAMETS, eds. *The Modern Composer and His World.* Toronto: University of Toronto Press, 1961.

BEESON, JACK. "Otto Luening," *American Composers Alliance Bulletin,* III, 3 (Autumn, 1953).

BEHRMAN, DAVID. "The Changing Landscape of Contemporary Music," *Bandwagon,* XIII, 5 (November, 1965).

BERGER, ARTHUR. "Music Written for Tape Recording," *American Composers Alliance Bulletin,* II, 4 (1952–53).

BERIO, LUCIANO. "The Studio di Fonologia Musicale of the Milan Radio," *Score,* 15 (March, 1956).

BINKLEY, ROBERT. "The New Rock and Music Education," *Music Educators Journal,* LV, 9 (May, 1969).

BOARDMAN, EUNICE. "New Sounds in the Classroom," *Music Educators Journal,* LV, 3 (November, 1968).

BOTTJE, WILL GAY. "Electronic Music—Creative Tool in the Classroom," *The School Musician,* 4 issues, April–October, 1970.

CAGE, JOHN. *Silence.* Middletown, Conn.: Wesleyan University Press, 1961.

———— and HILLER, LEJAREN. "*HPSCHD,*" *Source,* II, 2 (July, 1968).

CEELY, ROBERT. "Electronic Music Three Ways," *Electronic Music Review,* 1 (January, 1967).

CHAPIN, LOUIS. "The Future Started Here," *BMI: The Many Worlds of Music* (Summer, 1970).

CHILDS, BARNEY. "The Beginning of the Apocalypse?" *Kulchur,* IV, 15 (Autumn, 1964).

————. "The Newest Minstrelsy: A Dialogue," *Bandwagon,* XIII, 5 (November, 1965).

CHOU, WEN-CHUNG. "Varèse: A Sketch of the Man and His Music," *The Musical Quarterly,* LII, 2 (April, 1966).

COHEN, DAVID. "Computer-Generated Music," Southeastern Composers League *Newsletter,* December, 1966.

"Computer Performances of Music" (reports and discussion: J. K. Randall, Herbert Brün, Ercolino Ferretti, Godfrey Winham, Lejaren Hiller, David Lewin, Harold Shapiro), American Society of University Composers *Proceedings,* 1966.

"Computer Research" (forum: Milton Babbitt, J. K. Randall, Stefan Bauer-Mengelberg), *Perspectives of New Music,* III, 2 (Spring-Summer, 1965).

COPE, DAVID. *New Directions in Music.* Dubuque, Iowa: Wm. C. Brown, 1971.

COPPAGE, NOEL. "A Bad Year for Rock," *Stereo Review,* XXVI, 5 (May, 1971).

DANIEL, OLIVER. "The Science of Saying Nothing," *The Saturday Review,* XLIX (April 30, 1966).

DENNIS, BRIAN. *Experimental Music in Schools.* London: Oxford University Press, 1970.

DOCKSTADTER, TOD. "Inside-Out: Electronic Rock," *Electronic Music Review,* 5 (January, 1968).

EATON, JOHN. "The Humanization of Electronic Music," *Music Educators Journal,* LV, 3 (November, 1968).

EATON, M. L. *Electronic Music: A Handbook of Sound Synthesis and Control.* Kansas City, Mo.: Orcus Publications, 1969.

EHLE, ROBERT C. "Inside the Moog Synthesizer," *Audio,* LIII (December, 1969).

————. "The Social World of Electronic Music," *Instrumentalist* (October, 1970).

EIMERT, HERBERT. "What Is Electronic Music?" *Die Reihe*, 1 (1955).

ELLIS, MERRILL. "Musique Concrète at Home, or How to Compose Electronic Music in Three Easy Lessons," *Music Educators Journal*, LV, 3 (November, 1968).

FEATHER, LEONARD. *The Book of Jazz*. New York: Horizon Press, 1965.

FELDMAN, MORTON. "Between Categories," *The Composer*, I, 2 (September, 1969).

————. "Boola Boola," *Source*, IV, 2 (July, 1970).

"Five Questions, 35 Answers" (joint interview: Earle Brown, Harold Budd, Philip Corner, Jim Fulkerson, William Hellermann, Karel Husa, Elliott Schwartz), *The Composer*, II, 4 (March, 1971).

"Four Views of the Music Department at the University of California, San Diego," *Synthesis*, I, 2 (July, 1971).

FOWLER, CHARLES. "An Interview with Milton Babbitt," *Music Educators Journal*, LV, 3 (November, 1968).

GOEYVAERTS, KAREL. "The Sound Material of Electronic Music," *Die Reihe*, 1 (1955).

"Groups" (joint discussion-interview: Davis New Music Ensemble, ONCE Group, Sonic Arts Group, Musica Elettronica Viva), *Source*, II, 1 (January, 1968).

HAGEMANN, VIRGINIA. "Electronic Composition in the Junior High School," *Music Educators Journal*, LV, 3 (November, 1968).

HARMAN, CARTER. "Music Moves into the Future," *BMI: The Many Worlds of Music* (Summer, 1970).

HASSELL, JOHN. "*Map 2*" (performance material and commentary), *Source*, III, 1 (January, 1969).

HILLER, LEJAREN. "Electronic Music at the University of Illinois," *Journal of Music Theory*, VII, 1 (Spring, 1963).

————. "Electronic Synthesis of Microtonal Music," American Society of University Composers *Proceedings*, 1967.

———— and ROBERT A. BAKER. "*Computer Cantata*: A Study in Compositional Method," *Perspectives of New Music*, III, 1 (Fall-Winter, 1964).

———— and LEONARD M. ISAACSON. *Experimental Music*. New York: McGraw-Hill, 1959.

HITCHCOCK, H. WILEY. *Music in the United States: A Historical Introduction*. Englewood Cliffs, N. J.: Prentice-Hall, 1969.

HOWE, HUBERT S., JR. "A General View of Compositional Procedure in Computer Sound Synthesis," American Society of University Composers *Proceedings*, 1968.

IVEY, JEAN EICHELBERGER. "Electronic Music Workshop for Teachers," *Music Educators Journal*, LV, 3 (November, 1968).

JOHNSON, WILL. "First Festival of Live-Electronic Music 1967," *Source*, II, 1 (January, 1968).

JUDD, FREDERICK C. *Electronic Music and Musique Concrète*. London: Neville Spearman, 1961.

KASAMETS, UDO. "Eight Edicts on Education with Eighteen Elaborations," *Source*, II, 2 (July, 1968).

KETOFF, PAUL. "The Synket," *Electronic Music Review*, 4 (October, 1967).
KOENIG, GOTTFRIED MICHAEL. "Studium im Studio," *Die Reihe*, 5 (1959).
KOSTELANETZ, RICHARD, ed. *John Cage*. New York: Praeger, 1970.
LIGETI, GYÖRGY. "Metamorphoses of Musical Form," *Die Reihe*, 7 (1960).
LONG, ROBERT. "The Color of Sound," *High Fidelity*, XXI, 3 (March, 1971).
LUCIER, ALVIN. "The Making of *North American Time Capsule 1967*," *Electronic Music Review*, 5 (January, 1968).
LUENING, OTTO. "Some Random Remarks About Electronic Music," *Journal of Music Theory*, VIII, 1 (1964).
————. "An Unfinished History of Electronic Music," *Music Educators Journal*, LV, 3 (November, 1968).
MARKS, J. *Rock and Other Four Letter Words*. New York: Bantam Books, 1969.
MELLERS, WILFRID. *Music in a New Found Land*, New York: Knopf, 1965.
MELTZER, R. *The Aesthetics of Rock*. New York: Something Else Press, 1970.
"Mixed-Media Composition" (panel discussion: Ross Lee Finney, George Cacciopo, Edwin London, Salvatore Martirano), American Society of University Composers *Proceedings*, 1968.
MODUGNO, ANNE. "Electronic Composition in the Senior High School," *Music Educators Journal*, LV, 3 (November, 1968).
"Moog Modulations" (group interview: Robert Moog, Chris Swansen, Paul Bley, Annette Peacock, and Sun Ra), *Down Beat*, XXXVII, 14 (July 23, 1970).
MUMMA, GORDON. "Alvin Lucier's Music for Solo Performer 1965," *Source*, I, 2 (July, 1967).
————. "What Is a Performance?" *Bandwagon*, XIII, 5 (November, 1965).
NEUHAUS, MAX. "Six Sound Oriented Pieces for Situations Other Than That of the Concert Hall," *Source*, III, 1 (January, 1969).
NORTON, RICHARD. "The Vision of Morton Subotnick," *Music Journal*, XXVIII (January, 1970).
OLIVEROS, PAULINE. "Some Sound Observations," *Source*, II, 1 (January, 1968).
————. "Tape Delay Techniques for Electronic Music Composition," *The Composer*, I, 3 (December, 1969).
PLEASANTS, HENRY. *Serious Music—and All That Jazz*. New York: Simon and Schuster, 1969.
POTTER, RALPH K. "New Scientific Tools for the Arts," *Journal of Aesthetics and Art Criticism*, X, 2 (December, 1951).
POUSSEUR, HENRI. "Formal Elements in a New Compositional Material," *Die Reihe*, 1 (1955).
POWELL, MEL. "Electronic Music and Musical Newness," *The American Scholar*, XXXV, 2 (Spring, 1966).
————. "Volley for Varèse," *The Saturday Review*, XLIII (December 31, 1960).
"Programmed Control" (symposium of reports: Robert A. Moog, Emmanuel Ghent, George W. Logemann, James Gabura, and Gustav Clamanga), *Electronic Music Review*, 1 (January, 1967).

PULFER, J. K. "Computer Aid for Musical Composers," *Computer Music Newsletter*, 2 (June, 1971).

RANDALL, J. K. "Electronic Music and Musical Tradition," *Music Educators Journal*, LV, 3 (November, 1968).

"Recent Developments in Electronic Music" (panel discussion: Hubert S. Howe, John Clough, David Cohen, Emmanuel Ghent, Max Mathews, and Robert Moog), American Society of University Composers *Proceedings*, 1969.

A Report on an Experimental General Music Program, Department of Music, University of California, San Diego, 1969.

SALZMAN, ERIC. *Twentieth Century Music: An Introduction*. Englewood Cliffs, N. J.: Prentice-Hall, 1967.

————. "A Whole New Classical Ballgame," *Stereo Review*, XXVI, 3 (March, 1971).

SCHAEFFER, MYRON. "The Electronic Music Studio of the University of Toronto," *Journal of Music Theory*, VIII, 1 (Spring, 1963).

SCHAFER, R. MURRAY. "A Basic Course," *Source*, III, 1 (January, 1969).

————. *The Composer in the Classroom*. Don Mills, Ontario: BMI Canada, Ltd., 1967.

————. *Ear Cleaning*. Don Mills, Ontario: BMI Canada, Ltd., 1967.

SCHERCHEN, HERMANN. "The Musical Past and the Electronic Future," *The Saturday Review*, XLVII (October 31, 1964).

SCHULLER, GUNTHER. "Conversations with Varèse," *Perspectives of New Music*, III, 2 (Spring-Summer, 1965).

————. "The New German Music for Radio," *The Saturday Review*, XLV (January 13, 1962).

SCHWARTZ, ELLIOTT. "Elevator Music," *The Composer*, II, 2 (September, 1970).

———— and BARNEY CHILDS, eds. *Contemporary Composers on Contemporary Music*. New York: Holt, Rinehart and Winston, 1967.

SEAWRIGHT, JAMES. "What Goes into an Electronic Music Studio," *Music Educators Journal*, LV, 3 (November, 1968).

SELF, GEORGE. *New Sounds in Class*. London: Universal Editions, 1967.

SHAW, ARNOLD. *The Rock Revolution*. New York: Macmillan, 1969; rev. ed., New York: Paperback Library, 1971.

"Short Answers to Difficult Questions" (panel interview: Lukas Foss, John Cage, Iannis Xenakis), *The Composer*, II, 2 (September, 1970).

SMITH-BRINDLE, REGINALD. "The Lunatic Fringe: I. Concrete Music. II. Electronic Music. III. Computation Composition," *The Musical Times*, XCVII (1956).

STOCKHAUSEN, KARLHEINZ. "Actualia," *Die Reihe*, 1 (1955).

————. "Electronic and Instrumental Music," *Die Reihe*, 5 (1959).

————. "Not a Special Day," *The Composer*, I, 2 (September, 1969).

STRANGE, ALLEN. "Tape Piece," *The Composer*, II, 1 (June, 1970).

STUCKENSCHMIDT, H. H. "Contemporary Techniques in Music," *The Musical Quarterly*, XLIX, 1 (January, 1963).

————. "The Third Stage," *Die Reihe*, 1 (1955).

————. *Twentieth Century Music*. New York: McGraw-Hill, 1969.

SUBOTNICK, MORTON. "Extending the Stuff Music Is Made of," *Music Educators Journal*, LV, 3 (November, 1968).

————. "The Synthesizer: Is It the Ultimate Musical Weapon?" *Recording Engineer/Producer*, I, 1 (April-May, 1970).

"Synthesizers" (comparative survey of the entire range of available instruments), *Synthesis*, I, 2 (July, 1971).

TALLMADGE, WILLIAM H. "The Composer's Machine," *Journal of Aesthetics and Art Criticism*, XIX, 3 (1961).

"Tape Recording" (symposium of reports: Robert A. Moog, Walter Carlos, Benjamin Folkman, Gordon Mumma, etc.), *Electronic Music Review*, 6 (April, 1968).

TENNEY, JAMES. "Sound Generation by Means of a Digital Computer," *Journal of Music Theory*, VII, 1 (Spring, 1963).

TURETZKY, BERTRAM. "The Solo-Ensemble Piece," *The Composer*, II, 3 (December, 1970).

USSACHEVSKY, VLADIMIR. "As Europe Takes to Tape," *American Composers Alliance Bulletin*, III, 3 (1953).

————. "The Making of Four Miniatures: An Analysis," *Music Educators Journal*, LV, 3 (November, 1968).

————. "Notes on *A Piece for Tape Recorder*," *The Musical Quarterly*, XLVI, 2 (April, 1960).

VEGA, AURELIO DE LA. "Regarding Electronic Music," *Tempo*, 75 (Winter, 1965–66).

VERCOE, BARRY L. "Electronic Sounds and the Sensitive Performer," *Music Educators Journal*, LV, 3 (November, 1968).

————. "The Music 360 Language for Sound Synthesis," *Computer Music Newsletter*, 2 (June, 1971).

VERKEN, MONIQUE. "An Interview with Frederick Rzewski," *The Drama Review*, XIV, 1 (Fall, 1969).

XENAKIS, IANNIS. "Free Stochastic Music from the Computer," *Gravesaner Blätter* (*Gravesano Review*), 26 (1965).

YATES, PETER. *Twentieth Century Music*. New York: Pantheon Books, 1967.

ZAPPA, FRANK. "Edgar Varèse: Idol of My Youth," *Stereo Review*, XXVI, 6 (June, 1971).

Discography

"AMM" Group of London (Cornelius Cardew, Lou Gare, Christopher Hobbs, Eddie Prevost, Keith Rowe), Mainstream MS-5002.

APPLETON, JON. *Syntonic Menagerie (Chef d'Oeuvre, Nyckelharpan, Infantasy, Georganna's Fancy, The Visitation, Newark Airport Rock, Spuyten Duyvil, Second Scene Unobserved, Times Square Times Ten)*, Flying Dutchman FDS-103.

———— and DON CHERRY. *Human Music.* Flying Dutchman FDS-121.

AREL, BÜLENT. *Electronic Music No. 1; Music for a Sacred Service (Prelude and Postlude); Fragment,* Son Nova 3.

————. *Stereo Electronic Music No. 1,* Columbia MS-6566.

Ars Nova group, Elektra EKS-74020.

ASHLEY, ROBERT. *The Wolfman,* Composer-Performer Edition (see Bibliography).

AUSTIN, LARRY. *Accidents.* Composer-Performer Edition (see Bibliography).

BABBITT, MILTON. *All Set** (jazz ensemble), Columbia C2S-831.

————. *Composition for Synthesizer,* Columbia MS-6566.

————. *Ensembles for Synthesizer,* Columbia MS-7051.

————. *Philomel* (soprano, recorded soprano, and synthesized sound), Deutsche Grammophon 0654-083 (AR Series).

BADINGS, HENK. *Capriccio for Violin and Two Sound Tracks; Genese; Evolutions,* Limelight 86055.

THE BEATLES. *The Beatles,* Apple SWBO-101.

————. *Sgt. Pepper's Lonely Hearts Club Band,* Capitol SMAS-2653.

BEAVER, PAUL; and BERNARD KRAUSE. *The Nonesuch Guide to Electronic Music,* Nonesuch HC-73018.

BEDFORD, DAVID. *Come in Here Child* (soprano voice and amplified piano), Mainstream MS-5001.

BERIO, LUCIANO. *Sinfonia** (orchestra and voices), Columbia MS-7268.

————. *Thema (Ommagio a Joyce),* Vox Turnabout TV-34177 and Mercury SR2-9123.

————. *Visage,* Vox Turnabout 34046S.

BRANT, HENRY. *Millennium II** (brass and percussion ensemble, soprano voice), Lehigh University RINC-1103. Also includes spoken commentary by the composer on spatial music.

BROWN, EARLE. *Four Systems* (realization by Max Neuhaus for four amplified cymbals), Columbia MS-7139.
BRÜN, HERBERT. *Futility 1964* (speaker and tape), Heliodor HS-25047.
BUSSOTTI, SYLVANO. *Coeur pour batteur—Positively Yes* (electronic realization by Max Neuhaus), Columbia MS-7139.
CAGE, JOHN. *Aria with Fontana Mix*, Mainstream MS-5005.
————. *Cartridge Music*, Mainstream MS-5015 and Deutsche Grammophon 137009.
————. *Fontana Mix* (magnetic tape version), Vox Turnabout 34046S.
————. *Fontana Mix—Feed* (electronic realization by Max Neuhaus), Columbia MS-7139.
————. *Imaginary Landscape No. 1; Williams Mix*, Avakian 1 (in 3-record set commemorating the twenty-five-year retrospective Cage concert of 1958, available only from George Avakian, 285 Central Park West, New York 10025).
————. *Variations II*, Columbia MS-7051.
————. *Variations IV*, Everest 3132.
————. *Variations IV, Volume II*, Everest 3230.
———— and LEJAREN HILLER. *HPSCHD*, Nonesuch H-71224.
CALE, JOHN, and TERRY RILEY. *Church of Anthrax*, Columbia C-30131.
CARLOS, WALTER. *Dialogues for Piano and Two Loudspeakers; Variations for Flute and Electronic Sound*, Vox Turnabout 34004S.
————. *Switched-on Bach* (realizations of Brandenburg Concerto No. 3, Chorale Prelude "Wachet Auf," etc.), Columbia MS-7194.
————. *The Well-tempered Synthesizer* (realizations of Scarlatti sonatas, Handel *Water Music*, etc.), Columbia MS-7286.
DAVIDOVSKY, MARIO. *Electronic Study No. 1*, Columbia MS-6566.
————. *Study No. 2*, Son Nova 3.
————. *Synchronisms No. 1* (flute and tape); *Synchronisms No. 2* (ensemble and tape); *Synchronisms No. 3* (cello and tape), CRI S-204.
DOCKSTADTER, TOD. *Drone*; *Two Fragments from Apocalypse*; *Water Music*, Owl ORLP-7.
————. *Eight Electronic Pieces*, Folkways FM-3434 (monaural).
————. *Luna Park*; *Traveling Music*; *Apocalypse*, Owl ORLP-6.
————. *Quatermass*, Owl ORLP-8.
DODGE, CHARLES. *Changes*, Nonesuch H-71245.
————. *Earth's Magnetic Field*, Nonesuch H-71250.
DRUCKMAN, JACOB. *Animus I* (trombone and electronic tape), Vox Turnabout TV-34177.
————. *Animus III* (clarinet and electronic tape), Nonesuch H-71253.
EATON, JOHN. *Songs for R.P.B.* (soprano, Syn-Ket, and piano); *Piece for Solo Syn-Ket No. 3*, Decca DL-710154.
EIMERT, HERBERT. *Epitaph*; *Sechs Studien*, Wergo WER-60014.
————. *Sélection I*, Mercury SR2-9123.
EL DABH, HALIM. *Leiyla and the Poet*, Columbia MS-6566.
ELLIS, DON, and orchestra. *Electric Bath*, Columbia CS-9585.
ERB, DONALD. *In No Strange Land* (trombone, doublebass, and tape); *Reconaissance* (instrumental ensemble and two Moog synthesizers), Nonesuch H-71223.

ERICKSON, ROBERT. *Ricercar à 3* (contrabass), Ars Nova/Ars Antiqua AN-1001.
———. *Ricercar à 5* (trombone), Deutsche Grammophon 0654-084 (AR Series).
FELDMAN, MORTON. *The King of Denmark** (percussion), Columbia MS-7139.
FERRARI, LUC. *Visage V*, Mercury SR2-9123.
FOSS, LUKAS. *Echoi* (clarinet, cello, piano, and percussion), Heliodor 2549001.
———. *Geod* (orchestra), Candide 31042.
———. *Paradigm* (amplified instrumental ensemble), Deutsche Grammophon DG-2543005.
GABURO, KENNETH. *Lemon Drops; For Harry*, Heliodor HS-25047.
———. *Music for Voices, Instruments & Electronic Sounds (Antiphony III: Pearl-White Moments; Exit Music I: The Wasting of Lucrecetzia; Antiphony IV: Poised; Exit Music II: Fat Millie's Lament)*, Nonesuch H-71199.
GERHARD, ROBERTO. *Collages (Symphony No. 3 for Electronic Tape and Orchestra)*, Angel S-36558.
THE GRATEFUL DEAD. *Live/Dead*, Warner Bros., Seven Arts 2WS-1830.
HELLERMANN, WILLIAM. *Ariel*, Vox Turnabout 34301S.
HENDRIX, JIMI. *The Jimi Hendrix Experience*, Reprise RS-6261.
HENRY, PIERRE. *Mass for the Present Time (The Voyage*—extract; *The Green Queen; Variations for a Door and a Sigh*—extracts), Philips 4FE8004.
———. *Variations for a Door and a Sigh*, Limelight 86059.
———. *Le Voyage*, Mercury SR-90482.
HILLER, LEJAREN. *Computer Music* (tape and percussion); *Suite for Two Pianos and Tape; Avalanche* (theater piece including tapes), Heliodor 2549006.
———. *Machine Music* (piano, percussion, and tape), Heliodor HS-25047.
ICHYANAGI, TOSHI. *Extended Voices* (chorus and synthesizers), Odyssey 32-16-0156.
IVEY, JEAN EICHELBERGER. *Pinball*, Folkways FM-33436.
JOHNSTON, BEN. *Casta Bertram*, Nonesuch H-71237.
JOLIVET, ANDRÉ. *Concerto for Ondes Martenot and Orchestra*, Westminster XWN-18360 (monaural).
KAGEL, MAURICIO. *Transición I*, Mercury SR2-9123.
———. *Transición II* (piano, percussion, and two tapes), Mainstream MS-5003.
KIRCHNER, LEON. *String Quartet No. 3* (including electronic tape), Columbia MS-7284.
KOENIG, GOTTFRIED MICHAEL. *Terminus II; Function Gruen*, Deutsche Grammophon 137011 SLPM.
LeCAINE, HUGH. *Dripsody*, Folkways FM-33436.
LIGETI, GYÖRGY. *Atmosphères** (orchestra), Columbia MS-6733 and Wergo WER-60022.
LUCIER, ALVIN. *North American Time Capsule 1967* (chorus and Sylvania Vocoder), Odyssey 32-16-0156.

LUENING, OTTO. *Concerted Piece for Electronic Sounds and Orchestra*, CRI 227 USD.

——. *Gargoyles* (violin and tape), Columbia MS-6566.

——. *Tape Music: An Historic Concert* (*Fantasy in Space*; *Invention on 12 Notes*; *Legend*; *Low Speed*; *Lyric Scene*; *Moonflight*), Desto 6466.

—— and VLADIMIR USSACHEVSKY. *Incantation*, Desto 6466.

—— and VLADIMIR USSACHEVSKY. *A Poem in Cycles and Bells* (tape recorder and orchestra); *Suite from "King Lear,"* CRI 112 (monaural).

—— and VLADIMIR USSACHEVSKY. *Rhapsodic Variations for Tape Recorder and Orchestra*, Louisville 545-5 (monaural).

MALOVEC, JOZEF. *Orthogenesis*, Vox Turnabout 34301S.

MARTIRANO, SALVATORE. *L's GA* (gassed-masked politico, helium bomb, and two-channel tape), Polydor 24-5001.

——. *Underworld* (chamber ensemble and tape), Heliodor HS-25047.

MESSIAEN, OLIVIER. *Trois petites liturgies de la présence divine*, Music Guild S-142.

——. *Turangalîla-Symphonie*, RCA Victor LSC-7051.

MIMAROGLU, ILHAN. *Le Tombeau d'Edgar Poe*; *Intermezzo*; *Bowery Bum* (*Study After Jean Dubuffet*), Vox Turnabout TV-34004S

THE MOTHERS OF INVENTION. *Freak Out!*, Verve 6-5005-2X.

——. *Uncle Meat*, Bizarre 2MS-2024.

MUMMA, GORDON. *Mesa* (for Cybersonic Bandoneon), Odyssey 32-16-0158.

——. *Music from the Venezia Space Theatre*, Advance FGR-5 (monaural).

"The Music Improvisation Company," ECM 1005 (Munich, Germany).

"Musica Elettronica Viva" Ensemble of Rome (Alan Bryant, Alvin Curran, Frederic Rzewski, Richard Teitelbaum, Ivan Vandor). *Spacecraft*, Mainstream MS-5002.

OLIVEROS, PAULINE. *I of IV*, Odyssey 32-16-0160.

——. *Sound Patterns** (chorus), Odyssey 32-16-0156.

Panorama of Musique Concrète (*Railway Study*; *Symphonie pour un homme seul; Veil of Orpheus*, etc.), London, Ducretet-Thomson DTL-93090 and DTL-93121. Released under sponsorship of the International Music Council, UNESCO (monaural).

PENDERECKI, KRZYSZTOF. *Fluorescences** (orchestra); *Sonate for Cello and Orchestra,** Wergo WER-60020.

POUSSEUR, HENRI. *Rimes pour différentes sources sonores* (orchestra and tape), RCA Victrola VICS-1239.

——. *Scambi* (*Exchanges*), Mercury SR2-9123.

——. *Trois visages de Liège*, Columbia MS-7051.

POWELL, MEL. *Events* (tape recorder); *Second Electronic Setting*, CRI 227 USD.

RANDALL, J. K. *Lyric Variations for Violin and Computer*, Vanguard Cardinal C-10057.

——. *Quartets in Pairs*; *Quartersines*; *Mudgett: monologues by a mass murderer*, Nonesuch H-71245.

REICH, STEVE. *Come Out*, Odyssey 32-16-0160.

——. *Violin Phase*; *It's Gonna Rain*, Columbia MS-7265.

RILEY, TERRY. *In C*,* Columbia MS-7178.
———. *Poppy No Good and the Phantom Band; A Rainbow in Curved Air*, Columbia MS-7315.
RUDIN, ANDREW. *Tragoedia* (Moog synthesizer), Nonesuch H-71198.
SAHL, MICHAEL. *A Mitzvah for the Dead* (violin and tape), Vanguard Cardinal C-10057.
———. *Tropes on the Salve Regina*, Lyrichord LLST-7210.
SALZMAN, ERIC. *The Nude Paper Sermon* (tropes for actor, Renaissance consort, chorus, and electronics), Nonesuch H-71231.
SCHWARTZ, ELLIOTT. *Aria No. 4* (bassoon and tape), Advance FGR-7 (monaural).
———. *Interruptions* (woodwind quintet and tape loop), Advance FGR-11.
SMILEY, PRIL. *Eclipse*, Vox Turnabout 34301S.
STOCKHAUSEN, KARLHEINZ. *Gesang der Jünglinge*, Deutsche Grammophon 138811 SLPM.
———. *Hymnen: Anthems for Electronic and Concrete Sounds*, Deutsche Grammophon 139-421/22 SLPM.
———. *Mikrophonie I* (tam-tam, two microphones, two filters, and Potentiometers); *Mikrophonie II* (choir, Hammond organ, and ring modulators), Columbia MS-7355.
———. *Opus 1970*, Deutsche Grammophon 139-461-SLPM.
———. *Prozession* (tam-tam, viola, Elektronium, piano, filters, and Potentiometers), Candide CE-31001.
———. *Studie I; Studie II*, Deutsche Grammophon 16133 (monaural).
SUBOTNICK, MORTON. *Silver Apples of the Moon*, Nonesuch H-71174.
———. *Touch*, Columbia MS-7316.
———. *The Wild Bull*, Nonesuch H-71208.
TAKEMITSU, TORU. *Water Music; Vocalism Ai (Love)*, RCA Victrola VICS-1334.
TAVENER, JOHN. *The Whale* (chorus, orchestra, and soloists), Apple SMAS-3369.
THE UNITED STATES OF AMERICA GROUP, Columbia CS-9614.
USSACHEVSKY, VLADIMIR. *Creation-Prologue*, Columbia MS-6566.
———. *Metamorphosis; Linear Contrasts; Improvisation No. 4711*, Son Nova 3.
———. *Of Wood and Brass; Wireless Fantasy*, CRI 227 USD.
———. *A Piece for Tape Recorder*, CRI 112 (monaural).
———. *Sonic Contours*, Desto 6466.
VARÈSE, EDGARD. *Déserts* (instrumental ensemble and tape), Columbia MS-6362.
———. *Poème électronique*, Columbia MS-6146..
VERCOE, BARRY. *Synthesism*, Nonesuch H-71245.
WEBBER, ANDREW LLOYD, and TIM RICE. *Jesus Christ Superstar*, Decca DXSA-7206.
WHITTENBERG, CHARLES. *Electronic Study II with Contrabass*, Advance FGR-1 (monaural).
WILLIAMS, TONY. *Emergency!*, Polydor 25-3001.
WILSON, OLLY. *Cetus*, Vox Turnabout 34301S.

WUORINEN, CHARLES. *Time's Encomium* (electronic music synthesizer), Nonesuch H-71225.

XENAKIS, IANNIS. *Electro-Acoustic Music* (*Bohor I, Concret P-H II, Diamorphoses II, Orient-Occident III*), Nonesuch H-71246.

————. *Metastasis;* Pithoprakta,** Vanguard Cardinal VCS-10030.

————. *Orient-Occident,* Mercury SR2-9123.

ZAWINUL, JOE. *Zawinul,* Atlantic SD-1579.

Index

Index

306 *Index*

DATE DUE

GAYLORD	PRINTED IN U.S.A.